Black Images of America
1784–1870

THE NORTON ESSAYS IN AMERICAN HISTORY

Under the general editorship of
HAROLD M. HYMAN
William P. Hobby Professor of American History
Rice University

EISENHOWER AND BERLIN, 1945: THE DECISION
TO HALT AT THE ELBE *Stephen E. Ambrose*

THE MONEY QUESTION DURING RECONSTRUCTION
Walter T. K. Nugent

ANDREW JACKSON AND THE BANK WAR
Robert V. Remini

THE GREAT BULL MARKET: WALL STREET IN THE 1920's
Robert Sobel

THE JACKSONIAN ECONOMY *Peter Temin*

A NEW ENGLAND TOWN: THE FIRST HUNDRED YEARS
Kenneth A. Lockridge

DIPLOMACY FOR VICTORY: FDR AND UNCONDITIONAL
SURRENDER *Raymond G. O'Connor*

THE ORIGINS OF AMERICAN INTERVENTION IN THE
FIRST WORLD WAR *Ross Gregory*

THE IMPEACHMENT AND TRIAL OF ANDREW JOHNSON
Michael Les Benedict

THE GENET MISSION *Harry Ammon*

THE POLITICS OF NORMALCY: GOVERNMENTAL
THEORY AND PRACTICE IN THE HARDING–COOLIDGE ERA
Robert Murray

THE FAILURE OF THE NRA *Bernard Bellush*

A HISTORY OF THE ICC: FROM PANACEA TO PALLIATIVE
Ari and Olive
Hoogenboom

BLACK IMAGES OF AMERICA 1784–1870
Leonard I. Sweet

Black Images of
America
1784–1870

Leonard I. Sweet

New York W · W · NORTON & COMPANY · INC ·

Library of Congress Cataloging in Publication Data

Sweet, Leonard I
    Black images of America, 1784–1870.

    (The Norton essays in American history)
    Bibliography: p.
    Includes index.
    1. Negroes—Historiography. 2. Slavery in the
United States—Historiography. I. Title.
E184.65.s84   973'.04'96073   75–40248

ISBN 0–393–05569–8
ISBN 0–393–09195–3 pbk.

1 2 3 4 5 6 7 8 9 0

For Joan

Contents

Acknowledgments   *ix*

1   Introduction   1

2   George Bancroft, Father of American History, wherein America's self-image is set forth and examined in the light of images of America accepted by other select white historians in the nineteenth century   7

3   Samuel Hopkins, Father of African Colonization, wherein the ideals of American history are accommodated to the reality of slavery, and early blacks react to that accommodation   23

4   The Black Response to the Colonizationist Image of America, wherein blacks expose the motives of white colonizationists, enumerate their conception of the historic image of America, and enunciate their felt relationship to America and American ideals   35

5   The Destiny of Black Americans, wherein blacks interpret the experience of slavery, the meaning of history, and the nature of their identity with and contributions to American history   69

6   The Goals of Black Separatism, wherein is discussed the black justification of "exclusivist tendencies," the relationship between separation and integration, and the views of America which were operative in black separatism   125

7 The Role of Blacks in American History, wherein blacks affirm their dedication to the ideals of America, their appropriation of the American model in their struggle for elevation and equality, and their special status as "testers" of America's commitment to her avowed values 148

8 Conclusion 168

A Bibliographical Review 185

Index 207

Acknowledgments

WITH ROUGHLY 435,000 books presently in print in the United States, the publication of another one is less an occasion for pride than it is of humility and gratitude, especially toward those institutions and individuals who have aided the thousands of authors like myself and our endless importunities. Several libraries have borne my pressing requests with courtesy and hospitality: the University of Rochester, the Rochester Center for Theological Studies, the Schomburg Collection of the 135th Street Branch of the New York Public Library, the Library of Congress, and the Buffalo-Erie County Historical Library.

I am almost embarrassed to admit how much I owe to Professor Winthrop S. Hudson of the University of Rochester and Colgate Rochester Divinity School. Only he knows the extent to which I have picked his brain and poached his perspectives. I also stand in great debt to Professor Milton Berman of the University of Rochester, whose door was always open for helpful advice and assistance, and to Professor David Levin of the University of Virginia, who gave the chapter on Bancroft a kind but critical reading. Senior Editor James Mairs and General Editor Harold Hyman offered many judicious suggestions to improve the quality of the manuscript. My numerous research jaunts to New York City were made especially pleasant by the gracious hospitality of Dr. Arthur P. Whitney, Deputy General Secretary of the American Bible Society. The concern, sensitivity, and encouragement of Luther M. Ridgeway speeded up the process of writing. Dr. B. David Wilson exercised his proofreading abilities on portions of the manuscript, and Eleanor Lussow of the library staff at Colgate Rochester Divinity School radiated charm and patience as she found no request too major or minor. The labor of typing was lifted from my shoulders by Georgianna White, who suffered more than any typist should decently have to suffer and yet never failed to grin inspiringly and give wise words of counsel. Brenda Reeves typed with dispatch a revised manuscript, and Connie Johnston typed the final revisions with efficiency and cheerfulness. Thanks to the skill of Eula B. White of the State University College of New York at Geneseo, I was exempted from the exacting task of preparing an index.

When asked the secret of his writing ability, Somerset Maugham is reported to have replied: "Placing my posterior extremities in a chair and resisting the first fifteen temptations to get up." My wife, Joan, and son, Leonard Jr., were responsible for at least a dozen of those first fifteen temptations. Only a wife knows what it is to live with a writer who occupies much space but little time. Without her understanding and support, none of this would have been possible.

1

Introduction

UNLIKE THE BLACK intelligentsia in the decades after World War I, the articulate blacks of the nineteenth century exhibited little puzzlement over their identity. At the second annual meeting of W. E. B. Du Bois's Niagara Movement, which met at Harper's Ferry in the summer of 1906, Reverdy C. Ransom appropriately chose as his topic "The Spirit of John Brown." After portraying Brown as a latter-day Puritan in disposition, demeanor, and deed, Ransom went on to summarize Afro-American history in the nineteenth century: "There is not now, and never has been, any discussion among the Negroes as to the place they hope to occupy within this nation. But there is a division among them as to method and the choice of ways leading to the coveted goal."[1]

This study is an attempt to evaluate Ransom's thesis in terms of what nineteenth-century black leaders said about themselves, about their identity, about their relationship to America, and about their involvement in American history. The views they expressed are examined against the backdrop of the white image of America depicted by a representative white historian, George Bancroft, who elucidated the common vision of America and its vocation. In a unique way, Bancroft's immensely popular writings summed up the major nineteenth-century intellectual themes of the ideal image of America and the mission and destiny of America in the

1. Reverdy C. Ransom, *The Spirit of Freedom and Justice: Orations and Speeches* (Nashville, 1926), 18, 22.

1

world. The attempt to accommodate these American ideals to the reality of slavery is exemplified by the subordinate voice of the father of African colonization, Samuel Hopkins, who sought to provide white America with a way out of its basic contradictions and dilemmas.

The initial examination of George Bancroft's representative conception of America and of Samuel Hopkins's representative arbitration of the American ideal with the American reality sets the stage for a look at how black leaders conceived of America's self-image vis-à-vis the American creed, American conduct, and American society.

On the major themes of American history, mission, and destiny, black leaders wrote like white historians. Black leaders making history and white historians (typified by George Bancroft) writing history shared a common belief system, a common "configuration of ideas and attitudes in which the elements are bound together by some form of constraint of functional interdependence."[2] From the internal dynamics of a shared belief system, various combinations and permutations were drawn by white and black leaders, depending on the centrality of idea-elements within the belief system and the range of objects that were referents for the ideas in the belief system.

Black elites shared with their white counterparts a providential understanding of history that envisioned America playing a special role in the advancement of mankind.[3] Most

2. Philip E. Converse, "The Nature of Belief Systems in Mass Publics," in *Ideology and Discontent,* ed. David E. Apter (New York, 1964), 207.

3. There has been little attempt to determine the existence of anything resembling a continental shelf between black masses and the active leadership stratum of blacks. It would take another study to plumb a vertical ordering of influential actors and mass beliefs starting from visible black elites and trickling down to local elites and mass beliefs—although it is suggestive that the united efforts of the two most influential black leaders of the 1840s, Frederick Douglass and Charles Lenox Remond, could not prevent the 1843 national black convention from supporting the Liberty Party. (See Howard H. Bell, "National Negro

black leaders throughout the century were convinced that they had a particular role to play in American history, whether as "testers" of America's commitment to her avowed values or as a people who, because of their history of suffering, offered the infusion of a moral and spiritual dimension lacking in America's history. Black leaders refused to accept the white leaders' panacea of colonization because it contradicted the ideal image of America; because they refused to abandon the claim to American nationality which they earned with their blood, sweat, and tears; because they believed that America would one day live up to her airy abstractions; and because they refused to desert their brethren in bonds.

On many subjects black leaders presented a panorama of perspectives, and one must be careful not to maximize consensus and solidarity at the expense of minimizing disagreements. Kelly Miller summarized the differing black approaches to the race problem in America: "Frederick Douglass said, 'Get White,' Marcus Garvey said, 'Get out,' Booker T. Washington said, 'Get along.' "[4] On any given issue, blacks displayed as wide a range of opinion as did other Americans. The question of the Spanish-American War and

---

Conventions of the Middle 1840s: Moral Suasion versus Political Action," *Journal of Negro History,* XLII [October 1957]: 249 ff.) It is evident from an analysis of school textbooks and readers that the white children of the nation were systematically indoctrinated in the image of America projected by Bancroft and other white historians, and there is much evidence to indicate that this indoctrination was successful. (See Ruth Miller Elson, *Guardians of Tradition: American Schoolbooks of the Nineteenth Century* [Lincoln, Nebraska, 1964], and Paul C. Nagel, *This Sacred Trust: American Nationality 1798–1898* [New York, 1971].) In contrast to what is known of the white community in America, little attempt thus far has been made to determine if a similar continental shelf existed in the relationship of the active leadership stratum of blacks to the opinions and images of the black masses. For a pioneer effort in this direction, see Jane H. Pease and William H. Pease, *They Who Would Be Free: Blacks' Search for Freedom, 1830–1861* (New York, 1974) 285–97.

4. Quoted in Emma Lou Thornbrough, *T. Thomas Fortune: Militant Journalist* (Chicago, 1972), 368.

imperialism, for example, prompted black responses which ran the gamut from the expansionistic fervor of E. E. Cooper, editor of the Washington *Colored American,* to the anti-imperialist anti-Americanism of the veteran colonizationist Bishop Henry McNeal Turner.[5] Range should not be mistaken for frequency, however, and on most issues blacks exhibited sufficient consistency in their views to allow for generalization.

Black leaders at times indulged in carping criticism of one another, but these contretemps did not usually involve major disagreement. David Ruggles sued the editors of the *Colored American* for libel, categorizing its readers as the scum of the black community. William Wells Brown characterized the emigrationist Martin R. Delany as a tactless, conceited, racist braggart. In 1853 Frederick Douglass termed Charles Lenox Remond, Robert Purvis, and William C. Nell "my bitterest enemies" and also engaged in verbal vendettas with John Mercer Langston. James Theodore Holly, who supported Langston, in turn accused Douglass of being guilty of "the blackest treason." Friction also developed between James McCune Smith and Henry Highland Garnet, and between William Wells Brown and Henry Highland Garnet.[6] Still the bickering of black leaders was no sharper or of no longer duration than that of whites in corresponding positions, and in most cases these factional feuds revolved more around personality than policy. The sharing of larger themes should not be obscured by whimsical, parochial tensions.

Black leaders knew who they were. They were black,

5. Willard B. Gatewood, "Black Americans and the Quest for Empire, 1898–1903," *The Journal of Southern History,* XXXVIII (November 1972): 548–49.

6. *Colored American,* 12 September 1840; William E. Farrison, *William Wells Brown: Author and Reformer* (Chicago, 1969), 345; *Liberator,* 16 August 1853; John W. Cromwell, *The Negro in American History* (Washington, D.C., 1914; reprinted New York, 1969), 36; and John Mercer Langston, *From the Virginia Plantation to the National Capitol* (Hartford, Connecticut, 1894; reprinted New York, 1969), 466–69.

they were Americans, and they were committed to the cause of emancipation, elevation, and equality—a cause that would purify American ideals and redeem America's destiny as a beacon to the oppressed. Blacks appropriated the American Revolutionary model in their abolitionist crusade and understood the Civil War as a continuation of the struggle initiated in 1776. Yet the black image of America entailed the black self-image, since whites excluded blacks from their image of America. If blacks were to refute the white denial of their American nationality, they first had to refute the negative image which whites had of blacks. Put in positive terms, black nationalism was indispensable to black assertions of America nationality. Black nationalism provided the creative thrust for black demands of American nationality.

Blacks were nationalistic about their color and about their capabilities. Nevertheless, their nationalism did not preempt their demands for inclusion as Americans. Afro-American history in the nineteenth century is the struggle for integration into American life, not separation from it. Black institutional separatism was justified basically as a means to the end of integration. At the same time that blacks recognized that separatist demands seemed to contradict the ideal of equality which their ancestors had helped to establish in the American Revolution, they also realized that without their own independent actions to secure their emancipation, elevation, and equality, black identity, equality, and self-confidence would be no more than an artificial product of white abolitionist tutelage.

The black nationalism that expressed itself in the nineteenth century can best be interpreted not as a pathological reaction to white racism or to the failure of white nationalism, but as a sentiment which emerged from within the black experience and consciousness. Articulate blacks professed confidence in their abilities and pride in their color, in their contribution to American history, and in the superiority of American ideals. Thus blacks combined two contrapuntal but harmonious themes in the nineteenth century. They asserted their identity as blacks and their identity as Americans. And they did not see any contradiction between the two—between being both black and American.

The twentieth-century puzzlement over black identity was occasioned by the drastic shift in black leadership views after World War I. Black alienation from the American vision proceeded from the growing awareness of the hopeless contradictions between profession and practice, ideals and realities, myths and actualities. Black Americans were bitterly disillusioned by the outcome at home and abroad of the "war to end war" and the war to "make the world safe for democracy." They had hoped that the enthusiastic loyalty of blacks to the American war effort—not to mention the millennial vision of the war itself—would make it a war to end racism and a war to make America safe for blacks. The aftermath of disillusionment was matched only by the ensuing despair. Where nineteenth-century black leaders had once seen a pure ideal reduced to a racist reality, post-World War I black leaders saw a racist reality lifted to an ideal. The image of America had lost the allegiance of innocence. But black Americans did not lament or linger at its passing. A "New Negro" was already engrossed in discovering distinctly black images, black ideals, and black myths.

2

George Bancroft,
Father of
American History

~~~~~~

More than any other American, George Bancroft is the personal embodiment of the historic spirit of these United States.

HERBERT BAXTER ADAMS

IN THE SPRING of 1886, the fledgling American Historical Association departed from what was to be its usual custom of meeting in Saratoga Springs, New York. Instead it made a "pilgrimage" to Washington, D.C., workshop of the aging George Bancroft, "there to seek and obtain his patriarchal blessing." The eighty-six year old Bancroft had been elected the second president of the Association the year before, and Herbert Baxter Adams deemed the pilgrimage a fitting and proper respect to the "Nestor of American history."[1] The

1. See Herbert Baxter Adams, "Secretary's Report," *American Historical Association Papers, II* (April 1886): 6–7. During his lifetime, Bancroft was as read and respected in Europe as he was in America, and his European friends and correspondents constitute a catalog of the intellectual giants of the nineteenth century. Frederic Bancroft, who was no relation to George Bancroft, discovered the magic of the Bancroft name when he found all the doors of visitation closed to Leopold von Ranke until Frederic Bancroft posed as George Bancroft's nephew, whereupon the aged master Leopold von Ranke ushered Frederic Bancroft immediately into his study. (See Jacob E. Cooke, *Frederic Bancroft, Historian* [Norman, Oklahoma, 1957], 27. See also Jennings B. Sanders, *Historical*

esteem of Bancroft reflected by this pilgrimage was no passing sentiment, and the title conferred upon him as the father of American history has remained almost axiomatic for writers on American historiography. Yet the manner in which Bancroft fathered American history has often been misunderstood, for historians have not always given due weight to Bancroft's wide-ranging historiographical and intellectual influence.

Almost all schools of American historiography have stood in Bancroft's debt. His providential understanding of American history and progress was perpetuated well into the twentieth century by the writings of such eminent white historians as John Fiske, Woodrow Wilson, and Edward Channing. Bancroft's treatment of Roger Williams was imitated by Vernon Louis Parrington and James Ernst.[2] Moreover, by insisting that progress in American history depended upon the existence of a frontier, Bancroft exhibited an environmentalism that foreshadowed the work of Frederick Jackson Turner.[3] Mention could also be made of the way in which Bancroft early "began to grope his way toward a conception of the function of partisan conflict"; his adumbration of Herbert Baxter Adams's "germ theory"; and his early avowal that a pure democracy existed in the seventeenth and eighteenth centuries, an original assessment which has sub-

Interpretations and American Historianship [Yellow Springs, Ohio, 1968], 12–13, for an assessment which does not do justice to Bancroft's international reputation.)

2. LeRoy Moore, Jr., "Roger Williams and the Historians," *Church History,* XXXII (December 1963): 432–51.

3. It is an error to describe John Bach McMaster as "the first national historian to appreciate the importance of the West" (see William T. Hutchinson, "John Bach McMaster," in *The Marcus W. Jernegan Essays in American Historiography,* ed. William T. Hutchinson [Chicago, 1937], 138; and M. G. Kraus, *A History of American History* [New York, 1937], 390, 394). As David Levin noted, to Bancroft "Tennessee frontiersmen proved, what Frederick Jackson Turner later asserted in language surprisingly similar to Bancroft's . . . that 'political wisdom is not sealed up in rolls and parchments. It welled up in the forest, like the waters from the hillside.' " (See David Levin, *History as Romantic Art* [Stanford, California, 1959], 38.)

sequently been reaffirmed by B. Katherine Brown and Robert E. Brown.[4]

In short, Bancroft was more than "the greatest apologist of Jacksonian democracy."[5] His historical writings, which J. F. Jameson tersely remarked "voted for Jackson,"[6] also voted for

4. Richard Hofstadter, *The Idea of a Party System* (Berkeley, 1970), 259–60; Levin, *History,* 81 ff; Michael G. Kammon, ed., *Politics and Society in Colonial America: Democracy or Deference?* (New York, 1967), 11–15, 29–40, 67–75. Whether Bancroft directly influenced later historians remains inconclusive, for, as David Levin has rightly reminded me, continuity does not necessarily mean influence. The important point, central to any venture into intellectual history, is that Bancroft espoused a cluster of Puritan beliefs about American history that were widely shared—and even presupposed—by men like Tom Paine and Robert Owen who, although not in the mainstream of American religious thought, could still share the mainstream views about the timeliness of America's discovery, chosen status, and asylum image. (See Winthrop S. Hudson, ed., *Nationalism and Religion in America* [New York, 1970], 55; see also Robert Owen's address to Congress upon the invitation of Henry Clay on 25 February 1825 and his 1826 "Declaration of Mental Independence," quoted in O. C. Johnson, *Robert Owen* [New York, 1970], 74.)

5. David W. Noble, *The Eternal Adam and the New World Garden* (New York, 1968), 6–7. The two best treatments of Bancroft can be found in David Noble's *Historians Against History: The Frontier Thesis and the National Covenant in American Historical Writing Since 1830* (Minneapolis, 1965) and Russell B. Nye, *George Bancroft, Brahmin Rebel* (New York, 1944). Both Noble and Nye depart from the exclusively Jacksonian interpretation of Bancroft. Nye accepts the conventional view that Bancroft rejected Puritan historiographical categories and stresses the "transcendentalistic" presuppositions to Bancroft's Jacksonian persuasion. Building on Nye, Noble emphasizes Bancroft's reaction against the Enlightenment and his basically Puritan outlook. Nevertheless, while acknowledging Bancroft's fundamental belief that America was a covenanted nation, Noble overlooks the relation of Bancroft's well-known continentalism to that covenant and neglects Bancroft's pervasive millennialist beliefs. Furthermore, neither Noble nor Nye appreciate the extensive influence of this "Brahmin Rebel" (a label Bancroft earned, incidentally, by his political affiliation rather than by his historical writing).

6. John Franklin Jameson, *The History of Historical Writing in America* (Boston, 1891), 107. Bancroft's own contemporaries, including Henry Hallam, Thomas Carlyle, and Leopold von Ranke, also stressed Bancroft's excessive adulation of American democracy. (See M. A. DeWolfe Howe, *The Life and Letters of George Bancroft,* Vol. II [New

God in the manner of the Puritans. If Bancroft's history was
Jacksonian, it was Jacksonian in a way that was acceptable
to Whigs. In short, at bottom it was neither Jacksonian nor
Whig but an American approach to history that displayed
marked continuity to the earlier New England tradition of
American historiography.

I

As the father of American history and the most widely
respected nineteenth-century interpreter of America to white
Americans, George Bancroft projected an American self-
image that featured four major themes. First, Bancroft retained the Puritan conviction of an unfailing, divine Providence governing the affairs of men. Second, related to this
providential view of history was his belief in the inevitability
of progress. Third was an unquestioning acceptance of the
notion that Americans were an elect people chosen and covenanted by God to effect his purposes for the world. Finally,
rooted in this covenantal view of the nation's vocation,
Bancroft exhibited great confidence in America's mission and
destiny in the world and a conviction of the millennial sway
of the democratic philosophy.

All of Bancroft's writings were composed within a context which viewed God as the prime mover of history.
According to Bancroft, God had established from time im-
memorial a blueprint for mankind, and through history this
plan has been gradually revealed and realized. In a char-
acteristically sweeping metaphor, Bancroft asserted that

York, 1908], 106, 226, 183.) For subsequent historians besides Jameson
who followed the lead of Bancroft's contemporaries, portraying Bancroft
as the great apologist for Jacksonian democracy, see G. P. Gooch, *History and Historians in the Nineteenth Century* (Boston, 1959), 377;
Kraus, *American History,* 238; and John Spencer Bassett, *The Middle
Group of American Historians* (New York, 1917), 203. Henry Adams,
in an 1875 review of a new edition of George Bancroft's *History of the
United States,* deprecated the Jackonsian bias in Bancroft's writings. (See
North American Review, CXX [April 1875]: 424–37.)

history "sees the footsteps of Providential Intelligence everywhere," footsteps which are easily read "along the line of the centuries."[7] Bancroft's philosophy of history, which later was shared by Woodrow Wilson, the "Presbyterian Priest" of American historians, boasted as its cardinal tenet the determination of all events by divinely established law.[8] Nothing happens by chance or contingency.[9] Given this philosophy of history (which had been popularized by John Foxe's *Book of Martyrs* and was avowedly continued in the colonial histories of New England)[10] and Bancroft's stated goal of writing the great American "epic of liberty,"[11] it is not surprising that Bancroft viewed God's control over human events as never more visibly manifested than in the creation of this "new empire of democracy."[12]

While the concept of God as the prime mover of history was the fundamental assertion, it was the belief in progress that supplied the most vivid illustration of this working phi-

7. George Bancroft, *History of the United States,* Vol. IV 20th ed. (Boston, 1868), 10. (Hereafter cited as *History.*) Bancroft, *History,* Vol. V 18th ed. (Boston, 1869), 23.

8. George Bancroft, *Memorial Address of the Life and Character of Abraham Lincoln* (Washington, 1886), 3. Woodrow Wilson's overriding sense of Providence in America's development is reflected in the following remarks to his secretary: "I believe in divine providence. . . . It is my faith that no body of men, however they concert their power or their influence, can defeat this great world enterprise, which, after all, is the enterprise of divine mercy, peace, and goodwill." (Quoted in Harold Garnet Black, *The True Woodrow Wilson* [New York, 1946], 189.) See also Arthur S. Link's account of Wilson's providential outlook in *Wilson the Diplomatist* (Baltimore, 1957), 12.

9. George Bancroft, "On Self Government," *American Historical Association Papers,* II (April 1886):7; George Bancroft, *Literary and Historical Miscellanies* (New York, 1855), 500. George Bancroft, *History of the Formation of the Constitution of the United States of America,* Vol. II (New York, 1882), 3. (Hereafter cited as *History of Constitution.*)

10. William Haller, *Foxe's Book of Martyrs and the Elect Nation* (London, 1963).

11. Howe, *Letters,* II: 321.

12. Bancroft, *History,* IV: 15.

losophy of history. Bancroft's conception of the divine plan for humanity involved the gradual perfection of mankind. For this purpose God equipped man with "reason," empowering him to intuit the truths of liberty, justice, and equality.[13] Viewing Roger Williams and Jonathan Edwards as the two great apostles of progress, Bancroft believed that the progressive spiral pointed toward a worldwide conversion to democratic principles. In this sense Bancroft was writing another "History of the Work of Redemption," or, in James Truslow Adams's equally observing phrase, a history of the "kingdom of Heaven."[14]

Bancroft emphasized two aspects of progress. First, being divinely devised, it is inevitable. Articulating a view that Woodrow Wilson later stressed, Bancroft argued that the forces of oppression had always failed because they tried to constrain that which God had ordained—free inquiry and equality.[15] Second, "the measure of the progress of civilization is the progress of the people."[16] Bancroft believed that history, with the progressive actualization of democratic principles as its central theme, served as its own critic. To the degree that freedom was allowed to exist, there had been progress. Conversely, to the extent that freedom was stifled and the people were not allowed to govern themselves, there had been a dark and debased period. In the long run, however, reason and freedom had triumphed increasingly, until finally they were established as twin cornerstones in the New World. Hence, progress meant to Bancroft a growing perception of democratic truths, culminating in the formation of America, and eventually leading to the millennium in which

13. Bancroft, *History*, Vol. III 20th ed. (Boston, 1868), 5; *Historical Miscellanies*, 422. For an excellent discussion of "Nature, Progress and Moral Judgement" in Bancroft, see Levin, *History*, 24–45.

14. Bancroft, *History*, III: 399; James Truslow Adams, "History and Lower Criticism," *Atlantic Monthly*, CXXXII (1923): 310.

15. Bancroft, *Historical Miscellanies*, 434, 482, 485; *History*, III: 398; IV: 10.

16. Bancroft, *Historical Miscellanies*, 427.

the democratic philosophy would be universally accepted.[17]

The third feature of Bancroft's history was a covenantal view of the nation's vocation that relied heavily both on Old Testament imagery and on the Hebraic understanding of history—and Bancroft was quick to point out the parallels.[18] The idea of a national covenant that one finds in Hebraic history had been central to Puritan thought, but there had been a shift in interpretation, first from the election of the old Israel to the election of England, and then from the election of England to the election of America. This latter shift had begun early, being clearly evident in the thought of Jonathan Edwards. And it persisted in the thinking of as late a figure as Woodrow Wilson.[19]

Bancroft served as a vehicle for perpetuating this myth, affirming that America had been chosen to complete God's final plan for mankind, that is, to inaugurate the millennial rule of democracy. Not just the New England settlements (which early colonial historians believed would lead the English nation to a renewal of its covenant and vocation), but the southern colonies as well were described in covenant terminology, as evidenced by the allusion to Tennessee as the "land of promise," and to the Carolinas as the "American Canaan, that flowed with milk and honey."[20] To Bancroft, the New World was the "new Israel" redivivus, and the colonists were the "chosen emissaries of God"

17. For further evidence of this interpretation, see Bancroft, *History,* IV: 8; V: 193; Vol. VIII 6th ed. (Boston, 1868), 120.

18. See e.g., Bancroft, *History,* III: 73.

19. Wilson saw Americans as "the custodians, in some degree, of the principles which have made men free and governments just." (George McLean Harper, *President Wilson's Addresses* [New York, 1918], 35.) Also, in his address to Congress concerning the League of Nations, he exclaimed: "The stage is set, the destiny disclosed. It has come about by no plan of our conceiving, but by the hand of God who led us in this way. We cannot turn back. We can only go forward with lifted eyes and freshened spirit, to follow the vision. It was of this that we dreamed at our birth. America shall in truth show the way." (Cited by Link, *Wilson the Diplomatist,* 131–32.)

20. Bancroft, *History,* Vol. I (Boston, 1834), 414; Vol. VI 16th ed. (Boston, 1869), 380; III: 17.

who, "like Moses, escaped from Egyptian bondage to the wilderness," where, in a promised land, the "new gospel of freedom" might be lived and proclaimed.[21]

God's decision to establish a covenant with the people of the New World in preference to the nations of the Old World posed no mystery to Bancroft. The millennial role was assigned to the Western Hemisphere precisely because it was unsettled and undefiled by ancient customs and conflicts. The Old World, wedded to evil institutions, could not easily free itself from "the dictates of authority and the jars of insulated interests."[22] The opposite was true of America's pristine setting. In the New World where, in the European traveler Chevalier's words, "the past has never taken deep root,"[23] the chaff could be winnowed from the European experience and a new nation could be built with the good grain that remained.

To fulfill her destiny, all America needed was to heed the lessons of history, for Bancroft insisted the "wrecks of the past were her warnings."[24] Democratic ideas, such as mixed government, checks and balances, and voluntarism, were sifted from past error and incorporated into the American system. Furthermore, determinants from many sources, not only the English, molded the new republic. "Annihilate the past of any one leading nation of the world, and our destiny would have been changed."[25] No major nation was denied a beneficent effect

21. *Ibid.,* I: 347, 362–63; Vol. X (Boston, 1874), 528; III: 74, 451–52.

22. Bancroft, *History,* IV: 4.

23. Michael Chevalier, *Society, Manners and Politics in the United States: Being a Series of Letters on North America* (New York, 1969), 80. (Originally published in Boston, 1839.) See also p. 33, where Chevalier speaks of America's "instinctive perception of the future and its aversions to the past."

24. Bancroft, *Address on Lincoln,* 4; *History,* IV: 12, 55; Vol. VII 10th ed. (Boston, 1869): 295; Vol. IX 4th ed. (Boston, 1866): 499. For a more elaborate discussion of this point, see Bancroft's "On Self Government," 8.

25. Bancroft, *Historical Miscellanies,* 508. This theme was a favorite of the German immigrant Carl Schurz, who stressed the composite con-

on America's development.

Although many tributaries fed into the American stream, Bancroft felt that one was stronger than all the others—the Anglo-Saxon. Indeed, England's contributions to America and the ages were viewed as surpassing those of all other nations. The mother country, as the chief repository of liberty in Europe, was the best breeder of men worthy to settle the New World. For centuries England and her Parliament had nurtured a growing political and intellectual freedom. In the end, however, England had been unable to fully escape the arbitrary rule of the past, and consequently her institutions bore the imprint both of liberty and of oppression. The intention of the colonists was to purify England's own liberties by purging the latter element from the English institutions transplanted to virgin soil, where they would be untrammeled by the influence of nobility, royalty, and prelacy.[26] The new republic, though freed from the yoke of England, was heavily endowed by her and in the end was to be instrumental in England's recovery of her own liberties.

If America had culled the superior ideas and innovations from history and had begun her career, in the words of the Swiss theologian-historian, Philip Schaff, "with the results of Europe's two-thousand years' course of civilization," she did not so much change as culminate history. Time and again Bancroft (like Wilson at a later time) reiterated the contention that America's relation to the past was one of consummation, not revolution.[27] Even the War of Independence

---

tribution of various nationalities in making America "the great repository of the last hopes of suffering mankind." (Quoted in Arthur A. Ekirch, *The Idea of Progress in America, 1815–1860* [New York, 1944], 93.)

26. Bancroft, *History,* III:13; VII: 23; V: 32, 236; V: 367, 54; IV: 459; III: 74.

27. Philip Schaff, *America: A Sketch of Its Political, Social, and Religious Character* (New York, 1855; reprinted Cambridge, Massachusetts, 1966 [ed. Perry Miller]), 17; Bancroft, *History of Constitution,* I 3; *History,* IX: 258. Wilson repeatedly stressed that "America was created to unite mankind. . . . We came to America . . . to better the ideals of men, to make them see finer things than they had seen before,

could not properly be called a revolt from Britain, "for it came naturally from the applications of English principles." [28]

The fourth feature of the American self-image as depicted by Bancroft was a firm belief in mission and destiny. Bancroft recognized that with election came responsibility, not fatalistic determinism. Through the "medium of men," God effects his plans. Men are his agents, his instrumentalities.

In Bancroft's eyes, America's responsibility involved the divine expectation that she keep this New World paradise pure and untainted from the dross of European medievalism.[29] Important to this mission was the existence of a western frontier, where, according to a view that Frederick Jackson Turner made famous,[30] a relentless though receding filter of nature could test American ideals against American practices and could prevent European influences from indis-

---

to get rid of the things that divide and to make sure of the things that unite." (Harper, *Addresses*, 151.)

28. Bancroft, *History*, X: 37; IX: 283. Bancroft's views in this area have been the subject of some misunderstanding. He did not deny that "the Founding Fathers had any serious political ideals in their heads at all" (Irving Kristol, "American Historians and the Democratic Idea," *The American Scholar*, XXXIX [Winter 1969]: 89–104) but that the Founding Fathers followed only one particular political ideal. He admitted that "they moulded their design by a creative power of their own, but nothing was introduced that did not already exist or was not a natural development of a well-known principle. The materials for building the American Constitution were the gifts of the ages." (*History of Constitution*, II: 322.)

29. Noble, *Historians Against History*, 30. One is reminded here of Louis Hartz's contention, in *The Liberal Tradition in America* (New York, 1953), that America's lack of exposure to a medieval heritage explains, to a large degree, her uniqueness.

30. Here again, one should not overlook Woodrow Wilson's kindred interpretation of the frontier to Bancroft and Turner. During his years at Johns Hopkins, Wilson nurtured a friendship with Turner which included the sharing of corresponding ideas on the importance of the frontier in explaining American history. (See letter to Turner, 23 August, 1889, in Ray Stannard Baker's *Woodrow Wilson: Life and Letters*, Vol. III [New York, 1927], 125.) Wilson's analysis of the role of the frontier can be found in his *History of the American People*, Vol. III (New York, 1902), 270 ff.

criminately corroding American ideals and institutions. Though the Atlantic might not continue to serve effectively as such a filter, the Alleghenies, the plains, and the Rockies would. As the "Jacksonian Tocqueville," Francis Grund, put it, "The West— not the East continually troubled with European visions—is ultimately destined to sway the country." [31]

Bancroft interpreted the Jacksonian era and the Civil War in similar terms. In the case of the former, a western, natural, and unmolested political theory of democracy decontaminated eastern modes of political thought that had become saturated with harmful European ideas.[32] (Woodrow Wilson would later voice a similar sentiment: "He [Jackson] impersonated the agencies which were to nationalize the government. Those agencies may be summarily indicated in two words, 'the West.' ")[33] Thirty years later, when the United States was threatened to the point of destruction by the ancient evil of slavery, God raised up another avatar of the frontier, Abraham Lincoln, who, like Jackson, "was in every way a child of nature, a child of the West, a child of America."[34] Bancroft joined John Lothrop Motley, Carl Schurz, and Charles Dana in supporting Lincoln's plan for compensated emancipation and all other ideas aimed to "insure universal emancipation, and thus complete the work which the Revolution began."[35] Woodrow Wilson's thesis that there was no pure American nation until after the Civil War, which so profoundly influenced historical interpretation, was presaged by Bancroft's

31. Francis Grund, *Aristocracy in America* (London, 1839), 300–301. (Reissued by Harper and Brothers, 1959.) John William Ward has effectively dealt with the theme of Nature (*i.e.,* frontier) in *Andrew Jackson: Symbol for an Age* (New York 1955), especially 24–45.
32. Bancroft, *Historical Miscellanies,* 462–63, 471–73.
33. Woodrow Wilson, *Division and Reunion* (New York, 1894), 25.
34. Bancroft, *Address on Lincoln,* 16, 17.
35. *Lincoln Papers,* Library of Congress, 7 March 1862. Cited by Lorraine A. Williams, "Northern Intellectual Reaction to the Policy of Emancipation," *Journal of Negro History,* XLVI (July 1961): 179–80; George William Curtis, ed., *The Correspondence of John Lothrop Motley,* Vol. II (New York, 1889), 65.

"completion of the Revolution" motif and by black leaders' conception of slavery as a cancerous growth, gradually eating away the very fiber of the nation.

According to Bancroft, the Jacksonian "Revolution" and the Civil War were but repristinations of the democratic ideals of the American Revolution, prodded by the continual reenactment along the frontier of the original American experience. What would happen when the frontier disappeared never bothered Bancroft—a dilemma that Turner solved by finding a new frontier in the rejuvenation of the old, conquered, spent frontier, and which Woodrow Wilson solved by envisioning America's next frontier around the globe.[36]

II

Bancroft's image of America was not exhausted by these themes of Providence, progress, election, and responsibility. Rather, they all combined to culminate in a glorious millennial vision. The importance Bancroft placed on America's obligation not to get trapped by European history, for example, was closely tied to his grand impressions of America's millennial mission in the world. Under the aegis of the New World, a new and final age was breaking forth in which divine principles—that is, democracy—would rule the world. All of Europe expectantly watched the unfolding experiment of the Americans, and "invoked success on their endeavor as the only hope for renovating the life of the civilized world.[37]

While the American people must be "sifted grain," still Bancroft emphasized their larger responsibilities to mankind as a whole. The men who shaped the nation did not desire freedom and justice only for themselves; their millennial role

36. Frederick Jackson Turner, "The West and American Ideals," *The Frontier in American History* (New York, 1920), 293–94; Wilson, *Papers,* IX: 365; X: 574–76, cited by William Appleton Williams, "Wilson," *New York Review of Books* (2 December 1971): 64.

37. Bancroft, *History of Constitution,* II: 367; *History,* IV: 12.

meant that they carried the burden of the whole human race. They had built America, fully intending that "humanity was to make for itself a new existence," by using her high example. The struggle for American independence was linked to a wider struggle of all mankind to gain freedom from oppression and tyranny.[38] Even the Founding Fathers, while crafting the Constitution, "knew themselves to be the forerunners of reform for the civilized world."[39] According to Bancroft, America's success was not her own; it was all humanity's. If she failed in her mission to initiate the millennium and vindicate the rule of the people, the world's last hope would have expired. But Providence planned America's triumph, and from her witness "the human race drew hope."[40] As David Noble put it, "the American experience could stand as a beacon of inspiration to the rest of humanity which was still trapped by its history."[41]

Bancroft firmly believed that the expansion of democratic principles over the globe would be the inevitable result of the New World's example. Insisting that "America never made herself a spreader of her own system," Bancroft conceived of majoritarianism as an irrepressible force, latent in the mind of all mankind, that would spread itself by contagion.[42] America's role in the millennium was primarily a passive and "recessive" one; to stand as a hallmark of liberty and equality.[43] Since America manifested the true unity of all races through her belief in one redeeming God and through her synthesis of those positive democratic prin-

38. Bancroft, *History,* VII: 356; X: 140; IV: 5, 462; X: 41.
39. Bancroft, *History of Constitution,* II: 4.
40. Bancroft, *History,* X: 36; IV: 371; *Address on Lincoln,* 5.
41. Noble, *Historians Against History,* 31; Bancroft, *History,* VIII: 474.
42. Bancroft, *History,* VIII: 474. In a letter (10 July 1840) Bancroft wrote: "The progress of Democracy is like the irresistible movement of the Mississippi towards the sea. . . . The onward course of the mighty mass of waters is as certain as the law of gravitation." (Howe, *Letters,* I: 234.)
43. Bancroft, *Historical Miscellanies,* 512, 513; *History,* II: 465.

ciples that had pervaded the histories of all nations, the universal adoption of democratic procedures and inauguration of the millennium was guaranteed, for "the mind tends not only towards unity, but universality."[44] Bancroft did concede something to a more active role, however, writing to James Buchanan in 1848 that America should not sit idly by while "the old world is shaking off its chains and enthroning the masses."[45] But the nation was primarily called to exercise a priestly function. Her millennial mission was to witness, not to coerce. This was Woodrow Wilson's basic point when he said of the United States that "she was born to serve mankind."[46]

Though not an imperialist, George Bancroft was certainly an avid continentalist. America was to him not only justified in expanding westward; her chosen calling compelled her to stretch the rule of democracy to the Pacific and to complete her manifest destiny.

Bancroft's unabashed honesty in espousing continentalism reflected a total dedication to his Puritan philosophy of history. Not only did the colonists perceive America as the sanctuary for those oppressed by religion, dynasties, and territorial designs. They also envisioned America as the high priest, preaching to the world the gospel of democracy. Bancroft displayed both a fervent chiliastic belief in universal democracy as the final page of God's blueprint for mankind and an intense conviction that America was destined by God

44. Bancroft, *Historical Miscellanies,* 507, 511. Bancroft assigned a curious importance to Christianity as the initiator of this idea. He wrote: "To have asserted clearly the unity of mankind was the distinctive glory of the Christian religion. No more were the nations to be severed by the worship of exclusive deities. The world was instructed that all men are one blood; that for all there is but one divine nature and but one moral law; and the renovating faith taught the singleness of the race, of which it embodied the aspirations and guided the advancements." (Bancroft, *History,* IV: 7.)

45. Howe, *Letters,* II: 33.

46. Ray Stannard Baker, *The Public Papers of Woodrow Wilson* (New York, 1927), 53.

to serve as the lodestar of democracy, drawing all nations unto herself by her brilliance alone. These assumptions led Bancroft to question how America could expand by example, when the example she portrayed was not complete—when the rule of democracy was not virile enough in the promised land to span the continent.

III

Bancroft's secretary observed that "things concerning God and his country were his patrimony."[47] Contrary to most discussions of Bancroft, the father of American history was more than a Jacksonian chauvinist, progressive optimist, and uncritical glorifier of "his country." Indeed, Bancroft was the universal man for white Americans—the bearer of a tradition that was shared by Jacksonian and Whig alike. Bancroft espoused for white Americans a self-image that recognized America as a covenanted nation, God's preeminent role in her development, and the world's imminent progress towards the millennium through her example. Significantly, this view of America as a chosen nation served to bridle in some ways Bancroft's chauvinism. To whom much is given, much is required, and Bancroft could be quite harsh on "his country" when she relapsed or transgressed in her millennial role, as in the case of slavery.

Bancroft, throughout the better part of the nineteenth century, continued to explain American development by means of providential activity on behalf of a chosen people who would redeem the world. The long tradition of this American self-image, which began in the historical school of William Bradford, Cotton Mather, and Jonathan Edwards, persisted with general approbation throughout the nineteenth century.

Richard Hofstadter observed that Bancroft's volumes "still stand as the greatest monument of the American historical

---

47. See Austin Scott's comment in *The Warner Library: The World's Best Literature,* Vol. III Univ. ed. (New York, 1917), 1433.

self-consciousness of the nineteenth century."[48] In a similar vein, Herbert Baxter Adams asserted that "more than any other American, George Bancroft is the personal embodiment of the historic spirit in these United States."[49] If Adams and Hofstadter were correct in their estimation of Bancroft—and the immense popularity of his writings suggest that they were— Bancroft is a suitable foil to use first in examining the extent to which white Americans, typified by Samuel Hopkins, included blacks in the ideal American image symbolized by Bancroft. And second, Bancroft provides an appropriate background from which to examine the extent to which black Americans in the nineteenth century shared the image of America popularized by Bancroft and the solution to the white dilemma of what to do about the black presence in the picture of the ideal American image proposed by Hopkins. Slavery constituted a glaring violation of America's millennial vocation, and the response of Samuel Hopkins to this violation exemplified an initial attempt to grapple with the black contradiction of America's professed self-image.

48. Richard Hofstadter, *The Progressive Historians* (New York, 1969), 19.
49. See Adams, "Secretary's Report," 6–7.

3

Samuel Hopkins, Father of African Colonization

ON APRIL 8, 1773 Samuel Hopkins, the pastor of Newport, Rhode Island's First Congregational Church, visited "his archrival," Ezra Stiles, and asked him to cosponsor a project for educating and ordaining two black parishioners, John Quamine and Bristol Yamma, as missionaries to Guinea. In the course of Hopkins's visit, Stiles, the pastor of Newport's prestigious and affluent Second Congregational Church (and later president of Yale College), consented to interview one of the hopeful missionaries four days later, simply as a professional courtesy. Stiles granted the interview with John Quamine reluctantly, for the plan smacked too much of a plot to export Hopkins's doctrinal "peculiarities" to poor, defenseless Africa. The "peculiarities" which Stiles found so disturbing were the doctrinal tenets which Jonathan Edwards had elaborated, tenets which were associated too much with the enthusiasm of backcountry revivals to win favor among the more staid pastors of coastal New England. Stiles had little taste for furthering any project that might end in the promotion of emotional frenzy rather than calm good-order maintained by conventional orthodoxy.

Stiles's initially dim view of the African project was echoed a few months later when Charles Chauncy of Boston wrote to Stiles that as far as he was concerned "negroes had better continue in paganism than embrace Mr. H——'s scheme" of theology.[1] For John Quamine, however, success in answering Stiles's questions on the Bible and in reading from the Gospel of John and the Psalms was of more personal concern than just winning support for a general scheme to forward the Kingdom of God on earth by exposing "pagan peoples" in "heathen lands" to the light of Christianity. It was his brothers and sisters who were the "pagans," and it was his birthplace that was "heathen Africa."

John Quamine was ten years old when his father, a wealthy African chieftain from Annamaboe on the African Gold Coast, determined that his son should be exposed to the educational benefits of an American schooling. He commissioned a sea captain to transport his son to Rhode Island and back. But when Quamine arrived in Newport, a major slave market, the sea captain brought him not to the school where Quamine's father supposed he would receive an "English education" but to the trading block. Slavery was to be the "English education" of this chieftain's son.

In his interview with Stiles, Quamine explained how he gradually abandoned his "paganism," fell "under serious impressions of religion" (1761), became a Christian (1764), and in 1765 obtained his freedom when he joined Newport's First Congregational Church (five years before Hopkins became its pastor). When Stiles commented that Quamine possessed everything that a black man could desire, Quamine responded "that ever since he tasted the grace of the Lord

---

1. Chauncy to Stiles, 6 October 1773, in Edwards A. Park, ed., *The Works of Samuel Hopkins,* Vol. I (Boston, 1854), 133, 129 ff.; Franklin Bowditch Dexter, ed., *The Literary Digest of Ezra Stiles,* Vol. I (New York, 1901), 363.

Jesus, he had felt earnest desire or wish that his relations and countrymen in Africa might also come to the knowledge of, and taste the same blessed things."[2]

Although Stiles observed that Quamine needed "much improvement to qualify him for the gospel ministry," he did consent to sign a circular appeal written by Hopkins for the purpose of raising funds for evangelizing Africa by means of black Christian missionaries like Quamine and Yamma.[3] Stiles contended, however, that this "African Mission," as Hopkins dubbed it, would stand a greater chance of success if a society were formed that could round up thirty or forty properly trained blacks who were "inspired with the Spirit of Martyrdom."[4] Within a short period of time the appeal brought in sufficient funds to proceed with the project, and on November 22, 1774, Bristol Yamma and John Quamine were dispatched to Princeton College to receive the necessary theological training for their missionary endeavor.

Even before these two prospective missionaries left for Princeton, the airing of the missionary idea stimulated other blacks to surface and pledge their support. One of the first to respond was Phyllis Wheatley, the black poet, who began to correspond with Hopkins about the African Mission. Abandoning the customary constraints of her neo-classical poetry, she rejoiced in a letter from Boston in February 1774:

Methinks, Rev. Sir, this is the beginning of that happy period foretold by the Prophets, when all shall know the Lord from the least to the greatest and that without the assistance of human Art or Eloquence. My heart expands with sympathetic joy to see at distant time the thick cloud of ignorance dispersing from the face of my benighted country. . . . O that they could partake of the crumbs, the

2. Hopkins, *Works,* I: 130.
3. *Ibid.,* 131–32.
4. Stiles believed that the project would command greater attention if it were expanded to include the Indians, since "it is our bounden duty as Christians and successors on their territory to spare no expense towards effectually carrying the Gospel among them and continuing the offer of grace till they shall have vanished and their Nations shall all be swept off the Earth." (Dexter, ed., *Literary Digest,* I: 364, n. 1.)

precious crumbs, which fall from the table of these distinguished children of the Kingdom.[5]

The American Revolution directed attention to "the shocking, the intolerable . . . gross, barefaced inconsistence" between preachments about civil and religious liberty and the practice of enslaving Africans, a fact which Stiles and Hopkins noted on April 10, 1776 in their second financial appeal for the African Mission, and a theme which Hopkins forcefully framed into "A Dialogue Concerning the Slavery of the Africans . . . Dedicated to the Honorable Continental Congress" and sent in early 1776 to each member of the Continental Congress and to other leading lights throughout the colonies.[6]

At the same time, however, the Revolutionary War diverted time and energy from the mechanics of implementing their plans. Thus Phyllis Wheatley's excitement and the hope generated among other blacks by the proposed African Mission were soon quelled by the outbreak of war. The evangelization of Africa through black missionaries would have to wait. Sadly, the wait was too long for the original candidate, John Quamine, who was killed in an early naval battle in the fall of 1778. He had become a privateer in the war not only to "serve his country" but also to earn enough money to buy his wife's freedom.[7] His death exemplified the tension in the life of many blacks who labored under the push of American Christianity and the pull of American slavery.

The Revolutionary hiatus which interrupted Hopkins's African missionary venture provided an occasion for Hopkins

5. Wheatley to Hopkins, 9 February 1774, in Benjamin Quarles, "Documents: A Phyllis Wheatley Letter," *Journal of Negro History,* XXXIII (October 1948): 464; see also Hopkins, *Works,* I: 127–28, for 6 May 1774 letter from Wheatley.

6. *To the Public, There has been a Design Formed to send the Gospel to Guinea* (Newport, R.I., 1776); Hopkins, *Works,* I: 547–94; see also David A. Swift, "Samuel Hopkins: Calvinist Social Concern in Eighteenth-Century New England," *Journal of Presbyterian History,* XLVII (April 1969): 31–54.

7. Hopkins, *Works,* I: 153; Dexter, ed., *Literary Digest,* II: 378.

to rethink his plans for African evangelization. By 1784, he had abandoned his black-missionary enterprise in favor of a full-fledged African colonizationism. This transformation was the result of what Hopkins interpreted as the imperfect fruits of independence. In the mind of this early champion of black equality, slavery and the slave trade were glaring contradictions to the professed ideals of the Revolution. As the objectives of the rebelling colonists narrowed from what Hopkins saw as the noble affirmations of universal liberty, freedom, and equality to the scandal of limiting these rights to whites only Hopkins's view of the Revolution soured. In an unusual twist of interpretation, Hopkins asserted that God had ordained the Revolution to punish the colonists for their sin of slavery.

A covenanted community which persists in flaunting its sin in the face of God incurs the wrath of the Almighty, and Hopkins had come to view the war in such terms. Without any repentance for their participation in the slave trade, God had first demonstrated his displeasure by causing the impressment of American seamen, an obvious parallel to the seizure of Africans and the traffic in slaves. In similar fashion, God had utilized the tyranny of King, ministers, and Parliament to sensitize the American conscience to the tyranny of slavery.

In the aftermath of the conflict, Americans continued to ignore the lessons that the Lord had sought to teach them and perpetuated on blacks what had formerly been inflicted on them. "If this was a Heaven-daring crime of the first magnitude before the war with Britain," Hopkins wrote with intensity, "how much more criminal must we be *now,* when, instead of regarding the admonitions of Heaven and the light and conviction set before us, and repenting and reforming, we persist in this cruel practice!"[8] Cataloging the complaints and calamities which had befallen Americans in these *"evil times"* since the war, Hopkins traced their source back to a

8. See Hopkins's "The Slave Trade and Slavery" (1787), in Hopkins, *Works,* II: 618–19.

God whose favor with his people had waned with their persistent prodigality.[9] What had begun with so much promise had ended only in massive hypocrisy, and Hopkins queried how much more God would tolerate from a covenanted people who had "the blood of the Africans on our own hands and on our own children."[10]

At the same time that Hopkins feared that God's judgment and vengeance would be visited on the new nation for its sin of slavery (a sin which Hopkins cited as proof that the sixth vial spoken of in Revelation 16:12–16 was being poured out on the earth), Hopkins despaired of whites ever granting blacks their freedom and equality.[11] The intractable prejudice of Americans was to be matched by the inevitable outpouring of divine anger on the nation.

This dilemma, coupled with the influence of English colonizationists such as Granville Sharp and the Quaker William Thornton,[12] transformed Hopkins's plan for Christianizing Africa with a few black missionaries into a plan for colonizing Africa with all black Americans. Hopkins proposed that at first Africa be colonized only by selective black religious congregations, which could lay the groundwork for Christianizing and civilizing the continent with spiritual religion, republican institutions, and bourgeois morality.[13] With the success of these advance colonies in converting the

9. For an exposition of Hopkins's doctrine of "disinterested benevolence," see his *Inquiry into the Nature of True Holiness* (Newport, Rhode Island, 1773), 40–43.

10. Hopkins, *Works,* II: 624; see also David S. Lovejoy, "Samuel Hopkins: Religion, Slavery, and the Revolution," *New England Quarterly,* XL (June 1967): 235.

11. See Hopkins's "Discourse upon the Slave Trade and the Slavery of the Africans, Delivered Before the Providence Society for Abolishing the Slave Trade, etc. . . . at their Annual Meeting, May 17, 1793," in Hopkins, *Works,* II: 604–06; also *Works,* I: 145.

12. P. J. Staudenraus, *The African Colonization Movement 1816–1865* (New York, 1961), 5; see Hopkins's letter to Granville Sharp, 15 January 1789 in *Works,* I: 140–42.

13. Hopkins, *Works,* I: 150, 139.

heathen Africans into "a civilized, Christian, happy people," the excitement would spread among the black population at home and there would be a voluntary exodus of all blacks to the land of their ancestors.

This will gradually draw off all the blacks in New England, and even in the Middle and Southern States, as fast as they can be set free, by which this nation will be delivered from that which, in the view of every discerning man, is a great calamity, and inconsistent with the good of society; and is now really a great injury to most of the white inhabitants, especially in the Southern States.[14]

With the removal of the blemish on America's image, America would thus forestall further divine chastisement for her most insufferable sin and fulfill her destiny as a chosen people.

What had begun before the war as a missionary project of disinterested benevolence became, after the disillusioning incompleteness of the Revolution, a self-interested benevolent project designed to free America of a cause of divine chastisement. Thus missionary emigrationism, which had its origin in Hopkins's concern for the redemption of Africa, was transformed in the crucible of national "patriotism" into colonizationism. Justice to Africa was no longer an end; it was a means to another end, the deterring of divine judgment on American racism. In short, Hopkins reconciled himself to the fact that American nationalism was racist, and its racism national. Given this assumption, the only solution that Hopkins could envision to obviate the peril of America and the plight of blacks was colonization in Africa. Colonization would preserve American nationality and at the same time provide for an African nationality, structured along Christian lines.

The more Hopkins thought about colonization, the more promise it seemed to offer. In the end, he outlined nearly every argument later used by the American Colonization Society to justify the colonization of blacks in Africa. It

14. *Ibid.,* I: 144–45.

would Christianize and civilize a pagan people. It would open up commercial routes with new markets. It would stop the slave trade. It would restore to blacks equality in their "native land." It would establish a distinct feeling of "nationality" among blacks, a prerequisite to their moral, social, and political elevation. It would ward off the wrath of God on America. It would repay a debt to Africa. (Since slavery was a national sin, the entire nation should bear responsibility for its removal, which Hopkins saw possible in governmental assistance to the scheme.) Finally, it would make Americans "active instruments" in hastening the millennium when "all men shall be united into one family and Kingdom under Christ the Savior; and the meek shall inherit the earth, and delight themselves in the abundance of peace."[15]

Just as the Newport black community had responded positively to Hopkins's missionary emigrationism before the war, born out of a desire to elevate Africa, so now they enthusiastically endorsed his plan of African colonization, born out of a desire to elevate Africa and escape America. In September 1789 a black parishioner of Ezra Stiles named Salmar Nubia ("alias Jack Mason") and thirty-nine other members of the Union Society of Africans in Newport, Rhode Island, suggested to the newly formed Philadelphia Free Society that since God had brought them from the "heathenish darkness and

---

15. *Ibid.,* I: 138–50; II: 593–609. For later evidence of the way white colonizationists stressed the need for a development of black nationality, see Rev. F. Freeman, *Africa's Redemption the Salvation of our Country* (New York, 1852; reprinted Freeport, New York, 1969), 302–3; and Jacob Dewees, *The Great Future of America and Africa* (Philadelphia, 1854; reprinted Freeport, New York, 1971), 49, 99, *passim.* Later, colonizationists simply expanded the reasons for colonization introduced by Hopkins, with the exception of the economic justification, proferred by John Adams Dix, that colonization would buttress American economy by replacing slave labor with free labor. It never occurred to Senator Dix that freeing the slaves might have the same effect. (See his 1830 address "On African Colonization," in Chauncey M. Depew, ed., *The Library of Oratory Ancient and Modern,* Vol. VI [New York, 1902], 262–73.)

barbarity" of Africa to "a strange land, attended with many disadvantages and evils which are likely to continue on us and our children, while we and they live in this country," and since God had raised up some whites to "befriend the Africans . . . by proposing and endeavoring to effect their return to their own country," so it would seem fitting for "all the blacks in America" to celebrate publicly and privately the first Tuesday in July as a day of fasting and prayer, always acknowledging "the righteousness of God in bringing all these evils on us" and ever praying that "he would in his wise and good Providence prosper the way for our returning to Africa" as colonizers and Christianizers. The Philadelphia Free African Society, on the other hand, immediately opposed the suggestion, rebuking the Union Society's pessimism about the future of blacks in America, countering their inchoate African nationalism with the assertion that "every pious man is a good citizen of the whole world," while at the same time blessing those who might, for whatever reason, "apprehend a divine injunction" to return to Africa for missionary purposes.[16]

In spite of the rebuke from their black brethren in Philadelphia, the Newport blacks, nourished by Hopkins's speeches and sermons supporting colonization, were not easily discouraged. Thus, Caleb Gardner, a member of Hopkins's church, a music teacher in Newport, and a man of some repute for his musical compositions and abilities, throughout his life sought to maintain fluency in his native African tongue should the opportunity to return to his native land arise. Although Hopkins did not live to see it, tangible institutional expression was given his colonization scheme with the organization of the American Colonization Society in 1816. Ten years later, on January 4, 1826, the first contingent

16. Hopkins, *Works,* I: 136; Rev. William Douglass, *Annals of the First African Church in the United States of America, Now Styled the African Episcopal Church of St. Thomas, Philadelphia* (Philadelphia, 1862), 25–29.

was dispatched. Seventy-year-old Caleb Gardner and eighty-year-old Salmar Nubia, both serving as "deacons" of a religious congregation incorporated the month before, set sail from Boston with sixteen other Rhode Island blacks on the brig *Vine,* destined for Monrovia, Liberia.[17]

What John Quamine and Bristol Yamma had begun as missionary emigrationists, Caleb Gardner and Salmar Nubia had completed as African colonizers. One of the black colonizers explained upon embarking the ship that "I go to set an example to the youth of my race. I go to encourage the young. They can never be elevated here. I have tried it sixty years—it is in vain. Could I by my example lead them to set sail, and I die the next day, I should be satisfied." The missionary enterprise which Phyllis Wheatley had hailed in 1773 as an opportunity for Africa to "partake of the crumbs, the precious crumbs, which fall from the table of these distinguished children of the Kingdom" had ended in 1825 with the anthem, written and composed by Caleb Gardner and sung by the colonizers before they departed for Africa, on the same theme but with a different variation:

> The word that came to Jeremiah
> from the Lord, saying: Write
> thou all the words which I have
> spoken unto thee in a book. For
> lo! the days come, saith the
> Lord, that I will bring again
> the captivity of my people Israel
> and Judah, saith the Lord; and
> I will cause them to return to
> the land that I gave to their
> fathers, and they shall possess
> it. Therefore, fear thou not,
> O my servant Jacob, saith the
> Lord; neither be dismayed, O
> Israel; for lo! I will save
> thee from afar, and thy seed
> from their captivity, and Jacob

17. Hopkins, *Works,* I: 154.

shall return and be in rest and
quiet, and none shall make him
afraid. Amen. Hear the words
of the Lord, O ye African race,
hear the words of promise. But
it is not meet to take the
children's bread and cast it to
dogs. Truth, Lord, yet the dogs
eat of the crumbs that fall from
their masters table. O African,
trust in the Lord. Amen.
Hallelujah. Praise the Lord.
Praise ye the Lord. Hallelujah.
Amen.[18]

The path pursued by Samuel Hopkins and his black parishioners in Newport, Rhode Island, typified the way in which
many black and white Americans would later grapple with
the basic social question that confronted American society
in the nineteenth century—the relationship of blacks to
American life. The motives which prompted the tribal chieftain to send his son to America partially anticipate the later
perspective on slavery revealed by many blacks as they tried
to make sense of the slave experience. John Quamine illustrates the immense pride with which blacks looked upon
their Revolutionary role in the creation of the American nation and the dual interest of blacks in the redemption of
their African ancestors and in the reformation of their
"adopted country." Caleb Gardner and Salmar Nubia illus-
trate the fervent desire to return to Africa of those blacks
who were convinced that America was and always would be
a white man's country—not just as missionaries but as permanent colonizers. The correspondence between the African
Union Society of Newport, Rhode Island, and the Free African
Society of Philadelphia reveal the early dispute among free
blacks over the future of the race in America and the attempt by the most disillusioned segment of black leadership

18. *Ibid.,* 156.

to organize and mobilize black opinion in favor of colonization, even to the point of creating a rival celebration to the Fourth of July. Samuel Hopkins, the man who first conceived the idea of colonization, illustrates the dilemma of many whites who, concerned both for the welfare of blacks and for the well-being of the nation, sacrificed the former for the latter. Hopkins's rationale for colonizing blacks in Africa presages how the American Colonization Society, nearly thirty years later, would try and put a little bit into its colonization proposals for everyone: slave, slaveholder, slaveless, and freed slave. Finally, Hopkin's interpretation of the unfinished nature of the American Revolution presages the outlook on American history of many nineteenth-century black leaders, like Frederick Douglass, and of white historians, like George Bancroft.

4

The Black Response to the Colonizationist Image of America

By birth we are American citizens—by the facts of history and the admission of American statesmen. We are American citizens —by the courage and fidelity displayed by our ancestors in defending the liberties and in achieving the independence of our land, we are American citizens. Among the colored people we can point, with pride and hope, to men of education and refinement, who have become such despite the most unfavorable influence. We can point to mechanics, farmers, merchants, teachers, ministers, doctors, lawyers, editors and authors against whose progress the concentrated energies of American prejudice have proven quite unavailing.

RESOLUTION PASSED BY THE LARGEST ANTEBELLUM BLACK CONVENTION, ROCHESTER, NEW YORK, JULY 6–8, 1853

HENRY WARD BEECHER spoke for most white Americans when he announced that "if I had been God, I would not have made them [Negroes] at all; but since He who is wiser than all of us put together has seen fit to make them, and bring them here, what are you going to do with them?"[1] Ac-

1. Quoted in Emma Willard, *The African in America, To Find His True Position, and Place Him in It, The Via Media on which the North and South Might Meet in a Permanent and Happy Settlement* (n.p., n.d.), 1. A similar query can be found in Richard Fuller, *Our Duty to the African Race: An Address Delivered at Washington, D.C. January 21, 1851* (Baltimore, 1851), 4.

cording to Frederick Douglass, the answer of most Americans who bothered even asking the question of "what they shall do with us" was the same as Hopkins's solution—"Be gone."[2]

The formation of the American Colonization Society was in keeping with Douglass's observation.[3] Founded in 1816 by a New Jersey clergyman named Robert Finley, the ostensible purpose of the American Colonization Society was to forward the crusade for the Redeemer's Kingdom.[4] The colonization vision was the establishment of a black Christian empire in Africa paralleling the white Christian empire in America, thereby providing twin beacons of light in anticipation of the day when the spirit of true Christianity would rule the globe.

2. Of course, Douglass believed that the only legitimate answer to the question was an affirmation of self-determination: "Do nothing with us." (See Philip S. Foner, ed., *The Life and Writings of Frederick Douglass*, 4 vols. [New York, 1955], II: 169; IV: 164.) Archibald Alexander began his *History of Colonization on the Western Coast of Africa* (Philadelphia, 1846) declaring that "the best method of disposing of the free people of colour" was a topic of "Momentous consequence" (1).

3. William Lloyd Garrison, *Thoughts on African Colonization, or an Impartial Exhibition of the Doctrines, Principles and Purposes of the American Colonization Society. Together with the Resolutions, Addresses and Remonstrances of the Free People of Color* (Boston, 1832; reprinted New York, 1968), 102–3. Hoping to capitalize on the fear of slave revolts generated by Nat Turner's insurrection, Robert Finley toured Baltimore in 1832, trying to drum up support for colonization. Finley complained that while whites (boosted by their visions of black bands of rebels bent on murder and revenge) were generally enthusiastic about colonization, blacks were downright hostile about the idea. So hostile, in fact, that the Maryland Colonization Society gave up going into the western shore region of Maryland to recruit black emigrants. (See Penelope Campbell, *Maryland in Africa: The Maryland State Colonization Society* [Chicago, 1971], 39–40, 42.) Charles I. Foster argues that white colonization sentiment peaked during the furor over Turner's insurrection. (See his "Colonization of Free Negroes in Liberia, 1816–1835," *Journal of Negro History,* XXXVIII [January 1953]: 55.) Richard C. Wade has shown in his case study of how Cincinnati whites dealt with the problem of the free black in white society that hostility towards blacks, which was reflected in the growth of colonization societies, increased as the free black population grew. (See his "Negro in Cincinnati, 1800–1830," *Journal of Negro History,* XXXIX [January 1954]: 53–57.)

4. Staudenraus makes this connection between colonization and millennialism in his *African Colonization,* 42–67, 150–68.

Inspired by dreams of a multifaceted Christian empire spanning the globe, white colonizationists responded to a twofold summons: to forward the realization of this empire by the contagion of America's own example and to hasten the happy day by the further expedient of an African colonization project spearheaded by black Americans. Men like Henry Clay could look forward to the day when western Africa would boast mini-American black republics, and the Reverend F. Freeman unabashedly declared that to colonize the blacks was the only step of Christian patriotism available, for the American Colonization Socity "is preparing the way for the final REDEMPTION of *Africa,* and for the universal sway of THE KINGDOM OF THE LORD JESUS! *Who will presume to stay its progress?* To detach from its holy influence is TREASON TO OUR COUNTRY—MOST UNMERCIFUL TO AFRICA—SACRILEGE IN THE VIEW OF HEAVEN!"[5]

In their attempt to sell the colonizationist product as an essential part of American national policy, the organizers and officials of the American Colonization Society proved themselves masters in the art of effective publicity and promotional techniques. Their most clever advertising device consisted of giving public-opinion makers exalted honorary positions that required nothing more than their signatures. The list of officers at one time or another boasted the names of James Madison, John Randolph, Andrew Jackson, Daniel Webster, Henry Clay, Francis Scott Key, John Marshall, Richard Rush, William Henry Seward, Matthew Carey, Edward Everett, General Winfield Scott, and many more, thus making it appear as if national leadership as a whole had been persuaded to climb aboard the colonizationist bandwagon.[6]

The wooing of the black community by the American Colonization Society was less easy, necessitating more sophis-

5. Henry Clay is quoted in Garrison, *Thoughts on African Colonization,* "Appendix" (no pagination); Freeman, *Africa's Redemption,* 296.

6. As late as 1849, when Henry Clay was President of the American Colonization Society ("He is President of nothing else," chided Frederick Douglass), Douglass lamented that "almost every respectable man belongs to it, either by direct membership or by affinity." (See

ticated tactics, since, as a society director admitted, "the free people of color, taken as a community, look on our undertaking with disaffection."[7] The most common strategy of the colonizationists was to lure influential black leaders with the prospect of power, wealth, and prestige if only they would lead the exodus to Liberia. When this proved unsuccessful, the society tried more subtle and disingenuous tactics. The crafty Elliott Cresson, for example, proposed that since the opinion of the wealthy Philadelphia sailmaker and Revolutionary War veteran James Forten "has great weight with our colored population," Forten should be offered "great commercial advantages" if only he would establish a trading line between Philadelphia and Liberia, thereby in some way associating his prestige with the colonization endeavor.[8]

Thwarted even in the use of economics and flattery, the colonizationists finally resorted to threats against free blacks and to indoctrinating the minds of black children through the publication of a small primer written by John H. B. Latrobe, a Baltimore attorney and Maryland's leading colonization spokesman. Featuring testimonials of black colonists, the primer stressed the existence of Africa as the "only natural home" of black peoples and the folly of the puerile optimism that blacks would someday attain equal status with whites in America. The primer concluded with a hymn:

> Land of our fathers, Af-ri-ca,
> We turn our thoughts to thee—
> To gain thy shores we'll gladly bear
> The storm upon the sea.[9]

Foner, ed., *Douglass,* I: 390.) For the extent of clerical involvement in colonization, see John R. Bodo, *The Protestant Clergy and Public Issues, 1812–1848* (Princeton, New Jersey, 1954), 119: "No single group was more devoted to its program than the theocrats."

7. *Fifteenth Annual Report of the American Colonization Society* (Washington, D.C., 1833), xiii–ix.

8. Staudenraus, *African Colonization,* 190.

9. *Ibid.* This little poem can also be found in *Claims of the Africans: or The History of the American Colonization Society* (Boston, 1872),

The attribution to blacks of "gladness" and willingness to return to Africa was for the most part gratuitous, for there is evidence to suggest that some blacks were threatened with imprisonment and even death if they balked at colonization. In January 1835, for example, a group of thirty-three slaves belonging to a Charles County, Maryland, family were freed, subjecting them to an 1832 law which provided for the removal from the state of manumitted slaves. When an official of the Maryland State Colonization Society tried to recruit the thirty-three blacks as emigrants they refused, whereupon the official informed them that if they did not go to Liberia they would ultimately be starved, jailed, or hanged. Much to his exasperation, they still refused to be persuaded.[10]

To the puzzlement of the white colonizationists, the group to whom their benevolence was directed seldom responded, except in anger. In cities like New York, Philadelphia, Richmond, Charleston, and Cincinnati, where the black community was large and alert, black leaders, almost to a person, denounced the scheme as a "gigantic fraud" and an "evil trick," refusing to be intimidated by the ostentatious display of what the fugitive-slave preacher, teacher, and author, James W. C. Pennington, termed "a diseased public opinion" among their white benefactors.[11] Instead, black leaders attempted to mobilize public opinion on their own by organizing mass meetings of blacks in local, state, and national conventions to demonstrate black opposition to the society. The organization of the American Colonization Society in December 1816 thus provided the occasion for a rallying cry to be sounded, summoning the blacks to their first mass meeting, to be held in Philadelphia scarcely a month later. The commotion over the meaning, meth-

145. This anonymous children's textbook, published by the Massachusetts Sabbath School Union, is a dialogue between children and their parents on the merits of colonization. At the end of each chapter is a series of questions on which the child could be quizzed.

10. Campbell, *Maryland in Africa,* 104–06.

11. Staudenraus, *African Colonization,* 188–89, 191; Pennington to *Liberator,* 5 March 1852.

ods, and motives of the American Colonization Society did more to generate black solidarity and engender a sense of identity among the black community than any other single issue in the first half of the nineteenth century. Blacks were so united in their uproar against colonization, furthermore, that they compelled many white abolitionists to listen and to change their tune.

The black historian, novelist, and Harvard-trained physician, Martin R. Delany, looked back with pride on the history of the abolitionist movement in America, for it demonstrated that "Anti-Slavery took its rise among *colored men*" and that "our Anti-Slavery brethren were converts of the colored men in behalf of their elevation."[12] Delany did not give specific historical details, but the black newspaper *Freedom's Journal* (1827) antedated by four years Garrison's the *Liberator* (1831), and Garrison credited the wealthy Philadelphia sailmaker and temperance, peace, and women's-rights advocate, James Forten, with being instrumental in convincing him of black equality. More important, the pioneering leadership of blacks in the anti-slavery movement was most apparent in the shift of posture which they forced upon white anti-slavery leaders. Before blacks spoke out against colonization, it had promenaded hand-in-hand with anti-slavery as two steps in a single cause.

If Archibald Alexander, the first major nineteenth-century historian of colonization and the first dean of Princeton Seminary, is right in arguing that abolitionism as a forceful movement to be reckoned with originated in the commotion over colonization, then blacks, indeed, fathered the abolitionist movement.[13] It was not until after the black community

12. Martin R. Delany, *The Condition, Elevation, Emigration, and Destiny of the Colored People of the United States* (New York, 1852), in Howard Brotz, ed., *Negro Social and Political Thought, 1850–1920* (New York, 1966), 44.
13. Alexander, *History of Colonization*, 380–81. It is interesting to note in this context the great influence of another proscribed sector of society—women. Lydia Maria Child's *Appeal in Favor of that Class of Americans called Africans* (1833) converted to the anti-slavery crusade

made clear its unalterable opposition to colonization that white abolitionist leaders such as William Lloyd Garrison, Arthur and Lewis Tappan, and Gerrit Smith, denounced the scheme. The English observer Edward Strutt Abdy, who was converted to an anti-colonizationist opinion by his close friend Peter Williams, posited that the nagging negatives of colonization ironically had "united the friends of the black man and sown dissension among his enemies." The black abolitionist William J. Watkins helped to coax Garrison from his pro-colonization position prior to the *Liberator* to his anti-colonization stance after 1831. The minister and editor Samuel E. Cornish received most of the credit for reasoning Gerrit Smith out of the colonizationist fold, and Arthur Tappan was finally won over to the anti-colonizationist persuasion when he was convinced that the majority of blacks rejected the idea and feared its implications.[14] If blacks had not vigorously exerted themselves in defiant protest against the colonization solution to the problem of the free black in American society, it seems fair to assume that the anti-slavery movement would have remained captivated by the logic of colonization.

While colonizationists prescribed black transplantation to Africa as the antidote to the nation's ills, most blacks labeled

such important leaders as Wendell Phillips, Thomas Wentworth Higginson, Charles Sumner, and William Ellery Channing. (See Alma Lutz, *Crusade for Freedom: Women of the Anti-slavery Movement* [Boston, 1926], 26.)

14. See Ray Allen Billington, "James Forten: Forgotten Abolitionist," in John Bracey, Jr., August Meier, and Elliott Rudwick, eds., *Blacks in the Abolitionist Movement* (Belmont, California, 1970), 5; Bertram Wyatt-Brown, *Lewis Tappan and the Evangelical War Against Slavery* (Cleveland, 1969), 88; Leon F. Litwack, *North of Slavery: The Negro in the Free States, 1790–1860* (Chicago, 1961), 26–27; Edward Strutt Abdy, *Journal of a Residence and Tour in the United States of North America from April, 1833 to October, 1834,* Vol. I (London, 1835), 123; and the New York *Anglo-African* (October 1859) as reproduced in Herbert Aptheker, ed., *A Documentary History of the Negro People in the United States* (New York, 1951), 99.

the antidote poison. The tendency of white Americans to boost colonization as a panacea was matched by the tendency of black Americans to blast the "anti-republican and anti-Christian" colonization schemes as the prime reason for their persistent subjugation.

A large public gathering of blacks in New York City in January, 1839 unanimously expressed its irreversible hostility to the American Colonization Society, which "is the source whence proceed most of the various prescriptions and oppressions under which we groan and suffer." Samuel E. Cornish of Newark and Theodore S. Wright of New York City, two black Presbyterian ministers, traced the way in which slavery induced prejudice, prejudice induced colonization, and colonization induced the perpetual oppression of free blacks. Concluding their denunciation of colonizationists as wolves in sheep's clothing, they condemned colonization as

a scheme which nourished an unreasonable and unchristian prejudice—which persuades legislators to continue their unjust enactments against us in all their rigor—which exposes us to the persecution of the proud profligate—which cuts us off from employment, and straitens our means of substance—which afflicts us with the feeling, that our condition is unstable, and prevents us from making systematic effort for our improvement, or for the advancement of our usefulness and happiness and that of our families.[15]

Likewise, grocer David Ruggles ended his vitriolic treatise exposing the "deathly scheme" of colonization by attributing to it the enervation of black Americans. Likening it to " '*a moral Upas tree,* beneath whose pestiferous shades all intellect must languish and all virtue die,' " Ruggles arraigned

15. Cited by Samuel E. Cornish and Theodore S. Wright, *The Colonization Scheme Considered, in its Rejection by the Colored People—in its Tendency to Uphold Caste—in its Unfitness for Christianizing and Civilizing the Aborignes of Africa, and for Putting a Stop to the African Slave Trade: In a Letter to the Honorable Benjamin F. Batter and the Honorable Theodore Frelinghuyser* (Newark, New Jersey, 1840), 4, 26. The *Colored American* (9 May 1840) endorsed Wright's and Cornish's book against colonization and encouraged its readers to buy and distribute it.

the American Colonization Society for producing "enactments hostile to *coloured schools,* and to our elevation in any other way, in *'this, our own, our native* land.' "[16]

Although Frederick Douglass did not succumb to the facile idea that the subterfuge of colonization explained in large measure the oppression of black Americans, he did impute to the colonization society the perpetuation of the basic motivation which impeded black elevation in America —the exclusion of blacks from an American destiny. Looking back in 1859 at the history of black oppression in America, he judged that "no one idea has given rise to more oppression and persecution toward the colored people of this country, than that which makes Africa, not America, their home." The "jesuitical" teachings of the American Colonization Society, Douglass believed, engendered a Jim Crow mentality "that elbows us off the sidewalk, and denies us the rights of citizenship."[17]

In sum, colonization was so widely anathematized that David Ruggles (from 1838 to 1840 editor and publisher of the short-lived *Mirror of Liberty*) could claim without hesitation to be speaking for all black citizens when he suggested that a stop should be put to any further discussion of the entire question of colonization. The majority of white public opinion might favor having blacks "banished to that Sepulchre, LIBERIA," but Ruggles was certain that every black American rejected "colonization to Africa as a remedy for slavery, or as a relief from its bitter fruits." He was convinced that he could without qualification "take it for granted that no two Americans at most, who are despised and oppressed

16. David Ruggles, *The "Extinguisher" Extinguished; or David M. Reese, M.D. "Used Up." Together with Some Remarks Upon a Late Production, entitled 'An Address on Slavery and Against Immediate Emancipation with a Plan of their Being Gradually Emancipated and Colonized in Thirty-Two Years. By Herman Howlett'* (New York, 1834), 40.

17. *Douglass' Monthly* (February 1859), in Foner, ed., *Douglass,* II: 443.

on account of the color of their skin, and whom this appeal shall reach, are in favor of the *American Colonization Society.*"[18]

For the most part, Ruggles's sweeping generalization proved accurate. Before the melancholy events of the 1850s, northern blacks arrayed themselves in a nearly solid phalanx against what black historian William C. Nell described as "the hydra-headed monster, Colonization" and against those whom the black abolitionist Charles Lenox Remond denounced as the "negro-hating colonizationists."[19] In general, black resistance to colonization was in direct proportion to the widespread conviction that black Americans had earned and deserved the right to be included as American citizens. The colonizationist attempt at the expatriation of black Americans was viewed as a thinly-veiled disguise for the exclusion of blacks from the privileges and just desserts of their labors in America and, more than this, for the extirpation of black peoples. In rejoinder to the colonizationists' program, black Americans demanded inclusion into American society. They were to be included, not as a "gift" from whites, but as a "right" grounded, as Frederick Douglass insisted, on their contributions to American history.[20]

I

The invocation of black participation in American history as an organic ingredient in the development of the nation gave impetus to a sense of black identity. Forced to examine the colonizationist claim that nothing was in the offing for them in America but everything would be theirs in Africa,

18. David Ruggles, "Appeals to the colored citizens of New York and elsewhere in behalf of the press," in Dorothy Porter, ed., *Early Negro Writing, 1760–1837* (Boston, 1971), 642, 645.

19. William C. Nell, *The Colored Patriots of the American Revolution* (Boston, 1855), 344; *Liberator,* 21 May 1841.

20. *North Star,* 26 January 1849, in Foner, ed., *Douglass,* I: 351–52; see also Douglass's speech on the American Colonization Society, given in Faneuil Hall, 8 June 1849, 394 ff. of Foner's volume.

blacks retraced their history in America and found that they had done nothing for Africa but everything for America.

Purporting to reflect the sentiments of "thirty thousand disfranchised citizens of Philadelphia," a memorial to the United States Congress, signed by the Philadelphia dentist James McCrummill and other black leaders, professed that blacks possessed "the highest claims to the privilege of citizenship, since the first blood shed upon the altar of American Republicanism, and consecrated its sail to liberty and independence, was that of Crispus Attucks, a 'colored man' "[21] When but a child, the black Baptist preacher Jeremiah Asher recalled reaching the conclusion, based on the tales of two black veterans of the American Revolution, that "I had more rights than any white man in the town." William J. Watkins, assistant editor of *Frederick Douglass' Paper* in 1855, queried his white audience, "Why should *you* be a chosen people more than me?" when both white and black shared a common revolutionary grave in the struggle for liberty and independence.[22] Blacks had done as much to fashion the American nation as most whites. This realization sometimes added a note of militancy to black opposition to colonization and to black assertion of American status.

In challenging her black brothers to assert their manhood in opposing colonization, the feminist orator Maria W. Stewart attacked the way in which "now that we have enriched their soil, and filled their coffers, they say that we are not capable of becoming like white men, and that we never

21. *Memorial of Thirty Thousand Disfranchised Citizens of Philadelphia, to the Honorable Senate and House of Representatives* (Philadelphia, 1855), 13.

22. Jeremiah Asher, *An Autobiography, With Details of a Visit to England, And Some Account of the History of the Meeting Street Baptist Church, Providence, Rhode Island, and of the Shiloh Baptist Church, Philadelphia, Pennsylvania* (Philadelphia, 1862), 5; William J. Watkins, *Our Rights as Men: An Address Delivered in Boston, Before the Legislative Committee on the Militia, February 24, 1853* (Boston, 1855), in Dorothy Porter, ed., *Negro Protest Pamphlets* (New York, 1969), 11–12.

can rise to respectability in this country. They would drive us to a strange land. But before I go, the bayonet shall pierce me through."[23] Equally militant was the action envisioned by the *Colored American*—unswerving agitation for "universal emancipation, and universal enfranchisement," and determined resistance to colonization. "Should we die in the pursuit," continued an editorial, "we will die *virtuous martyrs* in a holy cause."[24]

David Ruggles was even more explicit in counseling resistance to the officious efforts of the colonization society. Addressing all "Colored Americans," he admonished them:

Rise, brethren, rise! Strike for freedom, or die slaves! The storm of colonization has come upon our brethren in Maryland, and threatens to visit us throughout this land. Come up, and help us! In our cause, mere words are nothing—action is everything.[25]

Evidently many Maryland blacks anticipated Ruggles's call to action, for Maryland seemed to be a nursery for black revolts against the colonizationists. As soon as preparations for the voyage of the *Orion* to Liberia became known, free blacks in Maryland held public meetings against the expedition and repeatedly visited the homes of the prospective emigrants to try to persuade them against colonization. Not only had they whittled down by one-half the number of willing emigrants by the date of embarkation in the fall of 1831, but they followed the remaining colonizers on board and pleaded with them until the last minute to return to their homes. When the next group of black colonizers left in 1833, the tactics of the black citizens of Baltimore had graduated to violence. The Maryland Colonization Society had to ask Baltimore City officials to protect the black emigrants from being molested

23. See Maria Stewart's 1833 address in Porter, ed., *Early Negro Writing,* 133.
24. *Colored American,* 15 April 1837.
25. Printed in the *Liberator,* 13 August 1841, and in Carter G. Woodson, ed., *The Mind of the Negro as Reflected in Letters Written During the Crisis, 1800–1860* (Washington, D.C., 1926), 252.

by anti-colonizationist black agitators.[26] Thus it was entirely within the Maryland tradition of black anti-colonizationist activity that a Maryland convention of blacks meeting in 1859 to debate emigration featured an outburst of physical violence by those blacks who desired to remain at home.[27]

In 1844 James McCune Smith responded to the Sixth Census of the United States, released in 1841, which purported to reveal that the incidence of idiocy and insanity among the free black population was already eleven times higher than among the slaves. The response of the respected black doctor was voiced in an 1844 letter to the editor of the *New York Tribune.* "Freedom has not made us mad," he countered, "it has strengthened our minds by throwing us upon our own resources and has bound us to American institutions with a tenacity which nothing but death can overthrow."[28]

There was one "peculiar" American institution which bound itself to three million blacks with a tenacity which nothing but death could overthrow, and it was this institution that Frederick Douglass, perhaps speaking figuratively rather than literally, came to believe should be overthrown by death —not death of the slave, but of the slaveholder. In a devastating upbraiding of the American Colonization Society, Douglass shocked his white audience in Faneuil Hall, Boston, by declaring (in 1849) that if it were in the tradition of American history for a people to revolt against a three-penny tea tax, it should be equally welcome in the American tradition if "the sable arms which had been engaged in beautifying and adorning the South were engaged in spreading death and devastation there."[29]

26. Campbell, *Maryland in Africa,* 28, 44.
27. *Liberator,* 26 August 1859, and *Douglass' Monthly,* March 1859.
28. Smith to *New York Tribune,* 29 January 1844, was reprinted in the *Liberator,* 23 February 1844. See also David J. Rothman, *The Discovery of the Asylum: Social Order and Disorder in the New Republic* (Boston, 1971), 112, for a discussion of insanity viewed as a measure of progress.
29. Foner, ed., *Douglass,* I: 398–99.

It remained for the towering David Walker, however, to warn whites in a literal sense of a bloody end to slavery. In perhaps the most militant document to emerge from the abolitionist movement, Walker's 1829 "Appeal" intransigently insisted that blacks should remain in their native land, daring the colonizationists to come and get them and test black wrath.

Let no man of us budge one step, and let slave-holders come to beat us from our country. America is more our country, than it is the whites—we have enriched it with our *blood and tears*. The greatest riches in all America have arisen from our blood and tears:—and will they drive us from our property and homes, which we have earned with our blood? They must look sharp or this very thing will bring swift destruction upon them. The Americans have got so fat upon our blood and groans, that they have almost forgotten the God of armies. But let them go on.[30]

II

In defiance of the prevailing contention that there was something incompatible, if not inimical, in the juxtaposition of black and American, free northern blacks in the nineteenth century affirmed both their blackness and their identity as Americans. In contending that "we are strongly American in our character and disposition," the *Colored American* admitted that it could see "nothing to approve" in the American people's "relation to us" and "much to disapprove." Nevertheless, "we are attached to the American soil, and to American institutions."[31]

The development of a black press constituted a crucial role in this ethnic sense of dual identity as blacks and Americans. Although financial failures and mainly extensions of individual personalities, newspapers of, for, and by blacks provided not only a forum and an audience for black Ameri-

30. David Walker, *Walker's Appeal, in Four Articles, Together with a Preamble, to the Colored Citizens of the World, but in Particular, and very expressly to those of the United States of America,* 2nd ed. (Boston, 1830; reprinted New York, 1969), 76.
31. *Colored American,* 9 May 1840.

cans and an organ for unifying the black community, they also stood as virtually singular sources of information on American history and on the role of blacks in that history, both in the past and present. The first issue of the *Weekly Advocate* devoted its fourth page to "a valuable Geographical, Historical, and Statistical account of our own country," and subsequent issues featured front-page episodic treatments of American history, state-by-state histories, and biographies of the Founding Fathers.[32]

Such newspapers served to educate blacks in their involvement in American history as soldiers, as labor-producing slaves, as a persecuted minority, and as abolitionists, while simultaneously educating them in American history in general. In the newspapers' reporting of resistance to slavery, and assistance for the fugitive slave, blacks saw mirrored their manhood and dignity. In the recounting of the travails and traumas of a slave-labor class, blacks saw that their vested economic interests lay in America and that, in fact, they held a preemptive claim by labor to the fruits of their toil. In the recording of significant events and developments in the abolitionist movement, they heard both black and white voices raised for the removal of "the giant sin of oppression from our land," allowing them the luxury of hope. In the recital of their role in the American Revolution and in the War of 1812, blacks saw crimson proof of their participation in the creation and preservation of the American nation.

Finally, in the reconstruction of American history from a black perspective and in the recollection of a common heritage as slaves, a black newspaper entitled the *New Era* believed that the slave experience might serve as examples to America and "warnings against injustice, to be cited as sad examples of that perversion which noble principles may undergo, when the children drift from the teachings of the fathers, when expedience and wrong are substituted for

32. *Weekly Advocate,* January 1837 issues.

right."[33] In such a manner did these journals help to inculcate a sense of racial solidarity, a sense of black American history, a visceral conviction that blacks belonged in America as much as the whites, and a cerebral attachment to the ideals, at least, of the American nation. Regardless of the degree of militancy, which ranged from the moderate *Colored American* to "one of the most militant of black abolitionist papers," the *Weekly Anglo-African*,[34] the titles chosen by the black press before the Civil War lectured Americans in their dual identity as the *Disfranchised American*, the *Aliened American*, the *Colored Citizen*, and the *True American* (which wedded in 1850 with Stephen Myers's *Northern Star and Freeman's Advocate* to form the *Impartial Citizen*).[35]

The uncertainty over what black Americans should call themselves, which manifested itself in their periodical titles and editorials, can be attributed in large measure to the disdain with which they held anything associated with the colonizationists.[36] Because of the refusal of many of the organizers

33. *New Era*, 5 May 1870, in Martin E. Dann, ed., *The Black Press, 1827–1890: The Quest for National Identity* (New York, 1971), 58–59.

34. *Ibid.*, 78.

35. Cf. the comments of Junius C. Morel (a leader of the early convention movement) and John P. Thompson, describing why they wanted to entitle their proposed publication *The American* (*Liberator*, 2 July 1831).

36. Henry Highland Garnet deemed it "unprofitable" for blacks "to spend our golden moments in long and solemn debate upon the questions whether we shall be called 'Africans,' 'Colored Americans,' or 'Africo Americans,' or 'Blacks.' The question should be, my friends, *shall we arise and act like men, and cast off this terrible yoke?*" (See *The Past and the Present Condition and the Destiny of the Colored Race* [Troy, 1848], in Earl Ofari, *"Let Your Motto Be Resistance": The Life and Thought of Henry Highland Garnet* [Boston, 1972], Appendix, 173.) By the end of the nineteenth century, this "debate" over terminology had still not been settled. The journalist T. Thomas Fortune led the campaign for the designation "Afro-American," and he was supported by the National Federation of Afro-American Women and Professors J. W. E. Bowen and W. S. Scarborough. Fortune's friend Booker T. Washington insisted on the word "Negro" spelled with a capital *N*, and Washington was supported by W. E. B. Du Bois, Alexander Crummell, the American

of the American Colonization Society to call blacks anything but "Africans" since, as Robert Finley remarked, they were all "sons of Africa" and destined by God to dwell exclusively in "the land of their fathers,"[37] many blacks reluctantly abandoned the designation "African" or "Free African." One could legitimately speak of the Irish, the Swiss, the German, or the English presence in America without any implicit denial that one was an American. But with the widespread currency of the colonizationist cant that, as the Third Annual National Negro Convention noted, once an African, always an African,[38] the African ethnic label carried too much of a stigma for many blacks, who felt the need for an explicit dual identification affirming both African origin and American status. For this reason apellations such as "colored Americans" and "oppressed Americans" became popular among various black leaders.

At the 1835 black convention held in Philadelphia, William Whipper proposed a resolution, which was adopted unanimously, that the title "African" should be removed from the

---

Negro Academy, and a majority of black leaders, according to a sample poll published by the *New York Tribune* on 10 June 1906. (See Thornbrough, *T. Thomas Fortune,* 127, 131–35.)

37. P. J. Staudenraus, *African Colonization,* 19–20.

38. *Minutes and Proceedings of the Third Annual Convention for the Improvement of the Free People of Colour . . . 1833* (New York, 1833), 35. The conventional address was given by the president of the convention, Abraham D. Shadd. A convention of Rochester, New York, blacks, meeting in October 1831, adamantly insisted that "we do not consider Africa to be our home, any more than the present whites do England, Scotland, or Ireland." (See Garrison, *Thoughts on African Colonization,* "Sentiments of the People of Color,") 43. James McCune Smith wrote that "the people of those days rejoiced in their nationality, and hesitated not to call each other 'Africans,' or 'descendants of Africa'; it was in after years, when they set up their just protest against the American Colonization Society and its principles that the term 'African' fell into descries and finally discredit." (See Smith's introduction, "Sketch of the Life and Labor of Rev. Henry Highland Garnet," to Garnet's *Memorial Discourse: Delivered in the hall of the House of Representatives, Washington, D.C., On Sabbath, February 12, 1865* [Philadelphia, 1865], 24.)

names of churches, lodges, societies, and all black institutions.[39] Acutely sensitive to the slightest indication that they were other than Americans, the ultra-integrationist American Moral Reform Society opposed the term "African" or even "colored." They were Americans, but not yet full-fledged Americans. They were best described as "oppressed Americans."[40] The anti-colonizationist New York minister and former editor of the first black newspaper, *Freedom's Journal,* Samuel E. Cornish, demurred from this term's lackluster descriptiveness. "Oppressed Americans! *who are they!*" he scoffed. "Nonsense, brethren! You are COLORED AMERICANS. The Indians are RED AMERICANS, and the white people are WHITE AMERICANS, and *you are as good as they, and they are no better than you.*"[41]

In an attempt to end this dispute over terminology, which reflected the disputed status of blacks in American life, Cornish thus baptized the term "Colored American" in March 1837 (upon assuming editorial responsibilities for the *Weekly Advocate*) in the hope that it would become a common shibboleth among blacks in America. Explaining why the paper's name would be changed to the *Colored American,* the outgoing editor of the *Advocate,* Philip A. Bell, wrote that "it is short, emphatic and distinctive. We are *Americans,—colored* Americans, brethren,—and let it be our aim to make the title '*Colored American,*' as honorable, and as much respected before the world, as '*white Americans,*' or any other."[42]

Owned by Philip Bell, edited by Samuel Cornish, and initially subsidized by Arthur Tappan, the first editorial in

39. *Minutes of the Fifth Annual Convention for the Improvement of the Free People of Colour . . . 1835* (Philadelphia, 1835), 15.

40. Cromwell, *Negro in American History,* 35. The search for a proper designation for black Americans ran through the nineteenth century. As late as 1895 the editor of the *Afro-American* revealed his hatred of the word "Negro" and deemed acceptable only the phrases "colored" and "Afro-American." (See *Afro-American,* 3 August 1895.)

41. Quoted in Litwack, *North of Slavery,* 238.

42. *Weekly Advocate,* 25 February 1837.

the *Colored American* was entitled "Title of This Journal." Cornish acknowledged the "diversity of opinion" regarding the title, especially those blacks who wondered why it was necessary to "draw this cord of caste" by the word "colored." To justify the distinction of color, Cornish observed that there was a need for an inoffensive, distinctive name for a distinctive people. "We are written about, preached to, and prayed for, as *Negroes, Africans,* and *blacks,* all of which have been stereotyped as names of reproach, and on that account, if no other, are unacceptable." Yet the identification of color was not enough, for to carry the African color said nothing of one's nationality, notwithstanding the colonizationists.

Many would rob us of the endeared name, 'Americans,' a distinction more emphatically belonging to us, than five-sixths of this nation, and one that we will never yield. In complexion, in blood and nativity, we are decidedly more exclusively 'American' than our white brethren; hence the propriety of the name of our people, *Colored Americans,* and of identifying the name with all our institutions, in spite of our enemies, who would rob us of our nationality and reproach us as exoticks.[43]

This last charge, the colonizationist tag of "foreigners" and "exoticks," was particularly offensive to two of the most influential black leaders in the first third of the nineteenth century, Richard Allen and James Forten, both of whom pioneered in establishing independent black congregations and both of whom organized black protest meetings against colonization. Allen, in addressing an 1830 convention of free blacks, demonstrated that a sense of identity with the plight of Africa and a blatant identification with America were not mutually exclusive. The injury inflicted by America on Africa and on her "sons and daughters" would stand as monuments of gross wickedness, he stated. Yet "we who have been born and nurtured on this soil, we, whose habits, manners, and customs are the same in common with other Americans, can never consent to take our lives in our hands, and be the

43. *Colored American,* 4 March 1837.

bearers of the redress offered by that Society to that much afflicted country."[44] In 1833 James Forten, the veteran black abolitionist who had recruited twenty-five hundred black patriots from Philadelphia to defend the city against the threat of the British during the War of 1812, summed up with characteristic sarcasm his views on colonization as an old man:

Here I have dwelt until I am nearly seventy years of age, and have brought up and educated a family, as you see, thus far. Yet some ingenious gentlemen have recently discovered that I am still an African; that a continent, three thousand miles, and more, from the place where I was born is my native country. And I am advised to go home. Well, it may be so. Perhaps if I should only be set on the shores of that distant land, I should recognize all I might see there, and run at once to the old hut where my forefathers lived a hundred years ago.[45]

But it was not just because blacks were born here and had adopted the best of American values, customs, and beliefs that they demanded the right to call American home and rejected the claims of African nationality. With bracing forthrightness, black leaders flaunted their willing sacrifices in America's war efforts in the face of America's denial of their citizenship. An 1837 petition for male suffrage to the New York State legislature, signed by 365 black males, queried why citizenship rights should be granted within a few years to those immigrants who did nothing to earn it, when "we, *native* born

44. *Constitution of the American Society of Free Persons of Colour, for Improving their Condition in the United States; for Purchasing Lands; and for the Establishment of a Settlement in Upper Canada, also The Proceedings of the Convention, with their Address to The Free Persons of Colour in the United States* (Philadelphia, 1831), 10, in Porter, ed., *Early Negro Writing,* 179.

45. Quoted in Billington, "James Forten," 10. For examples of other such sentiment, see the letter of "A Colored American" to the editor of the *National Anti-Slavery Standard,* reprinted in the *Liberator,* 27 August 1859, and reproduced in Woodson, ed., *Mind of Negro,* 243–44, in which he contends that Africa "belongs to the Africans, and not to us. We are Americans; this is our country, and we have no claim on any other."

Americans, the children of the soil, are most of us shut off.[46] Similarly, Peter Williams, rector of New York City's St. Philip's Episcopal Church, posed in sharp relief the double standard by which blacks were judged in relation to other ethnic groups. Speaking at a Fourth of July celebration in 1830, Williams proclaimed:

We are NATIVES of this country; we ask only to be treated as well as FOREIGNERS. Not a few of our fathers suffered and bled to purchase its independence; we ask only to be treated as well as those who fought against it. We have toiled to cultivate it, and to raise it to its present prosperous condition; we ask only to share equal privileges with those who came from distant lands to enjoy the fruits of our labor.[47]

The insult was all the more grinding, Frederick Douglass exclaimed, when these same immigrants had the audacity to propose African colonization. If anything, European immigrants had the least right to be considered American, for most in no way knew about or had participated in American history. If the giving of one's "sweat and blood" for the American nation had anything to do with whether or not one

46. The *Weekly Advocate,* 27 February 1837, printed an "Extra" which featured the text of the three petitions submitted to the New York State legislature by a convention of black residens. A similar *Memorial of Thirty Thousand Disfranchised Citizens,* 13, rebuked Congress for giving rights to those who fought against the colonists in the Revolution, while depriving rights to those who fought for America. Charles Lenox Remond told a Massachusetts convention of blacks, which met the first week of August 1858, that he resented having to "ask for rights which every pale-faced vagabond from across the water could almost at once enjoy." (*Liberator,* 13 August 1858, cited by Aptheker, ed., *Documentary History,* 406.) For other examples of blacks who contrasted America's hospitality to foreigners with her hostility towards blacks, see Robert Ernst, "Negro Concepts of Americanism," *Journal of Negro History,* XXXIX (July 1954): 207 ff.; Robert Purvis, *Speeches and Letters* (n.p., n.d.), 17.

47. Peter Williams, *A Discourse Delivered in St. Philip's Church, for the Benefit of the Coloured Community of Wilberforce, in Upper Canada, on Fourth of July, 1830* (New York, 1830), quoted in Garrison, *Thoughts on African Colonization,* 66.

should be identified as an American, then only the cruelest hypocrisy could keep from blacks their rightful nationality.[48]

Scarcely a month after the formal organization of the American Colonization Society, nearly three thousand infuriated blacks assembled in "Mother Bethel" Church in Philadelphia. Denouncing the society's violation of the principles for which whites and blacks had joined hands in fighting in the American Revolution, the gathering resolved that "whereas our ancestors (not of choice) were the first successful cultivators of the wilds of America, we their descendants feel ourselves entitled to participate in the blessings of her luxuriant soil, which their blood and sweat manured."[49] In church after church where blacks gathered to discuss the motives and objectives of the American Colonization Society resolutions were regularly adopted similar to the one passed by a group of Providence, Rhode Island blacks. Meeting on October 31, 1831, they had announced "that as our fathers participated with the whites in their struggle for liberty and independence. . . . Therefore Resolved, That we will not leave our homes, nor the graves of our fathers, and this boasted land of liberty and Christian philanthropy."[50]

48. Foner, ed., *Douglass,* I: 394.
49. Garrison, *Thoughts on African Colonization,* "Sentiments of the People of Color," 9.
50. *Ibid.,* 45. For most blacks, both the solution and the sincerity of the colonizationists were suspect. If they were truly interested in improving the character and condition of the black population in America, contended Maria W. Stewart, they would "expend the money which they collect, in erecting a college to educate their injured sons in this land of gospel light and liberty." (Maria W. Stewart, "Address," in *Early Negro Writing,* ed. Porter, 133.) Peter Williams commented on the inconsistency of claiming to improve the condition of blacks in America by removing them from "where schools and colleges abound, where the gospel is preached at every corner, and where all the arts and sciences are verging fast to perfection" and displacing them "far from civilized society." (Peter Williams, "Discourse Delivered in St. Phillip's Church," in *Early Negro Writing,* ed. Porter, 297.) In short, the Philadelphia Annual Convention of the Free People of Color wryly observed that "if we must be sacrificed to their philanthropy, we would rather die at home" (see the report

Black orators and authors overflowed with bitterness toward those who belittled their contribution of "blood, sweat and tears" and their readiness to give of their blood in battle to defend the liberties of the country that enslaved them.[51] Richard Allen made it known to the readers of *Freedom's Journal* that he deemed it a slanderous affront to deny that America was "not our mother country," especially after "we had tilled the ground and made fortune for thousands."[52] Slave labor had also made a fortune for the nation, and after all that the slave had meant to the economic health of America, the black historian William Wells Brown stood incredulous before the colonizationist answer to the question of what to do with the freed slave.

Expatriate him for what? He has cleared the swamps of the south, and has put the soil under cultivation; he has built up her towns, and cities, and villages; he has enriched the north and Europe with his cotton, and sugar, and rice; and for this you would drive him out of the country! 'What shall be done with the slaves if they are freed?' You had better ask, 'What shall we do with the slaveholders if the slaves are freed?' The slave has shown himself better fitted to take care of himself than the slaveholder. He is the bone and sinew of the south; he is the producer, while the master is nothing but a consumer, and a very poor consumer at that.[53]

---

of the convention in Charles Stuart, *Remarks on the Colony of Liberia and the American Colonization Society* [London, 1832], 12, quoted in William H. Pease and Jane H. Pease, *Black Utopia: Negro Communal Experiments in America* [Madison, Wisconsin, 1963], 15).

51. Nathaniel Paul, "Speeches Delivered at the Anti-Colonization Meeting in Exeter Hall, London, 13 July 1833 . . ." in Porter, ed., *Early Negro Writing,* 251, 288. Paul had traveled to England to raise money for the Wilberforce Settlement in Upper Canada. For the importance attached to the role of blacks in fighting to preserve the nation, see the 25 January 1831 denunciation of colonization by a mass meeting of New York City blacks organized by Samuel Ennals and Philip A. Bell, and reported in the *Liberator,* 12 February 1831; see also Hosea Easton, *A Treatise on the Intellectual Character, and Civil and Political Condition of the Colored People of the United States* (Boston, 1837), 33–34.

52. *Freedom's Journal,* 2 November 1827.

53. William Wells Brown, *The Black Man, His Antecedents, His Genius, and His Achievements,* 2nd ed. (New York, 1863; reprinted New

Whether from an economic or a patriotic perspective, black lecturers like Brown, Henry Highland Garnet, and Sojourner Truth summoned up the history of the African contribution to the building of America and found that it equalled, if not exceeded, that of the Anglo-Saxons. And when white Americans, many of them "professors," advised blacks who resisted colonization that "were they in our place, they would do as the pilgrim fathers did, leave the country" and go to Africa, the *Colored American* informed them that their view of American history was distorted.[54]

John B. Vashon of Pittsburgh, who served in 1814 under General Winder in defense of the nation's capital against the British, reminded the *Liberator* that if America planned to fulfill her original destiny as an asylum for the oppressed of all climes and colors, she must open herself up as "a sanctuary of security and repose to the wearied and depressed African," especially since part of this weariment and depression arose from the labor and tears with which the slave had enriched the soil of his birth.[55] Since colonizationists based their plans for preserving the whiteness of the American asylum on the capricious differences in shades of complexion, Abraham Shadd wryly observed, in his presidential address to the third annual colored convention, that their plan could easily backfire, for on the criterion of color, black American colonizationists "may be again compelled to migrate to the land of their fathers in America."[56] Whenever colonization-

---

York, 1968), 46. See also Pease and Pease, *They Who Would Be Free,* 39.

54. *Colored American,* 15 April 1837.
55. *Liberator,* 31 March 1832.
56. *Minutes of the Third Annual Convention, 1833,* 35. To a young domestic woman in Washington, D.C., of a "yellowish tint," it simply "was not fair to send the Negro back after they had disfigured the colour." (See Jesse Torrey, *The American Slave Trade* [London, 1822], 118, cited by Benjamin Quarles, *Black Abolitionists* [New York, 1969], 7.)

ists informed blacks that *no trespassing* signs were posted over the pages of American history, black leaders informed colonizationists that they may as well "come here to agitate the emigration of the Jay's, the King's, the Adam's, the Otis's, the Hancock's, etc." as to attempt the removal of a group who had donated as much of themselves to the fashioning of American history as the Founding Fathers themselves.[57]

III

In rejecting the glib notion that colonizationists differed from abolitionists only on the means of abolishing slavery, black leaders countered that the colonization chimera enabled many whites to mask their pro-slavery and anti-black motivations behind an aura of respectability and benevolence. Black leaders like David Ruggles opposed more than just the methods of the colonizationists; they also disputed the undergirding motives of colonizationists.[58] They deemed the underlying assumption that motivated the colonizationist fervor— the assumption that the condition of blacks in America was "intolerably grievous," "irremediably hopeless," and that blacks would ever inhabit, in the words of Henry Clay, "the lowest strata of social gradation—aliens—political-moral-social-aliens, strangers, though natives"[59]—as an affront to their standing as Americans, as Protestants, and as black men with pride in and concern for their race.

Completely apart from the fact that they deserved respect and the right to be called Americans through their labors and loyalty, blacks saw the issue confronting them as primarily one of confidence, optimism, self-assertion, and self-determination, versus one of despair, pessimism, and escapism. To stand firm against the tide of colonizationism sweeping the country (even Harriett Beecher Stowe, as Garrison notes in his

57. *Colored American,* 9 May 1840.
58. Ruggles, *"Extinguisher" Extinguished,* 28.
59. Quoted in Staudenraus, *African Colonization Movement,* 137.

review for the *Liberator*,[60] colonized George Harris off to
Liberia at the end of *Uncle Tom's Cabin*) became a test of
confidence in their manhood, in the principles upon which
America was founded, and in their Christianity.

A mass meeting of New York City blacks on January 25,
1831, denounced colonization because "we do not believe
that things will always continue the same. The time must
come when the Declaration of Independence will be felt in the
heart, as well as uttered from the mouth."[61] William Hamilton of New York, as chairman of the fourth annual national
Negro convention, admonished the fifty delegates from eight
states to "cheer up," since all British dominions would be
freed from the Antichrist of slavery next August, and "these
United States and her children, they will soon follow so good
an example" and wipe out "that beast whose mark has been
so long stamped on the forehead of the nation."[62] William C.
Nell castigated the colonization society for spreading the lie
that blacks could not be "elevated" in the United States, and
"A Colored Baltimorean" chided the colonizationist readers
of the *Liberator* with "What! has it come to this, that we must
not, in this Christian land, even indulge in *hope*?" When
Samuel Cornish heard that Francis Scott Key gave a speech
before the American Colonization Society detailing the hopelessness of the condition of blacks in America, he accused
Key of being a pagan and a hypocrite for believing that Satan
and stagnation could exert greater power than God and progress. How could a director of the American Bible Society

60. Wendell P. Garrison and Francis J. Garrison, *William Lloyd
Garrison*, Vol. III (New York, 1885–89), 362.
61. *Liberator*, 12 February 1831, cited by Aptheker, ed., *Documentary History*, 109.
62. *Minutes of the Fourth Annual Convention, for the Improvement
of the Free People of Colour . . . 1834* (New York, 1834), in Aptheker, ed., *Documentary History*, 156. See also *Minutes of the Third Annual Convention, 1833*, 27, where the comment was made that the
American Colonization Society was designed to deprive blacks of all
hope of being integrated into the American body politic.

believe in such anti-biblical principles? Cornish asked.[63] An optimistic trust in the validity of American democracy and Christianity served as the guard which checked the "undemocratic, unChristian, and unAmerican" colonizationist contention that America was destined to be a white man's country.

It should be kept in mind, however, that part of this hostility to white assertions of futility and despair arose because of its source. While "A Colored Philadelphian" wrote to the *Liberator* in 1831 that the notion that Africa was his true home was "the most absurd assertion" that he had ever heard, he still reserved the right to make this decision for himself, "—and if we do emigrate, it will be to a place of our own choice."[64] If blacks felt that they needed an aslyum, they would choose their own and would not accept a white-imposed asylum. Levi Coffin registered similar sentiments in his *Reminiscences,* as he told of his opposition back in the 1820s to southern "Manumission and Colonization Societies." To those emancipated blacks who felt "of their own free will" that expatriation was the only remedy, Coffin had no objection. But for whites to rule that there could be no emancipation without expatriation was an invasion of the right of self-determination.[65]

The Reverend Peter Williams (whose father, after his emancipation, operated a tobacco shop and had as his first servant the son of his former master) issued in 1834 an open letter to

63. Nell, *Colored Patriots,* 391; "A Colored Baltimorean" to the *Liberator,* 23 March 1833, in Woodson, ed., *Mind of Negro,* 238; *Rights of All,* 16 October 1829, as cited by Dann, ed., *Black Press,* 254. For similar repudiations of the assumption of hopelessness and its importance in black opposition to colonizing ventures, whether in the form of the American Colonization Society or the African Civilization Society, see Farrison, *Brown,* 309, 311–12.

64. *Liberator,* 12 February 1831, quoted in Woodson, ed., *Mind of Negro,* 224–25.

65. Levi Coffin, *Reminiscences of Levi Coffin, The Reputed President of the Underground Railroad; being a Brief History of the Labors of a Lifetime in Behalf of the Slave,* 3rd ed. (Cincinnati, 1898; reprinted New York, 1968), 75.

the citizens of New York. Acknowledging that "it was my greatest glory to be an American," Williams exuded optimism that "the time would come when they would all have abundant reason to rejoice in the glorious Declaration for "I could not, and do not believe that the principles of the Declaration of Independence, of American Independence, and of the Gospel of Christ, have not power sufficient to raise him, at some future day, to that rank of citizenship and equality towards which he aspired." Nevertheless, Williams upheld the right of each black man to decide this for himself, so long as in the process he was not duped by the colonizationist propaganda that the black man in America "must ever remain a degraded and oppressed being."[66]

In their reaction to the assumptions of the American Colonization Society, the dual identity of black Americans emerges again and again. Just as for most of them the creation of an "Americo-African empire" in Liberia became a symbol of white escapism from living up to the democratic and Christian foundations upon which America was first built, so emigrationism in general meant black escapism from racial realities and responsibilities and from the plight of their brethren still in bondage. To acquiesce in the basic platform of the American Colonization Society—that blacks could not survive in freedom in America—seemed to libel not only American democracy and black Americanism but, more importantly, black manhood and equality. In no uncertain terms, Frederick Douglass identified emigrationism with escapism. "You must be a man here," he challenged, "and force your way to intelligence, wealth and respectability. If you can't do that here, you can't do it there."[67] Similarly, in an editorial entitled "This Country Our Only Home," the *Colored American* could imagine no other place where black Americans might escape to raise

66. See letter of "Rev. Mr. Williams, To the Citizens of New York," *Mind of Negro* in Woodson, ed., 631–32. Also Abdy, *Journal of a Residence,* I: 46.
67. Foner, ed., *Douglass,* II: 173.

themselves politically, morally, and socially but to America, considering the fact that "most of our people" are "completely Americanized" and the fact that America stood as a lone asylum of ·liberty and opportunity, even if it were only to white people at the present.[68] Running away, regardless of the provocation, would only endorse the claims of the colonizationists and impair the effectiveness of those who remained to fight the battle. This is precisely what Reverend Theodore S. Wright argued had happened when he spoke to the New York State Anti-Slavery Society convention held in Utica on September 20, 1837. As he looked back on the history of the black man in the first third of the century, he delineated the era beginning with the arrival of the Reverend Robert Finley in Washington with his plan for the uplifting of American society tucked into his pocket as a "dark period" in their history and likened the colonizationist panacea of Negro deportation to a "great sponge" which "sponged up all the benevolent feelings which were then present," inflicting a severe setback to the anti-slavery movement.[69] And while white colonizers blandly insisted that their colonization scheme provided the only realistic hope for ending slavery in the United States, Samuel Cornish retorted, in the *Rights of All,* that interest in domestic abolition diminished in direct proportion to black interest in colonization.[70]

IV

Blacks proved even less willing to abandon their brethren in bonds than they did to abandon hope in the founding principles of democracy and Christianity. William Wells Brown, in a June 1861 guest editorial, entitled "Opposition to Emigration," in James Redpath's newly begun the *Pine and Palm,* objectively assessed the historic black antipathy to coloniza-

---

68. *Colored American,* 9 May 1840.
69. *Colored American,* 4 October 1837. For Douglass's views on the debilitating effects of the colonization proposal on black efforts at elevation, see Foner, ed., *Douglass,* II: 387–88.
70. *Rights of All,* 12 June 1829, reprinted in Dann, ed., *Black Press,* 250–51.

tion. "All objections to emigration appear to center in the feeling that we ought not to quit the land of our birth, and leave the slave in his chains."[71]

Most blacks accepted Richard Allen's assessment of colonization as a mere ruse of slaveholders to rid their slaves of the inspiring and potentially insurrectionary example of *"free men of colour enjoying liberty."*[72] Refusing to oblige, the first annual meeting of the American Moral Reform Society resolved "that we never will separate ourselves voluntarily from the slave population in this country; they are our brethren by the ties of consanguinity, of suffering and of wrong; and we feel that there is more virtue in suffering privations with them here, than in enjoying fancied advantages for a season."[73] Not only would free northern blacks not forsake their enslaved brothers and sisters, they also refused to glory excessively in their tenuous freedom. As James L. Smith, a freed southern slave residing in the north, wrote to William Lloyd Garrison in 1841: "Think you sir, that I can feel free, while millions of my countrymen are held in chains and fetters by this professed Christian nation?" And to his own rhetorical question, Smith replied: "No—I cannot feel free. I am still bound with my brethren, I feel the cruel lash, and their chains."[74]

71. Brown went on to admit that "this view of the case comes at first glance with some force, but on a closer examination, it will be found to have but little weight." (*Pine and Palm,* 2 June 1861, cited by Farrison, *Brown,* 334–35. This editorial was the closest Brown ever came to supporting emigration.)

72. Richard Allen to *Freedom's Journal,* 29 November 1827; see also "A Colored Philadelphian" to *Liberator,* 19 March 1831, cited by Woodson, ed., *Mind of Negro,* 228 .

73. *Minutes and Proceedings of the First Annual Meeting of the American Moral Reform Society . . . 1837* (Philadelphia, 1837), quoted in Porter, ed., *Early Negro Writing,* 220. See also Douglass's similar remarks in the *North Star,* 26 January 1849, in Foner, ed., *Douglass* I: 351.

74. *Liberator,* 26 March 1841; reprinted in Woodson, ed., *Mind of Negro,* 261. See also the similar remarks of David Nickens, "An Address to the Colored People of the United States," *Report of the Proceedings of the Colored National Convention . . . 1848* (Rochester, 1848), 18–29,

Until all blacks were free, no black was free, and no black should be lulled into considering himself free. The white historian George Bancroft and the first successful black politician, John Mercer Langston, took the reasoning one step further. No white man could consider himself free as long as slavery existed, for by depriving black Americans of their rights, Bancroft asserted that America was depriving "a foothold for the liberty of the white man to rest upon."[75]

There can be no dating of racial solidarity, for it was hammered on the anvil of suffering by cruel and oppressive slaveholders. But a sense of the kinship of all black Americans assumed many outward manifestations besides denunciations of colonization. For some, like Jupiter Hammon, black interrelatedness meant phillipics against immorality and ignorance amongst the race. For George Lawrence it meant the quest for racial unity and "social Love." For Absalom Jones and seventy-three others, it took the form of a petition to the President, Senate, and House of Representatives imploring them to abide by constitutional imperatives. Elected officials must represent all constituencies, including the slaves.[76]

---

reproduced in John H. Bracey, Jr., August Meier, and Elliott Rudwick, ed., *Black Nationalism in America* (New York, 1970), 54.

75. On 9 May 1855, in the same year he became the first black man elected to public office in the United States (elected clerk of a township near Oberlin College, where he made history by being the first black man to earn an advanced degree in theology), the Ohio abolitionist John Mercer Langston gave an address to the twenty-second anniversary celebration of the American Anti-Slavery Society, in which he told his audience that no American, white or black, could consider himself a free man as long as slavery existed. (See Langston, *Virginia Plantation,* 151, 153.) The remarks of George Bancroft were in response to the philosophy of the Dred Scott decision, quoted in George Livermore, *An Historical Research Respecting the Opinions of the Founders of the Republic on Negroes as Slaves, as Citizens, and as Soldiers. Read Before the Massachusetts Historical Society, August 14, 1862* (Boston, 1862; reprinted New York, 1969), 10.

76. Jupiter Hammon, *An Address to the Negroes in the State of New York* (New York, 1787), in Porter, ed., *Early Negro Writing,* 313–23; George Lawrence, *Oration on the Abolition of the Slave Trade De-*

Despite the attempts of whites to wedge apart the sealed bonds of affection between slaves and free blacks, and the natural status differences that pried them apart,[77] one cannot help but be impressed by the pervasiveness of this sense of solidarity between freemen and bondsmen. Indeed, free black identification with slaves supplied an emotional dimension to the opposition to colonization that assists in explaining why, of all the issues, colonization should be the catalyst for unifying the free black population of the North. Black unity expressed itself through black conventions and benevolent associations, which passed with ritual regularity resolutions like the one asserting "we never will separate ourselves voluntarily from the slave population in this country."[78] The grip of racial solidarity also helps to explain why a congregation of black citizens met at the Pittsburgh African Methodist Episcopal Church in September 1831 to declare that any black American who "allows himself to be colonized in Africa, or elsewhere" will be viewed as "a traitor to our cause"; why on December 16, 1839, black Philadelphians gathered to vent their hostility against the "SPECULATIVE, DETESTABLE AND TRAITOROUS" projects "which contemplate our removal from the land of our birth, and affection"; why John B. Vashon accused any black who colonized Liberia of being

---

livered on the First Day of January, 1813, in the African Methodist Episcopal Church (New York, 1813), quoted in Porter, ed., *Early Negro Writing,* 378; "Petition of Absalom Jones and Seventy-Three Others," as found in John Parrish, *Remarks on the Slavery of the Black People Addressed to the Citizens of the United States, Particularly to Those Who are in Legislative or Executive Stations in the General or State Governments; and Also to Such Individuals as Hold Them in Bondage* (Philadelphia, 1806), 49, reproduced in Porter, ed., *Early Negro Writing,* 330–32.

77. See Ira Berlin's penetrating analysis in *Slaves Without Masters: The Free Negro in the Antebellum South* (New York, 1974), 271–79.

78. *Minutes and Proceedings of the First Annual Meeting of the American Moral Reform Society,* quoted in Porter, ed., *Early Negro Writing,* 220.

guilty of selling out to slavery and of staining his hands with "the blood of his country men"; why blacks from Baltimore organized opposition throughout the state against colonization and stigmatized those who did emigrate as traitors to their race; and why the Bowdoin college graduate, John B. Russwurm, complained bitterly of "violent persecution" at the hands of friends when he announced his conversion to colonization in an editorial entitled "Our Rightful Place is in Africa."[79]

Russwurm had even greater cause to complain eight years later. In April 1837 the *Colored American* lambasted those *"base traitors"* who would abandon "the millions of our brethren, who are in bondage." A year later the magazine became more specific, singling out Russwurm as the black Benedict Arnold. This charge of treason was levied against Russwurm even by some of his warmest friends.[80] As late as 1853, Henry Ford Douglass of Columbus, Ohio, gave an index to the grassroots antipathy to colonization when he responded with exaggerated enthusiasm to a resolution adopted by the Ohio State Convention of Colored Freemen denouncing the American Colonization Society as "one of our worst enemies." His influence had been so "injured" by rumors which "misrepresented" his conditional support of colonization that Douglass felt compelled to visibly and vigorously reaffirm his hostility to the society.[81]

79. Garrison, *Thoughts on African Colonization*, "Sentiments of the People of Color," 34–35, quoted in Cornish and Wright, *Colonization Scheme Considered*, 4–5; Vashon to the *Liberator*, 31 March 1832, quoted in Woodson, ed., *Mind of Negro*, 246; *Seventh Annual Report of the Board of Managers of the Maryland State Colonization Society* (Baltimore, 1839), 10; Quarles, *Black Abolitionists*, 7.

80. *Colored American*, 15 April 1837; 27 January 1838. The story of Russwurm's rejection by the black community is also told in Ruggles, *"Extinguisher" Extinguished*, 18.

81. See the organ of the Ohio State Anti-Slavery Society, the *Aliened American*, 9 April 1853. Douglass clarified his position by denouncing the "diabolical scheme" of colonization, while allowing that "under some circumstances colored men may advance their interest by emigration." The term "colonization" had been so anathematized that some groups

Blacks who abandoned faith in America and the fight against American slavery suffered the censure of ostracism by many of their brethren. They had committed "the unpardonable sin." According to David Walker's "Appeal," black colonizers were "traitors" to the black brotherhood.[82]

---

were pressured into abandoning it. The "Young Men's Colonization Society" changed in February 1837 to the "American Society for the Promotion of Education in Africa."

82. Walker, *Appeal,* 77. A meeting of the "Peace and Benevolent Society of Afric-Americans," held in New Haven, 7 August 1831, resolved that "any man who will be persuaded to leave his own country and go to Africa" will be considered "an enemy to his country and a traitor to his brethren." (Garrison, *Thoughts on African Colonization,* "Sentiments of the People of Color," 31.)

5

The Destiny of
Black Americans

'Twas mercy brought me from my Pagan land,
Taught my benighted soul to understand
That ther's a God, and ther's a Saviour too;
Once I redemption neither sought nor knew.
Some view our sable race with scornful eye,
"There colour is a diabolic die."
Remember, Christians, Negroes, black as Cain,
May be refin'd, and join th' angelic train.

PHYLLIS WHEATLEY

THE FIRST TWO articulate blacks in America—both poets —had a common concern. From the depths of shared experiences, they both asked the same question: Why slavery?

Phyllis Wheatley was the second woman in America to publish a book of poetry. Included in this volume was a poem entitled "On Being Brought From Africa to America," in which she confessed that "Mercy" had transported her to this country and had introduced her to the liberating experience and doctrine of Christianity. Five years later, in 1776, Jupiter Hammon repeated the motif in a dedicatory poem addressed to his fellow slave Phyllis Wheatley, praising divine providence for bringing her from pagan Africa to Christian America.

God's tender mercy brought thee here;
Tost o'er the raging main;

In Christian faith thou hast a share,
Worth all the gold of Spain.[1]

Yet the push of American Christianity, which enabled Wheatley to explain slavery, was matched by the pull of African descent, which never allowed her to justify slavery. "And can I then but pray," she queried of the Earl of Dartmouth, "Others may never feel tyrannic sway?"[2]

There is no evidence to suggest that any black American writer in the nineteenth century believed that God had willed that Africans be slaves to Americans. Frederick Douglass recalled that his "very first mental effort" when but a child had been the painful grappling with the question of why he was a slave to the white man. When told by his white master that God had ordained blacks to be slaves, Douglass wept in disbelief, intuitively sensing that God could not have done any such thing, for "it was not good to let old master cut the flesh off Esther, and make her cry so." Slavery was caused not by God, but by "the pride, the power, and avarice of man."[3] Slavery was not part of God's providential plan for blacks. It was man's willful and criminal cupidity that had enslaved a portion of those made in God's image. Still God was able to make even the wrath of men to praise him and to use despots to serve his ends. Not because of slavery but in spite of slavery, God's purpose for blacks would be realized. God could and would bring good out of evil, even the greatest evil. In the end, however, these were but empty abstractions. The

1. Phyllis Wheatley, *Poems on Various Subjects, Religious and Moral* (London, 1773), 18; Jupiter Hammon's poem is quoted in Leslie H. Fishel, Jr. and Benjamin Quarles, ed., *The Black American: A Documentary History,* (revised edition New York, 1970), 7. See also Phyllis Wheatley's letter to Obour Tanner (most likely a girl she travelled with in the 1761 slave passage to America), 19 May 1772, in Herbert G. Renfro, *Life and Works of Phyllis Wheatley* (Washington, D.C., 1916), 27.

2. Wheatley, *Poems on Various Subjects,* 74.

3. Frederick Douglass, *My Bondage and My Freedom* (New York and Auburn, 1855; reprinted New York, 1968), 28.

tormenting question remained: Why did God permit this greatest evil in the first place? The answer to the most fundamental of the existential questions of the black experience in America was answered, and yet remained unanswerable.

In the nineteenth century, no one—black or white—questioned the conviction that God had uniquely entrusted America with the mission of spreading Christianity and democracy. Black intellectuals, accepting a philosophy of history which rivaled the blind faith of white historians like George Bancroft in divine sovereignty over human history, asserted that history bore witness to God's design that America was to be the conveyer of true Christianity and civilization to the world. With this premise, white historians had busied themselves with answering the question of why God had chosen white Americans to fulfill this role. But black leaders were preoccupied with a more personal question—why God had allowed the supreme evil of slavery to be inflicted on the Africans by this allegedly "chosen people" in the first place.

According to Maria W. Stewart, Africans had forfeited their former pride and glory due to "our gross sins and abominations." In this view slavery became a means of punishing Africa for what the Reverend Daniel H. Peterson called its "disobedience, rebellion, and neglect of God," as well as a means God had chosen of reconciling the African people to himself.[4]

4. Maria W. Stewart, "An Address Delivered at the African Masonic Hall, Boston, February 27, 1833," in Porter, ed., *Early Negro Writing*, 130–31; Daniel H. Peterson, *The Looking Glass: Being a True Report of the Life, Travels, and Labors of the Rev. Daniel H. Peterson, a colored clergyman; embracing a period of time from the year 1812 to 1854, and including His Visit to Western Africa* (New York, 1854), 49–50. David Walker, in his "Appeal," stated his belief that "ignorance, the mother of treachery" is a misfortune "which God has suffered our fathers to be enveloped in for many ages, no doubt in consequence of their disobedience to their Maker." (See *Walker's Appeal, With a Brief Sketch of his Life. By Henry Highland Garnet. And also Garnet's Address to the Slaves of the United States of America* [New York, 1848; reprinted New York, 1969], 31–32.) Martin R. Delany, on the other hand, desired to "correct" the "long standing error among a large body of the colored people in this country, that the cause of our oppression and degradation,

Throughout the course of slavery, explained Theodore Wright, Charles B. Ray, and James McCune Smith to the three thousand New York black recipients of Gerrit Smith's gift of 140,000 acres of land enabling their eligibility for the franchise, "HE overruled the evil intentions of men for the benefit of mankind, by placing us in the midst of the path of progress, that we might work out the great problem of human equality."[5]

The minister, lawyer, Ohio politician, judge, and historian, George Washington Williams, was the first black historian to use extensive documentation because, as he noted in presenting his two volumes to the public in 1883, "while men with the reputation of [George] Bancroft and [Richard] Hildreth could pass unchallenged when disregarding largely the use of documents and the citation of authorities, I would find myself challenged by a large number of critics." In his *History of the Negro Race,* Williams distinguished the early imperial glory of primeval Africans from the present degraded "Negro type," who occupies "the lowest strata of the African race" because "he early turned from God" to idolatry, and in so doing he lost his civilization and "found the cold face of hate and the hurtful hand of the Caucasian against him." Nevertheless, American slavery "had the effect of calling

is the displeasure of God towards us, because of our unfaithfulness to Him. This is not true." (See Delany, *Condition, Elevation, Emigration,* in Brotz, ed., *Negro Social and Political Thought,* 51.)

5. Theodore Wright, Charles B. Ray, James McCune Smith, *An Address to the Three Thousand Colored Citizens of New York Who are the Owners of One Hundred and Twenty Thousand Acres of Land* (New York, 1846), 18. Robert Russa Morton, successor to Booker T. Washington, echoed a similar sentiment when he spoke at the dedication of the Lincoln Monument in Washington, D.C., on 30 May 1922. Informing the crowd that the eyes of the world were fixed on America's "great experiment of the ages" in ethnic cooperation and coexistence, he ventured that "in the providence of God the black race in America was thrust across the path of the onward-marching white race to demonstrate, not only for America, but for the World, whether the principles of freedom are of universal application, and ultimately to extend its blessings to all mankind." (Quoted in Benjamin E. Mays, *The Negro's God as Reflected in His Literature,* [New York, 1969], 202–03.)

into life many a slumbering and dying attribute in the Negro nature." As for the Anglo-Saxon, Williams wrote, "ye meant it unto evil, but God meant it unto good"—the elevation of the African race.[6] Yet the beneficial by-products of slavery— exposure to Christianity and civilization—in no way palliated the curse of slavery. All the pious ponderings in the world could not mitigate the wickedness of enslavement. The "Declaration of Sentiment," the singular substantial contribution of the American Moral Reform Society, condemned as sinful the sinister separation of their ancestors from their homeland, however great the subsequent advantages might be.[7]

Austin Steward, in his July 5, 1827, oration, detailed the progress of mankind and the progress of America. He then noted the bitter irony in the way God had used slavery, the abolition of which they were celebrating that day in New York State, to bring to black peoples "those best and noblest of his gifts to man, in their fairest and liveliest form." Like the captivity of the Israelites in Egypt, the suffering of slavery provided the means of redemption. Yet while rejoicing in how slavery had been made to serve the purpose of redemption, Steward cried out in exasperation, "I ask, Almighty God, are they who do such things thy chosen and favorite people?"[8]

6. George Washington Williams, *History of the Negro Race in America from 1619 to 1880* (New York, 1883), Vol. I, vii, 109, 110, 114. Williams made it clear, however, that "God often permits evil on the ground of man's free agency, but he does not commit evil" (113).

7. *Minutes and Proceedings of the First Annual Meeting of the American Moral Reform Society held at Philadelphia . . . from the Fourteenth to the Nineteenth of August, 1837* (Philadelphia, 1837), in Porter, ed., *Early Negro Writing,* 201. Samuel Hopkins, in his *Dialogue Concerning the Slavery of the Africans,* informed the members of the Continental Congress in 1776 that slavery could not be justified for its christianizing effects because spiritual enlightenment through enslavement grossly violated the commands of Christ. "He commands us to go and preach the gospel to all nations, to carry the gospel to them, and not to go and with violence bring them from their native country." (See Hopkins, *Works,* II: 557.)

8. Austin Steward, *Twenty-Two Years a Slave, and Forty Years a Freeman,* 4th ed. (Canandaigua, New York, 1867), 154–57.

On the same day and on the same occasion, another black orator, a Baptist pastor named Nathaniel Paul, asked the same question: "Why it was that thou didst look on with the calm indifference of an unconcerned spectator, when thy holy law was violated, thy divine authority despised, and a portion of thy own creatures reduced to a state of mere vasalage and misery?" God's reply came to Paul from the Book of Job: "It is my sovereign prerogative to bring good out of evil, and cause the wrath of man to praise me."[9]

Clearly, as James L. Smith concluded when he reflected in his autobiography on the apparent providential design behind American slavery, God often dealt with his people through suffering and hardship; even in the infamy of slavery, God had the power of "bringing good out of evil, light out of darkness."[10] Slave spirituals most clearly express this idea, that the stumbling block of suffering can be a stepping-stone to salvation.

A more extended discussion of the issue was provided by the Episcopal clergyman Alexander Crummell, who took a degree in Cambridge University in 1853 before going to Africa. He built a philosophy of history on the way in which God overrules the evil propensities of mankind and transforms those histories into "benignant providence." Although history seemed to be dominated by the "dark needs of man," Crum-

9. See Bishop L. H. Holsey, "Speech Delivered Before Several Conferences of the Methodist Episcopal Church, South," in *Autobiography, Sermons, Addresses, and Essays* (Atlanta, 1898), 242.

10. James L. Smith, *Autobiography* (Norwich, Connecticut, 1881), 215. In evaluating the Civil War, Smith expressed his belief that regardless of how much evil emerged in the conflict—evil that for Smith took the form of: Lincoln's stipulation that for various reasons only whites need apply to defend the country; northern "hatred" of the people for whom they were allegedly fighting; the government's hostility at the onset of the war toward freeing the slaves—yet the "guiding hand" of God overruled all these evils and worked them for the "noble purpose" of the black man. (See his *Autobiography,* 196 ff.) Harriet Tubman stated at the end of 1861 that "God's ahead of Massa Linkum. . . . God won't let Massa Linkum bent de South till he do the right thing." (Cited by James M. McPherson, *The Negro's Civil War: How American Negroes Felt and Acted During the War for the Union* [New York, 1965], 43.)

mell contended that if only the veil of eternity were lifted one could see "a higher, mightier, more masterful hand than theirs, although unseen;—distracting their evil counsels, and directing them to goodly issues. God, although not the author of sin, is, nevertheless, the omnipotent and gracious dispenser of it."[11] Rather than Providence having ordained the bitter scourge of slavery for the Africans, Crummell argued that Providence had ordered the evil so that it would work for the good of "Negro-land."

In contrast to the easy way in which white historians traced the divine footsteps through history, Alexander Crummell found that God revealed his mastery over history in a maze of mystery, irony, and paradox. The very people most responsible for enslaving Africans, the Anglo-Saxons, were inexplicably the people God had chosen for the "grand cause" of evangelizing and elevating black peoples. Although God had not destined Africans for slavery, he had destined them "to be given up to the English language, and hence to the influence of Anglo-Saxon life and civilization."[12] Slavery exemplified the way God employed evil means in history to accomplish such divine ends.

Revealing the extent to which even a spokesman for "the rising tide of nationalist sentiment" had assimilated English

11. Alexander Crummell, "The Promise of Civilization Along the West Coast of Africa," in *The Future of Africa: Being Addresses, Sermons, etc., etc., Delivered in the Republic of Liberia* (New York, 1862; reprinted New York, 1969), 125–26.

12. *Ibid.,* 122–23. For an analysis of the confusing conceptions of "civilization" in Crummell, and indeed in most nineteenth-century literature, see Wilson J. Moses, "Civilizing Missionary: A Study of Alexander Crummell," *The Journal of Negro History,* LX (April 1975): 229–51. See also Bishop Holsey's comment that through slavery in "Christian Europe and Christian America" blacks had benefited by the "spiritual and physical dynamos that must thrill the world with its propulsion and redemptive entities and agencies" (*Autobiography,* 242). Bishop Henry McNeal Turner, of the African Methodist Episcopal Church, in 1883 also revealed his belief that God had permitted slavery because the African needed schooling in American civilization and Christianity. (See Edwn S. Redkey, *Black Exodus: Black Nationalist and Back-to-Africa Movements, 1890–1910* [New Haven, Connecticut, 1969], 35–36.)

culture, in 1860 Alexander Crummell wrote an article on the superiority of Anglo-Saxon religion, political doctrine, and language entitled "The English Language in Liberia." Anglo-Saxon America was chosen by God to school Africans in religion and political principles, he explained, because

In truth, how could France or Spain train the Negro race to high ideas of liberty and of government, when all their modern history has been an almost hopeless effort, to learn the alphabet of freedom. . . . Indeed it is only under the influence of Anglo-Saxon principles that the children of Africa, despite their wrongs and injuries, have been able to open their eyes to the full, clear, quiet, heavens of freedom, far distant, though at times they were.[13]

The enigma of God's blessing Africans with Christianity and democracy by blighting them with slavery served not to lessen black hatred of slavery, but to heighten their awe of God's mysterious, providential workings in history. As sure as black Americans were that God ruled in the affairs of men, mysteriously using evil for good, so sure were they that the God of justice reigns on earth as well as in heaven, ineluctably bringing divine judgment on the evil.

According to Samuel Ringgold Ward, the "God of the Poor and the Needy," or the God who Frederick Douglass liked to call the "God of the oppressed," or the God who David Walker called "the God of the Etheopeans," would not tarry long in meting out deferred but "deserved judgments" upon the "Anglo-Saxon Spoilers."[14] In reminding white Americans that "God works in many ways his wonders to perform," David Walker

13. Bracey, Jr., Meier, and Rudwick, ed., *Black Nationalism in America*, 123; Crummell, "The English Language in Liberia," in *Future of Africa*, 37.

14. Remarks by Samuel Ringgold Ward, Corresponding Editor, "Home Department," of the *Aliened American*, 9 April 1853. For other indications that some blacks viewed God's chosen people as the oppressed throughout history, see Absalom Jones, *A Thanksgiving Sermon, preached January 1, 1808, in St. Thomas's or the African Episcopal Church, Philadelphia: On Account of the Abolition of the African Slave Trade, on that day, by the Congress of the United States* (Philadelphia, 1808), as reproduced in Porter, ed., *Early Negro Writing*, 338. In contrast to the Puritan settlers of Massachusetts, who used the Jewish folk

warned that God's justice demanded vengeance, and one could never be sure just how God's wrath would come on America. Destruction might come from the insurrection of the oppressed black Israelites, or perhaps from dissensions among the oppressors themselves. Whatever the means, Walker contented himself with the knowledge that soon the Red Sea would come in a sea of blood for those who rode roughshod over biblical jeremiads against slavery.[15]

While submitting to what Alexander Crummell termed the "severe providences of God," to Bishop L. H. Holsey of the Colored Methodist Episcopal Church, God's providential activity in history still remained mysterious and inscrutible, something "deeply hidden" and "intricate."[16] Several decades earlier, in 1844, James W. C. Pennington's open letter to his family in bondage had distinguished between God's permission of slavery and God's approval of slavery. After rapacious men had invented the slave system, Pennington wrote, God demonstrated his unspeakable providence by transforming evil into good. Yet the question remained: Why had God permitted the evil in the first place? "He could have brought about that very good in some other way." Since the resources at God's disposal were infinite, Pennington tortured himself with the question for which he could find no answer: "Could He not have made this great and wealthy nation without making its riches to consist in our blood, bones, and souls? And could He not also have given the gospel to us without making us slaves?"[17]

---

myth to explain their people's separateness, Timothy L. Smith argues that black preachers used the metaphor of a chosen people "to affirm a common humanity" and to identify as "God's chosen people servants who suffered for all." (See his "Slavery and Theology: The Emergence of Black Christian Consciousness in Nineteenth-Century America," *Church History*, 41 [December 1972]: 504.)

15. Walker, *Appeal,* 14.

16. Crummell, "The Duty of a Rising Christian State to Contribute to the World's Well-Being and Civilization," in *Future of Africa,* 75; Holsey, *Autobiography,* 243.

17. James W. C. Pennington, *The Fugitive Blacksmith; or, Events in the History of James W. C. Pennington, Pastor of a Presbyterian*

In similar fashion, Alexander Crummell rejected the "empty verbosity" of "vain babblers" who would seek to rationalize away the sting of slavery by attributing to it a "training for freedom" or a schooling for "free government." Thanks to the superintendency of divine providence, slavery was at the same time inherently evil and consequentially good, both a curse and a cure. Yet the cure did not arise intrinsically from the curse, but from God's redemptive reversal of the effects of the curse. To say that Christianity and free government were the "natural sequence, or legitimate result, or effect" of their "parent cause," slavery, would be as mindless as asserting that death authored life, sin authored salvation, pollution generated purity, or hell gave birth to heaven. When confronted with the gloomy history of American thralldom, one both praised the mysterious sovereignty of God in history and prayed that "the whole matter could be blotted out forever, as history and as a remembrance, and become a blank!"[18]

John W. E. Bowen, a black Methodist pastor in Washington, D.C., and later a professor at Gammon Theological Seminary, posed the same issue in the early 1890s in his "national sermon." Nearly every "sorrowful chapter" in the history of black peoples ends in the turbid mist of the impenetrable question mark, "Wherefore?" Black people should neither labor over the bitterness of slavery nor over the vindication of its existence. Suffice it to acknowledge that God had a destiny for black peoples and that eventually God would reveal his divine purpose behind the present mystery—slavery.[19]

Thus for many blacks the mystery of slavery was not

Church, New York, Formerly a Slave in the State of Maryland, United States, 2nd ed. (London, 1849), 76–77.

18. Crummell, "The Duty of a Rising State," in *Future of Africa,* 73.

19. John W. E. Bowen, *What Shall the Harvest Be? A National Sermon; Or, a Series of Plain Talks to the Colored People of America, on their Problems* (Washington, D.C., 1892), 32, 40–42.

without meaning, and the meaning went far beyond spiritual salvation and human progress. As the Pilgrims were compelled by God to settle America, not just to work out their own destiny but the destiny of the world, so black leaders translated the divine providence in bringing African people within the pale of progressive principles into a responsibility for blacks to share with Africans the salvation they had found in America.[20] In commemoration of the abolition of the slave trade on January 1, 1808, Absalom Jones preached a thanksgiving sermon in St. Thomas's African Episcopal Church in Philadelphia.[21] Acknowledging that the reasons why God had permitted Africans to be enslaved would "forever remain a mystery," Jones nevertheless conjectured that "perhaps his design was that a knowledge of the gospel might be acquired by some of their descendants, in order that they might become qualified to be the messenger of it, to the land of their fathers."[22]

The Reverend Peter Williams eulogized Captain Paul Cuffe as just such a "messenger" in his 1817 memorial sermon before the New York African Institution. In giving of his time and money to promoting Christian colonies in Africa, Cuffe "hoped, that our curse would be converted into a blessing, and Africa speedily brought to enjoy all the advantages of

20. This was, of course, a familiar theme in the rhetoric of white colonizationists. See Fuller, *Our Duty*, 8–9; also the argument by Daniel Webster that slavery had providentially educated blacks in Protestantism and democracy so that they could return to Africa and educate their forefathers, quoted in Freeman, *Africa's Redemption*, 325. See also Alexander, *History of Colonization*, 12; and Jacob Dewees, *Great Future*, 32 ff., 185–86.

21. In 1794, the year this church was formed, the trustees (who included Absalom Jones) asked Samuel Magaw, the rector of St. Paul's Episcopal Church in the city, to preach the dedicatory sermon. The white pastor advised the black congregation that gratitude to God was in order "for having directed, in his own wise Providence, that you should come from a land of Pagan darkness, to a land of Gospel light." In God's own inimitable way, Magaw continued, the evil intentions of men were altered for the good of God's children. (See William Douglass, *Annals of First African Church*, 76–77.)

22. Jones, *A Thanksgiving Sermon*, quoted in Porter, ed., *Early Negro Writing*, 340.

civilization and Christianity."[23] These twin advantages were
of such magnitude that two black preachers in the later years
of the nineteenth century could look back on the history of
American slavery and claim that whites had lost more from
slavery than blacks, for it was whites who lost their freedom.
The white emerged from slavery like the Egyptian, the "slave
of slaves," while the black emerged from slavery like the Israelite, clothed "with the rings and jewels of a better civilization,
and with the crown of truth upon his head, and with a wreath
of grace upon his brow and the golden cup of salvation in the
mouth of his sack." Thus, in the baffling fullness of God's providence, slavery would prove the instrument for regenerating black
Americans, who in turn would work for the redemption of
Africa.[24] While not absolving Americans from the crime of slavery, Alexander Crummell told a crowd of Liberians in 1860
that American slavery had been a priming ground where blacks
could learn "the noblest *theories* of liberty, the grandest *ideas*
of humanity" and translate what had to a considerable degree
been "abstractions *there*" into "realities *here*."[25]

In short, the fact of slavery was true; but it was not the
truth. Groping for meaning in the dark facts of the accursed
slave traffic, black leaders of differing racial dispositions seized
upon a similar providential understanding of history to make

23. Peter Williams, *A Discourse, Delivered on the Death of Captain
Paul Cuffe, Before the New York African Institution, In the African
Methodist Episcopal Zion Church, October 21, 1817* (New York, 1817),
15.

24. Bishop L. H. Holsey, *Autobiography*, 242–43; Daniel H. Peterson, *Looking Glass*, 49–50; Bishop Alexander Walters, *My Life and
Work* (New York, 1917), 172–73. On his graduation from Newton
Theological Seminary in June 1874, George Washington Williams delivered an oration entitled "Early Christianity in Africa," in which he
translated into the black experience Joseph's response to his brothers who
had enslaved him: "As for you, ye meant it unto evil, but God meant it
unto good; that we, after learning your arts and sciences, might return
to Egypt and deliver the rest of our brethren who are yet in the house
of bondage." (See his *History of Negro Race*, I: 114.)

25. Crummell, "The English Language in Liberia," in *Future of
Africa*, 51–52.

sense out of the horror of their passage to America. Fifty years before the "Tuskegee Wizard," Booker T. Washington, alluded to slavery as evidence of the way "Providence so often uses men and institutions to accomplish a purpose," the emigrationists James Theodore Holly and J. Dennis Harris recounted the providential purpose behind the influx of blacks into the New World. Relying on solar symbolism and the passage of "Civilization and Christianity . . . from East to the West," Holly believed with Harris that the "final purpose of negro slavery" was the building in Hayti of what each called respectively a "negro nationality" and "colored nationality." Providence had planned that an "Anglo-African" empire should beam back to Africa those progressive principles which an Anglo-American empire was beaming back to Europe.[26]

To delegates attending a special 1895 conference on Africa sponsored by Gammon Theological Seminary in Atlanta, this issue of the relationship of American blacks to the Christianization and civilization of Africa was of obviously pressing pertinence. Most of the papers read at the conference theorized that Providence had intended that blacks be brought to the New World so that Africa could be enlightened through returning black missionaries. Bishop Henry McNeal Turner, who never relented in his bitter attacks against what America had done to her black citizens, nevertheless could specify America as "a heaven-permitted, if not divine-sanctioned, manual laboring school" where blacks "might have direct contact with the mightiest race that ever trod the face of the globe."[27] Yet in explaining slavery, black Americans were

26. See Washington's *Up From Slavery,* as reprinted in Louis R. Harlan, ed., *The Booker T. Washington Papers,* Vol. I (Chicago, 1972), 222–23. Howard H. Bell, ed., *Black Separatism and the Caribbean 1860 by James Theodore Holly and J. Dennis Harris* (Ann Arbor, Michigan, 1970), 65, 178, 181–82.

27. J. W. E. Bowen, ed., *Africa and the American Negro. Addresses and Proceedings of the Congress on Africa Held under the Auspices of the Stewart Missionary Foundation for Africa of Gammon Theological Seminary in Connection with the Cotton States and International Exposi-*

careful not to explain it away. As Booker T. Washington noted in his autobiography, the motivations behind transplanting thousands of Africans in America were mercenary, not missionary.[28]

Paradoxically, it took one of the most integrationist-minded blacks in the nineteenth century to reject the providential interpretation of the African migration to America, and it took one of the most racially proud and African-oriented black men in the nineteenth century to come closest to granting divine sanction to chattel slavery and the slave trade. T. Thomas Fortune, who attended the 1895 Gammon Conference on Africa, had written in 1884 that he rejected as nonsense the attempt to make sense out of slavery by putting it into a providential framework as a school for the eventual evangelization of Africa. "The Lord, who is eminently just, had no hand in their forcible coming here; it was preeminently the work of the devil."[29]

Part of Fortune's hostility to the theory of providential design was that, in the thought of one such as Edward Wilmont Blyden, it implied that blacks were American residents only temporarily. Blyden, the brilliant scholar and "Pan-Negro Patriot" whose writings, whether on history, religion, or linguistics, proclaimed a pledge of allegiance to Africa, constructed a philosophy of history that interpreted historical dynamics in terms of providence, race, and suffering. Sharing as he did with his black brethren in America a peculiar sense of the mysterious operations of Providence in history, Blyden wrote that God had a "divine plan" to restore glory to Africa, and that it was an integral part of that plan that Africans be deported to the New World, where they could receive Christianity and other elements of western culture. The ultimate

---

tion December 13–15, 1895 (Atlanta, 1896; reprinted Miami, Florida, 1969), 195; also 13–14, 145–46, 208–09, *passim.*

28. Harlan, ed., *Washington Papers,* I: 223.

29. Timothy Thomas Fortune, *Black and White: Land, Labor and Politics in the South* (New York, 1884; reprinted New York, 1969), 143.

destiny that God had decreed for Africans, Blyden constantly insisted, was not to be worked out in white America, but in black Africa. The diaspora of Africans in the New World would end in the return of Christianized and westernized Negroes to Africa where a new and unparalleled civilization would be built.[30] As late as 1900 Blyden wrote:

To those who have lived any time in West Africa, three things are indisputably clear; first, that it was absolutely necessary that large numbers of the people should be taken into exile for discipline and training under a more advanced race; second, that they should be kept separate from the dominant race; third, that chosen spirits from among the exiles should in course of time return and settle among their brethren in the fatherland to guide them into the path of civilization.[31]

30. In an address to the American Colonization Society in 1880 on "Ethiopia Stretching Out Her Hands Unto God, or Africa's Service to The World," Blyden contended that abolition was decreed by God: "The ways of God are mysterious. We must walk by faith and not by sight. We hear His voice saying, 'This is the way; walk ye in it.' In the raising of this Society *and the doing away wth slavery* we can see almost visibly the hand of God displayed." (Cited by St. Clair Drake, *The Redemption of Africa and Black Religion* [Chicago, 1970], 55–60, 60–61.)

31. *Liberia Bulletin,* 16 (February 1900), as cited by Hollis R. Lynch, *Edward Wilmot Blyden: Pan-Negro Patriot 1832–1912* (London, 1967), 79–80. As Lynch notes, "This statement of 1900 represented a modification of his earlier viewpoint that an entire Negro exodus was inevitable." Henry McNeal Turner's providential understanding of history led him to impose a similar interpretation on slavery and the slave trade. He believed that the early colonists, fleeing from persecution themselves, came to the New World "to civilize the heathen and to build up an asylum for the oppressed of all nations." America was chosen by God to provide a "school" where blacks could learn Christianity, democracy, and other aspects of "moral and intellectual culture." In return for Christianity and civilization, blacks were to repay the white man with the fruits of their labor. For this reason, Turner affirmed that God briefly "sanctioned" the slave trade and "winked, or lidded his eyeballs, at the institution of slavery." Slavery thus became "a trust from God" and "a test of the white man's obedience" to the divine will and plan for elevating blacks. When America betrayed its sacred trust by suppressing rather than supporting black advancement, God brought judgment upon the nation in the form of the Civil War. Turner and Blyden, however, stopped just short of theocratic determinism in their providential philosophies of history. Ultimately neither could bring himself to declare firmly

Yet Blyden stopped just short of theocratic determination in his philosophy of history, for he never could bring himself to believe fully that the cruel means of African "regeneration" were predestined by Providence. "When we say that Providence decreed the means of Africa's enlightment," he wrote in the 1880s, "we do not say that He decreed the wickedness of the instruments." According to Blyden, "it was not the first time that wicked hands were suffered to execute a Divine purpose."[32] In fact, it would not be the last, for "All the advancements made to a better future by individuals or race, has been made through paths marked by suffering. This great law is written not only in the Bible, but upon all history."[33]

Both white and black writers in the nineteenth century subscribed to the same providential understanding of history which denied that history was a meaningless meandering of events. The black intellectual formulation of the concrete operations of this purposeful Providence in history, however, was suffused with a painfully profound sense of paradox, mystery, and tragedy that was missing in the ponderings of white historians.

I

Blacks who surveyed the mysterious ways in which Providence had wrested their spiritual, mental, and cultural enlightenment from the evil intentions of men, belabored the enormity of slavery's debilitating effects and psychological brutality only long enough to warn of impending divine judgment

---

that the cruel means of African "regeneration" were predestined by providence. In an 1883 letter to the *Christian Recorder,* Turner feebly tried to distinguish between American slavery as a "divine institution," which he denied, as opposed to a "providential institution," which he affirmed. (See Edwin S. Redkey, ed., *Respect Black: The Writings and Speeches of Henry McNeal Turner* [New York, 1971], 7–8, 42, 55.)

32. Drake, *Redemption of Africa,* 60. This is contrary to Lynch, who states that "in effect, [Blyden] gave divine sanction to the slave trade, [and] absolved those who had taken a part in it" (*Blyden,* 80).

33. Drake, *Redemption of Africa,* 63.

on the perpetrators of racial oppression. They then proceeded to proclaim with pride the exalted destiny that was theirs as black Americans. Blacks refused to succumb to the white stereotype of themselves (widely propogated by colonizationists such as Jacob Dewees) as innately too "weak," like the American Indian, to coexist alongside the aggressive, domineering, and industrious Anglo-Saxon. If the American Indians, the original owners of America, were powerless before the progressive path of the Anglo-Saxon, the argument went, how much more certain was the fate of the African?[34] Just such pronouncements, lamented the Maryland physician, James Hall (who edited the *Maryland Colonization Journal*), hardened the hearts of blacks against colonization. In a January 1847 editorial, "Why Don't the Colored People Go to Africa?" Hall suggested that there was more to the universal hostility to colonization than indolence, ignorance, love of America, or optimism in achieving social and political equality with whites. The source of black antipathies to African colonization, he averred, was pride. It was a defiant but delusive pride in their destiny in America, he felt, that blinded blacks from seeing that weaker races must survive, die, or flee. Taking it one step further, Hall reasoned that it was racial pride that quickened black resolve to prove that they were of no inferior metal and to claim for themselves a destiny as black Americans.[35]

From Richard Allen to W. E. B. Du Bois, black leaders read history as evidencing that Providence was working out a divine purpose for mankind, for America, and for black peoples. Spanning the nineteenth century, furthermore, was a universal assumption among Afro-Americans that America's destiny was somehow related to the destiny of Africans. For the majority of black leaders, from Frederick Douglass to W. E. B. Du Bois, black Americans had a proud destiny

34. Dewees, *Great Future*, 219; see also 174, 203, 229–30.
35. *Maryland Colonization Journal*, III: 19 (January 1847): 290–91, cited by Campbell, *Maryland in Africa*, 184.

both as blacks and as Americans. For Douglass, in 1854, the destiny of the black American was coincident with the destiny of the white American: "All the facts in his history mark him out for a destiny, united to America and Americans." For Henry Highland Garnet, in 1848, "this republic, and this continent, are to be the theatre in which the grand drama of our triumphant Destiny is to be executed." For W. E. B. Du Bois in 1897, the black identity crisis of "Am I an American or am I a Negro?" yielded two interlocking destinies: "We are Americans, not only by birth and by citizenship, but by our political ideals, our language, our religion. Further than that our Americanism does not go. At that point we are Negroes," with a unique destiny that precludes "absorption by the white American."[36]

When blacks needed historical proof that Providence had ordained for them a unique destiny, they pointed to all the trouble to which Providence had gone in overruling the evil motivations of man in their behalf and to the way in which they had flourished, in contrast to the dying American Indian and Sandwich Islander when exposed to the enterprising Anglo-Saxon. Frederick Douglass wrote in 1854 that the black man's "tawny brother, the Indian, dies under the flashing glance of the Anglo-Saxon. *Not* so the Negro; civilization cannot kill him. He accepts it—becomes a part of it."[37] The question

---

36. See Frederick Douglass's address delivered at Western Reserve College, 12 July 1854, entitled "The Claims of the Negro Ethnologically Considered," reproduced in Foner, ed., *Douglass*, II: 308; Garnet, *Past and Present Condition*, in Ofari, *"Let Your Motto Be Resistance,"* 197; W. E. B. Du Bois, "The Conservation of Races," in Julius Lester, ed., *The Seventh Son: The Thought and Writings of W. E. B. Du Bois*, Vol. I (New York, 1971), 182–83.

37. Frederick Douglass, "The Claims of the Negro Ethnologically Considered," in Foner, ed., *Douglass*, II: 308. A study of the image of the American Indians in the mind of black Americans would be fascinating. For example, in calling for blacks to unite, Maria W. Stewart challenged blacks to appropriate the example of the Indians, who "are more united than ourselves. Insult one of them, and you insult a thousand. They also have contended for their rights and privileges, and are held in higher repute than we are. . . ." (See Maria Stewart, "An Ad-

was to what degree the destiny of black Americans was to become a part of the destiny of white Americans. In other words, were black Americans destined to contribute anything unique both to the destiny of America and to the destiny of the world?

The disturbing topic of racial discreation frequently arrested the attention of black thinkers. Their speculations, especially about the native American Indian, were often guilty of the same racial stereotyping against which they were combating. The Rochester grocer and sometime leader of the Wilberforce Colony, Austin Steward, was haunted by the specter of the extinction of native Americans in the presence of Anglo-Saxons. Nevertheless, he saw in the survival of the black man in America proof "that the colored man has yet a prominent part to act in this highly favored Republic." In fact, Steward could find no reason for God's having created the black man if he were not created "to fulfill his destiny as a *negro,* to the glory of God." This meant for Steward that blacks had to "cease looking to the white man for example

---

dress Delivered Before the Afric-American Female Intelligence Society, of Boston," in *Productions of Mrs. Maria W. Stewart* [Boston, 1835], 60–61). David Walker believed that blacks should instill in whites the same fear of enslaving blacks that the Indians had inspired in whites. Whites did not enslave Indians because whites had learned from experience that if they did, Indians "would tear them from the earth. The Indians would not rest day or night, they would be up all times of night, cutting their cruel throats." (Walker, *Appeal,* 39, 74). Robert Purvis and Martin R. Delany believed that blacks and Indians should unite and make a common cause with each other, since their claims to America, by virtue of the red man's natural rights and by virtue of the black man's physical rights, surpassed that of the whites (see the correspondence between Robert Purvis and Senator S. C. Pomeroy, 29 August 1862, in Purvis, *Speeches and Letters,* 21–22; Delany, *Condition, Elevation, Emigration,* in Brotz, ed., *Negro Social and Political Thought,* 79). And for David Ruggles, the history of the encounter between the Indians and the Puritan colony demonstrated that Christian colonization, however exalted its goals, could only serve to impede the Christianizing and civilizing of the native population, whether in America or in Africa (Ruggles, *"Extinguisher" Extinguished,* 19).

and imitation." Rather, he exhorted, "stand boldly on your own national characteristics."[38] Similar admonishments filled Henry Highland Garnet's 1848 address entitled *The Past and the Present Condition and the Destiny of the Colored Race.* Whereas red men had fallen before the onward march of the white man, black men have "clung and grown with their oppressor, as the wild ivy entwines around the trees of the forest, nor can they be torn thence."[39]

Seven years before the publication of Charles Darwin's *Origin of the Species* (1859), Alexander Crummell purported to see God's purpose for the future of Africans in the way "weaker" races, like the American Indians, had been earmarked for extinction when placed in juxtaposition with the Anglo-Saxon emigrants. Admittedly it was a sorrowful sight to see the Anglo-Saxon funeral procession marching across the backs of "the weak portions of mankind" to the tune of "progress of civilization and enlightenment." Yet Crummell professed to see "amid all these sad general facts . . . one exception—the NEGRO!" God had intended that the black be brought into close proximity with whites so that the black "might seize upon civilization; that he might obtain hardiment of soul; that he might develop those singular vital forces, both of the living spirit and the hardy frame, in which I claim the Negro is unrivalled; and thus, himself, be enabled to go forth, the creator of new civilizations in distant quarters, and the founder, for Christ, of new churches!"[40] As we shall see, both Crummell and Du Bois agreed that the black man was given a great and glorious destiny as conveyors of a separate spiritual message that, in the words of Du Bois, is "destined to soften the whiteness of the Teutonic today."[41]

38. Steward, *Twenty-Two Years a Slave,* 231, 332.
39. Garnet, *Past and Present Condition,* in Ofari, *"Let Your Motto Be Resistance,"* 179.
40. See Alexander Crummell's 1854 Monrovian address "God and the Nation," his 1852 sermon "Hope for Africa," and his essay "The Progress of Civilization Along the West Coast of Africa" in *Future of Africa,* 320, 126–27.
41. Du Bois, "Conservation of Races," 181, 183.

Black Americans believed that they were doomed neither to destruction like the American Indian, nor to the degradation of slavery. They were destined for an exalted future as free Americans, equal to whites. It was one thing to lay claim to a destiny as black Americans. It was another to define that destiny in terms of its two components—black and American. If God had ordained a destiny for Afro-Americans, was that destiny to be interpreted in relationship to one's African origin, to one's American status, or to both? For the most part, black Americans in the first half of the nineteenth century simply affirmed that white Americans and black Americans had a common country, a common citizenship, and a common destiny. It remained for Martin R. Delany to challenge the black community to tighten its concept of black destiny and to reexamine its identity as black Americans.

When Martin R. Delany proclaimed, in his 1852 book entitled *The Condition, Elevation, Emigration, and Destiny of the Colored People of the United States,* that blacks were a "nation within a nation," he meant two things. First, blacks were an oppressed "class of people" who lived in a society where other classes of people deprived them of equal political, religious, and social rights. Second, a unique people called "Africo-Americans" (a term Delany used consistently when he edited the *Mystery* in the mid-1840s) were "singled out—although having merged in the habits and customs of our oppressors—as a distinct nation of people" by a people Alexis de Tocqueville called "Anglo-Americans." The issue at stake was the relationship between the black oppressed nation to the white oppressor nation. As far as the black oppressed nation was concerned there was no issue:

Our common country is the United States. Here were we born, here raised and educated; here are the scenes of childhood; the pleasant associations of our school going days; the loved enjoyments of our domestic and fireside relations, and the sacred graves of our departed fathers and mothers, and from here will we not be driven by any policy that may be schemed against us.

We are Americans, having a birthright citizenship—natural claims upon the country—claims common to all others of our fellow citizens—natural rights, which may, by virtue of unjust laws, be obstructed, but never can be annulled. Upon these do we place ourselves, as immovably fixed as the decrees of the living God.[42]

With regard to the white oppressor nation, the issue was equally well drawn.

The United States, untrue to her trust and unfaithful to her professed principles of republican equality, has also pursued a policy of political degradation to a large portion of her native born countrymen, and that class is the Colored People. Denied an equality not only of political, but of natural rights, in common with the rest of our fellow citizens, there is no species of degradation to which we are not subject.[43]

Delany summarized the relationship between the black and white "nations" by announcing that "we love our country, dearly love her, but she doesn't love us—she despises us, and bids us begone, driving us from her embraces." In spite of the fact that this black "nation" by its "industry and interest," by its "habits and customs," has as much a claim to equal privileges and status as "any portion of the American people," yet "we are politically not of them, but aliens to the laws and political privileges of the country." With blasted hopes in America, Delany urged blacks to emigrate from the United States—but not from America. "We must not leave this continent," Delany counseled, for "America is our destination and our home." The American continent was "designed by Providence as an asylum for all the various nations of the earth," and blacks had just as much of a right to claim the New World as an asylum as the whites.[44]

As a black American, Delany had reached a critical juncture. The Fugitive Slave Law of 1850, the turning point for some black and white abolitionists in their attitudes towards integration and emigration, raised fundamental ques-

---

42. Delany, *Condition, Elevation, Emigration,* 55.
43. *Ibid.,* 38–39.
44. *Ibid.,* 95, 64, 72, 79, 85. A few years later, Delany would change his mind concerning North America as a locale for black emigration.

tions about the foundation of American democracy. The unfilled potentialities of black Americans seemed hopelessly stifled by the racial injustices of white Americans. There seemed to be no prospect for the black American "nation" to be accepted as a constitutive element of the larger American nation. Thus the time had come for Delany to decide whether to fight it out, armed only with facile faith that someday America would practice her preachments, or to separate the black American aliened nation from the alienator nation and to strike out for a national destiny on one's own. When Delany found himself forced to choose between perpetual degradation of the black American nation or the exodus of the oppressed nation from the oppressor nation, Delany chose the latter. Elevation and emigration, he declared, over degradation and America. Delany even went so far as to say that if need be he would rather be "a Heathen *African,* than a Christian *slave,*" although he never felt the necessity of making this choice.[45] By emigrating, Delany envisioned the establishment of a black society that achieved the ideal democracy professed but not practiced by the white American nation.[46]

The response to Delany's black declaration of independence was immediate. William Lloyd Garrison gave a lengthy review of *Condition and Elevation* in the *Liberator,* decrying Delany's "tone of despondency," "spirit of caste," and "separatism."[47] In response, Delany denied that he favored "caste" and "separatism," claiming that he "would as willingly live among white men as black if I had an equal *possession and enjoyment* of privileges; but [I] shall never be reconciled to live among them, subservient to their will." Regarding his alleged "despondency," Delany admitted that it was indeed true since he had "no hopes in this country, no confidence in the

45. *Ibid.,* 83.
46. See Victor Ullman, *Martin R. Delany: The Beginnings of Black Nationalism* (Boston, 1971), 21.
47. *Liberator,* 14 May 1852.

American people."[48] What added embitterment to his despondency, however, was the chilly reception accorded Delany's book by black abolitionists he had always respected,
especially his former co-editor of the *North Star,* Frederick
Douglass. Douglass gave the book the death dismissal, refusing to even notice its publication in his paper. When Douglass
did get around to attacking it, the prime object of his censure
was Delany's posture of hopelessness. The issue revolved not
around whether blacks loved America more than they did
liberty and equality. This had already been answered hypo-
thetically time and again by black voices like that which gave
the opening speech at the Buffalo National Convention of 1843.
"We love our country, we love our fellow citizens—but we
love our liberty more."[49] The crucial question, wrote Douglass, is "can the white and colored people of this country be
blended into a common nationality, and enjoy together, in
the same country, under the same flag, the inestimable blessings of life, liberty and the pursuit of happiness, as neighborly
citizens of a common country? I answer most unhesitatingly,
I believe they can."[50]

Just as neither Douglass nor Delany abandoned their racial
identity, so neither Douglass nor Delany denied their identity
as Americans. The difference was that Delany believed that
white Americans would never accept black Americans as
black men or as Americans. Thus Delany felt forced to resolve that "dichotomy" which W. E. B. Du Bois testified had
plagued all his reflections: "how far can love for my oppressed
race accord with love for the oppressing country? And when
these loyalties diverge, where shall my soul find refuge?"[51]

48. *Ibid.,* 21 May 1852. Delany's response to Garrison's review can
also be found in Woodson, ed., *Mind of Negro,* 293.
49. *Minutes of the National Convention of Colored Citizens: Held
at Buffalo, on the 15th, 16th, 17th, 18th, and 19th of August, 1843, For
the Purpose of Considering Their Moral and Political Condition as
American Citizens* (New York, 1843), 5.
50. Quoted in Ullman, *Delany,* 145.
51. W. E. B. Du Bois, *Dusk of Dawn: An Essay Toward an Autobiography of a Race Concept* (New York, 1840), 169.

Delany never did find this haven completely, but at this point he believed that black Americans had to create their own national destiny apart from white Americans. His soul was imprisoned in a dungeon of despair, and Delany grasped at the first visible key—emigration. Douglass, unlike Delany, was never stuck at the crossroads where one had to decide between continuing on a path that went hopelessly nowhere or veering off into a path that hopefully went somewhere. Douglass believed, as Delany would later come to espouse after the onset of the Civil War, that through the agitations and exertions of black Americans, the divine purpose of their elevation could be realized in America.

The difference between Frederick Douglass and Martin Delany was summed up by Douglass: "I have always thanked God for making me a man, but Martin Delany always thanks God for making him a black man."[52] It was because Douglass

---

52. Quoted in Adelaide Cromwell Hill and Martin Kilson, ed., *Apropos of Africa: Afro-American Leaders and the Romance of Africa* (Garden City, New York, 1971), 25. As equally as many blacks stressed their identity as African descendants, they also stressed their kinship with the "universal family of man." To quote one of the favorite texts of black preachers, God had "made of one blood all nations of men for to dwell on the face of the earth." Daniel A. Payne, for example, began his speech before the Franckean Synod in June 1839: "SIR—I am opposed to slavery, not because it enslaves the black man, but because it enslaves man!" (See Douglas C. Stange, "Document: Bishop Daniel Alexander Payne's Protestation of American Slavery," *Journal of Negro History*, LII [January 1967]: 60.) Henry Highland Garnet apologized for the necessity of speaking in terms of race when he explained in *Past and Present Condition*, quoted in Ofari, *"Let Your Motto Be Resistance"* (161), that "in order to pursue my subject I must, for the sake of distinction, use some of the improper terms of our times. I shall, therefore, speak of races, when in fact there is but one race, as there was but one Adam." The *Aliened American* dedicated itself to creating a "universal conscience" and to speaking for and appealing to all "Humanity." (See Dann, ed., *Black Press*, 50.) For other examples of the black perception of universal identity and the way in which they embraced the doctrine of the oneness and affinity of all mankind, see Woodson, ed., *Mind of Negro*, 232; Benjamin T. Tanner, *An Apology for African Methodism* (Baltimore, 1867), 115–16; and *Anglo-African*, I (May 1859): 160, as cited by Aptheker, ed., *Documentary History*, 422–23; Foner, ed., *Douglass*, II: 293, 433, 434.

envisioned himself a man with black skin rather than a black man that he justified marrying a white woman, that he prophesied assimilation, and that he opposed Delany's suggestion that an ethnic quota system be adopted in filling governmental positions.[53] Nevertheless, while oppression, more than color, constituted the primary referent for Douglass's activities, he still took great pride in his color and even praised Delany, in 1862, for giving "our white fellow citizens the opportunity of seeing a brave self-conscious black man, one who does not cringe or cower at the thought of his hated color, but one who if he betrays any concern about his complexion at all, errs in the opposite direction."[54] Regardless of their dispute over emigration and separatism, both Douglass and Delany found common ground in their pride in race, which Delany articulated before the 1854 National Emigration Convention.

That we shall ever cherish our identity of origin and race, as preferable, in our estimation, to any other people. That the relative terms Negro, African, Black, Colored and Mulatto, when applied to us, shall ever be held with the same respect and pride; and synonymous with the terms Caucasian, White, Anglo-Saxon and European, when applied to that class of people.[55]

The mathematician, almanac maker, inventor of a clock, and expert violinist, Benjamin Banneker, introduced himself to Thomas Jefferson in 1791 by saying that, "Sir, I freely and cheerfully acknowledge that I am of the African race, and in that color which is natural to them of the deepest dye."[56] If

53. Foner, ed., *Douglass,* IV: 116–17, 410–11, 194–96, 280.
54. *Douglass' Monthly* (August 1862).
55. Quoted in Ullman, *Delany,* 170. Upon crossing the mountains from Philadelphia to Pittsburgh in February 1849, Delany paused to reflect upon his color: "Indeed it is only on the mountains that I can fully appreciate my existence as a man in America, my own native land. It is then and there my soul is lifted up, my bosom caused to swell with emotion, and I am lost in wonder at the dignity of my own nature. . . . I then perceive the likeness I bear to Him." (Quoted in Ullman, *Delany,* 100.)
56. Benjamin Banneker, *Copy of a Letter from Benjamin Banneker to the Secretary of State, with his Answer* (Philadelphia, 1792), in

Jefferson had been alive in 1829, he would have had to endure the less restrained and more censorious enthusiasm of a Boston clothing merchant and sales agent for *Freedom's Journal* who took pride in his blackness—David Walker. To think, Walker fumed (in what Quaker Benjamin Lundy described as the most inflammatory publication in history), that Jefferson had the swaggering pretension to call the color of blacks " 'unfortunate!' As though we are not as thankful to our God for having made us as it pleased himself as they (the whites) are for having made them white." Contrary to the white self-flattery that blacks desired white skins, Walker insisted that blacks desired only to be clad in the color which God had intended for them.[57]

Over and over again the esteem with which black Americans held their color was manifested in frequent, unapologetic acclamations of blackness. "I am not a white man," David Ruggles testified. "I am a black man." The black abolitionist "Sidney" wrote in the *Colored American* that black Americans suffered no shameful black "colorphobia," but instead took pride in their God-given color. If their dark skin bothered whites, Sidney retorted, he could not care less. That was the whites' problem.[58] The black abolitionist, physician,

---

Porter, ed., *Early Negro Writing,* 325. Frederick Douglass also was noted for his prowess on the violin, and in later life he delighted especially in playing "The Star-Spangled Banner."

57. Walker, *Appeal,* 19. It should be remembered, however, that some slaves did acquiesce in the negative color-image promulgated by slaveholders. As late as the 1880s, Eli Shepard found extant the "barbarous belief that, whereas God is indeed Creator of the dominant white race, they, poor blacks are the handiwork of Satan. This making a man contra to the commands of our Creator was the sin for which the devil, once an angel of high degree, was flung from heaven: 'Flung into hell,' declared my informant, the corn-vendor, 'en dar he be now tied ter de wheel er de chariot er fire! Chained ter de turnin' wheel er fire; en dar he gwine stay twel de great Risin' Day.' " (See Shepard's "Superstitions of the Negro," *Cosmopolitan,* V [March 1888]: 47–50, as reprinted in Bruce Jackson, ed., *The Negro and His Folklore in Nineteenth-Century Periodicals* [Austin, Texas, 1967], 248.)

58. Ruggles, *"Extinguisher" Extinguished,* 7; Sidney to *Colored*

and first black attorney admitted to the bar of the United States Supreme Court, John Swett Rock, stated that he could not be bothered by those who disliked his color. It was a waste of time to get irritated over someone who "lacks good taste." In fact, Rock conceded that he was not particularly pleased with the physical appearance of whites.

If old Mother Nature had held out as well as she commenced, we should have had fewer varieties in the races. When I contrast the

---

American, 13 March 1841. Some black leaders were particularly stung by the chafing notion that whatever good came out of the black community could be charged to the presence of white blood. (See, for example, John I. Gaines's remarks to this effect in an 1848 tribute to Martin R. Delany in Ullman, *Delany,* 93.) Special effort was made in the writings of black authors to identify those black leaders who could claim no white ancestry. William Wells Brown delighted in needling whites with the fact that Nat Turner's parents were "of unmixed African descent" (W. W. Brown, *The Negro in the American Rebellion: His Heroism and His Fidelity* [Boston, 1867], 19). The dramatization of Brown's 1860 claim that the masses of Negroes "regarded without pride their illicit blood relationships to white people (Farrison, *Brown,* 316) and the 1860 confession of H. Ford Douglass of Illinois that "I am proud of the Negro race, and I thank God that there does not course in my veins a single drop of Saxon blood" (*Liberator,* 13 July 1860) had occurred thirty years earlier. On April 9, 1816, at the Philadelphia conference of the African Methodist Episcopal connection, black Methodists gathered to elect their bishop. According to the minutes, Richard Allen was selected bishop. According to the behind-the-scenes accounts, as published in 1881 and 1888 autobiographies of two A. M. E. ministers, David Smith and Daniel A. Payne, there were two rival candidates for the office, Daniel Coker of Baltimore and Richard Allen of Philadelphia. In the morning, according to this tradition, Daniel Coker was actually elected to the episcopacy because of his superior mental endowments. But the turmoil and dissatisfaction over his ordination among a faction of the delegates prompted him to resign in favor of Allen. It seems that since Coker was "nearly white," due to his half-English and half-African parentage, many felt that the church would not properly be recognized as an independent black institution (if its first leaders were not of pure African ancestry). (See David Smith, *Biography of Rev. David Smith of the A. M. E. Church Being a Complete History, Embracing Over Sixty Years Labor in the Advancement of the Redeemer's Kingdom on Earth* [Xenia, Ohio, 1881; reprinted Freeport, New York, 1971], 33–34; and Daniel Alexander Payne, *Recollections of Seventy Years* [New York, n.d.; reprinted New York, 1968], 100–1.)

fine, tough, muscular system, the beautiful rich color, the full broad features, and the gracefully frizzled hair of the Negro, with the delicate physical organization, wan color, sharp features and lank hair of the Caucasian, I am inclined to believe that when the white man was created, nature was pretty well exhausted—but determined to keep up appearances, she pinched up his features and did the best she could under the circumstances.[59]

Even the Bible believed that black is beautiful, wrote Henry Highland Garnet as he quoted from the Song of Solomon (1:5–6a):

> I am black but comely,
> O ye daughters of Jerusalem,
> As the tents of Kedar,
> As the curtains of Solomon.
> Look not upon me, because I am black,
> Because the sun has looked upon me.

Here was a black woman, exuded Garnet, who "was beautiful, and like all handsome women, she knew it."[60]

One of the ways in which Afro-Americans demonstrated pride in their blackness was in their response to interracial marriage. As the Peases have shown, the subject of miscegenation "generated neither any commonly accepted solutions nor even very much debate."[61] But the grudging acceptance or willing endorsement of intermarriage denoted no reduction in racial esteem. The ambivalence towards blacks in nearly all the white abolitionists, most of whom distinguished between emancipation and racial social mixing, was largely absent in the self-image of blacks in the nineteenth century. David Ruggles asserted that he did not desire amalgamation, "nor does any colored man or woman of my acquaintance." But his "detestation" of intermarriage was nothing more than a personal preference in favor of blackness. Although he

---

59. *Liberator,* 12 March 1858.
60. Garnet, *Past and Present Condition,* 164. This quote from the Song of Solomon was used widely in black assertions of preference for blackness. See Foner, ed., *Douglass,* I: 380.
61. Pease and Pease, *They Who Would Be Free,* 104–5.

was not repelled by the color of whites, he was attracted to his own color, confessing that "nothing is more disgusting than to see my race bleached to a pallid and sickly hue by the lust of those cruel and fastidious white men." The antipathy to amalgamation arose, Ruggles insisted, not out of natural repugnance between whites and blacks but out of the fashions of public opinion and prejudices ingrained by education.[62]

Although both Garnet and Ruggles consistently opposed any legal blockage to interracial marriage, they vehemently denied that the door to American social and political equality was hinged on miscegenation. Austin Steward underscored this view, contending that it was the design of Providence to preserve blacks as "an unmixed and powerful race" who would stand with equal status as Americans and with equal pride in their blackness alongside the Anglo-Saxon in America. Even the Baltimore minister and educator Daniel Coker, who himself was of mixed racial heritage, denounced interracial sexual unions as "truly disgraceful to both colours" and announced that black men who wedded white women "are generally of the lowest class, and are despised by their own people." Similarly, Henry Bibb and Robert Purvis voiced their resentment at being nearly deprived of an ebony complexion by their white ancestors.[63] The one thing blacks

62. Ruggles, *"Extinguisher" Extinguished,* 12–17. Walker wrote in his *Appeal* (p. 19,) that "I would not give a *pinch of snuff* to be married to any white person I ever saw in all the days of my life."

63. Steward, *Twenty-Two Years a Slave,* 328, 332; Coker is quoted in Berlin, *Slaves Without Masters,* 281. For Purvis and Bibb, see *Liberator,* 19, 26 May 1854 and Henry Bibb, *Narrative of the Life and Adventures of Henry Bibb, An American Slave, written By Himself, With an Introduction by Lucius Matlack* (New York, 1849; reprinted Miami, Florida, 1969), 49. W. E. B. Du Bois also opposed the loss of racial identity through intermarriage. (See Lester, ed., *Seventh Son,* I: 181.) Racial identity, wrote Alexander Crummell in 1888, originates in the divine intentionality for mankind. Josiah Strong, the public defender of Anglo-Saxonism, may have written an "able, startling, striking tractate" when he composed *Our Country* (1885), but Crummell assailed Strong's assimilationist solution to the American race problem. "Dr. Strong evi-

seemed to have condemned utterly was the slighting of one's black parentage, and the black press was especially sensitive to any indication that white women were preferred over black women. In the late nineteenth century Frederick Douglass found this out when he was put on the defensive by his choice of a white wife. In the early twentieth century the world boxing champion, Jack Johnson, was raked through the pages of the black press because of his much-publicized weakness for blond, white women.[64] Any appearance of sycophancy to whiteness was denounced as unseemly and unmanly black behaviour.

For a few blacks, like Bishop Henry McNeal Turner, Edward Wilmont Blyden, and culminating in Marcus Garvey, pride in blackness overflowed into prejudice against whiteness. All believed that, in the words of Bishop Turner, "God is a Negro."[65] All entertained an almost irrational detestation of mulattoes, so much so that Blyden told a close friend that "when I am dead—write nothing on my tombstone but . . . 'He hated mulattoes.' " All endorsed the racial segregation

---

dently forgets," Crummell asserted, "that the principle of race is one of the most persistent of all things in the constitution of man." Its persistence was of such magnitude that the African Emigration Association petitioned Congress in 1886 for funds to aid black emigration, giving as one reason the preservation of blackness, "which is here losing its identity by inter-mixture with white races." (Alexander Crummell, *Africa and America* [Springfield, Massachusetts, 1891; reprinted Miami, Florida, 1969], 46–49.) Cited by Earl E. Thorpe, *The Mind of the Negro: An Intellectual History of Afro-Americans* (Westport, Connecticut, 1970; originally published Baton Rouge, Louisiana, 1961), 32.

64. Al-Tony Gilmore, "Jack Johnson and White Women: The National Impact," *The Journal of Negro History,* LVIII (January 1973): 22–23.

65. Redkey, *Black Exodus,* 40. Turner was not the first black man to say this. In the early 1830s Rev. Samuel H. Cox is reported to have called Jesus Christ a black man from his pulpit. (See Wyatt-Brown, *Lewis Tappan,* 116.) And the congregational clergyman Samuel R. Ward implied something of the sort when, between 1840 and 1850, he preached in nearly every open church, auditorium, and school in central and western New York that enslavement of blacks was the buying and selling of the image of God.

being promulgated by whites at the time.[66] And in general, all demonstrated that if one travels far enough in one direction around the ideological globe, one will end up on the very spot from whence one started. The majority of nineteenth-century black leaders, however, shared the assimilationist and integrationist sentiments of Douglass, William Wells Brown, Samual Ringgold Ward, and T. Thomas Fortune. They believed that racial blending was certainly not a prerequisite to black equality, and, in fact, was aesthetically inferior to pure blackness. Although logistically undesirable in the fight to obtain recognition of black equality, nevertheless they considered miscegenation as ultimately destined to constitute a giant step in the progress of mankind. More than anything else, wrote Brown, amalgamation "breaks down caste and teaches the brotherhood of man."[67]

II

The idea that dark skin pigmentation caused racial prejudice and oppression, a recurring theme among white racial theorists, was flatly rejected by black Americans. In the first place, blacks denied that there was anything in itself odious

---

66. Lynch, *Blyden,* 139, 117–18, 122.

67. For T. Thomas Fortune, editor of the *New York Age* and one of the founders of the Afro-American League, see his essay "The Nationalization of Africa," reprinted in Kilson and Hill, ed., *Apropos of Africa,* 357; also Thornbrough, *T. Thomas Fortune,* 129–31, where Fortune is said to have favored the phrase "Afro-American" because he believed that Africans as a distinct racial group were destined to be absorbed in the melting pot. For Ward, see his *Autobiography of a Fugitive Negro: His Anti-Slavery Labors in the United States, Canada, and England* (London, 1855; reprinted Chicago, 1970), 107. For Brown see *Anglo-African,* 6 February 1864. A few whites defended "amalgamationism": Louisa May Alcott, Lydia Maria Child, and Anna Dickinson through short stories and novels; Gilbert Havens from the pulpit; and Wendell Phillips and Theodore Parker in Fourth of July orations. The biographer Bertram Wyatt-Brown notes that even Lewis Tappan "was not concerned by black and white intermarriage—though he would have insisted that the partners had to be of the same religious persuasion." (See *Lewis Tappan,* 177.)

in the color black. The dispute in the pages of the *Colored American* over what black Americans should call themselves sparked an angry outcry from the black abolitionist Sidney when he read that the highly successful black lumber dealer and pacifist William Whipper had advocated abandoning the term "colored" in deference to white sensibilities which designated prejudices as the offspring of color. "Surely," taunted Sidney, "the term colored is not disgusting to Mr. W. and his friends? They cannot be ashamed of their identity with the negro race!" Why should blacks abandon pride in their color for the sake of helping prejudiced whites get over their color anxieties?[68] Sidney correctly foresaw that by accepting the white argument that color caused prejudice, one was in effect both justifying the prejudice and condemning the color.

In a consistent display of harmony among the ranks of the black leadership, men such as William Wells Brown, Henry Highland Garnet, Hosea Easton, Frederick Douglass, and Martin R. Delany echoed the resounding declaration of the irrepressible "Augustine"—"CONDITION and not *color,* is the chief cause of prejudice, under which we suffer."[69] Henry Highland Garnet wrote that "racial" prejudice simply did not exist, for there was nothing about the color of the African race that elicited prejudice.[70] If an innate, primordial revul-

68. *Colored American,* 13 March 1841.
69. "Augustine" to the *Colored American,* 16 February 1839. See also the 2 December 1837 issue of the *Colored American,* in which Augustine states that the sin of slavery gives birth to "the sin of that prejudice which grows out of slavery." Floyd Miller, in his article " 'The Father of Black Nationalism': Another Contender," *Civil War History,* XVII (December 1971): 310–19, has argued persuasively that "Augustine" was a pseudonym assumed by Lewis Woodson, a minister from Pittsburgh.
70. Garnet, *Past and Present Condition,* 181. *Douglass' Monthly,* June 1863, reported on the resolutions passed at a series of three meetings held at Henry Highland Garnet's church to recruit black volunteers, one of which resolved "that in determination to stand by the government in this war, we are not only deciding to stand by good government, but against slavery, the parent and fosterer of the unjust prejudice we have been the subjects of here in the North."

sion to the color black existed among whites, William Wells Brown chimed in, no one would wear black clothing and whites would not spend so much money on black dyes for gray hair.[71] Hosea Easton haughtily dismissed the absurdity of saying that color caused prejudice by noting that if such were the case, prejudice would be directly proportional to the degree of blackness.[72]

Martin R. Delany scorned the "sheer nonsense" in the idea that Africans were enslaved by the white man because whites hated the color black. Native Americans were oppressed by the whites before the blacks, he wrote, and they were red.[73] William Wells Brown recalled, with characteristic historical acumen, that even before the red man, at various times in history different races had been enslaved, including the Anglo-Saxons. Certainly Anglo-Saxons would not attribute their past enslavement to the fact that their whiteness was deemed particularly offensive.[74] In much the same

71. Brown, *Negro in American Rebellion,* 361–62. Harvey Newcomb wrote sardonically in 1837 that if whites are naturally repulsed by the color black, they should feel sufficiently safe from the " 'scare-crow' of Amalgamation." Newcomb devoted an entire chapter to proving that prejudice against blacks was not related to prejudice against blackness. (See Harvey Newcomb, *The 'Negro Pew': Being an Inquiry Concerning the Propriety of Distinctions in the House of God, on account of Color* [Boston, 1837; reprinted Freeport, New York, 1971], 17 ff., 102.)
72. Hosea Easton *Treatise,* 21–26, 37–38.
73. Delany, *Condition, Elevation, Emigration,* 42.
74. Cited by Farrison, *Brown,* 320. Alexander Walters, bishop of the African Methodist Episcopal Zion Church, also used the historical argument, which detailed the past enslavement of nearly all races, to disprove the correlation between color and discrimination. "Caste prejudice exists" because of "our previous condition of servitude." (See Walters, *Life and Work,* 205, 222.) In 1860, a voice of dissent was raised against this "popular idea" among blacks that "prejudice against color was connected with the idea of slavery." At a meeting at Cooper's Institute in New York City concerning the African Civilization Society, a local black minister, Dr. Asa Hague, argued that "nothing could be more incorrect, for in the sixth century, in the time of Justinian, slaves were white. In order to subdue this prejudice and elevate the race, there must be a nationalization; and in order to bring the community together, scattered as it is far and wide, one grand center must exist. The people

vein, the Reverend Thomas McCants Stewart, historian at the College of Liberia, cited the indiscriminate nature of oppression throughout history to demonstrate the innocence of color in the infamy of prejudice. Addressing an 1884 alumni convention at Hampton Institute, Stewart gave a panoramic glimpse into the historical enslavement of nearly all races. History proved, Stewart concluded, that prejudice was hitched to condition, not color.[75]

"No," exclaimed the man who never wearied of words on any subject, there did not exist any such thing as an "instinctive aversion of the white race for the colored race." Yet if, as Douglass contended, "prejudice really has nothing whatever to do with race or color," prejudice did have everything to do with oppression and slavery.[76] For it was slavery and the condition spawned by slavery that constituted the source of prejudice.

Blacks refused to trace the source of their oppression to their color not only because they rejected the assumption that their color was offensive. They also rejected the negative vision of themselves as brutes, savages, and inferior beings who, in the words of the colonizationist Robert Goodloe Harper, "are condemned to a hopeless state of inferiority and degradation by their color, which is an indelible mark of their origin and former condition, and establishes an impossible barrier between them and the whites."[77] Black leaders did

---

must have a nation, a commerce, a system of diplomacy." (See the *Weekly Anglo-African,* 17 November 1860.)

75. Stewart's address, which was later published in pamphlet form, is summarized in Harlan, ed., *Washington Papers,* II: 253–54.

76. Frederick Douglass, writing in *The North American Review,* CXXXII (June 1881), in Foner, ed., *Douglass,* IV: 349. For Douglass's earlier denial that there was an innate, primordial revulsion of whites to the color black, see his *Bondage and Freedom,* 402–5, and Foner, ed., *Douglass,* II: 129, where Douglass states that "we are then a persecuted people; not because we are *colored,* but simply because that color has for a series of years been coupled in the public mood with the degradation of slavery and servitude."

77. Robert Goodloe Harper, *A Letter from General Harper of Maryland to Elias Caldwell, Secretary of the American Society for Colo-*

not wait until Du Bois to decline the white assessment of themselves as, by reasons of race, inferior and/or destined to a state of inferiority. Instead, aroused black leaders during the first half of the nineteenth century launched what amounted to a three-pronged attack against the racial aspersions cast upon them by the white community. First, blacks undertook the task of educating all Americans in the reasons for whatever actual mental and moral degradation while at the same time affirming the innate mental, moral, and spiritual equality that blacks enjoyed with whites. Second, when white abolitionists appeared on the scene, blacks demanded a recognition of equality, although they were not to get it. Third, and most preeminently, blacks were engaged in discussing the elevation of the race, in devising the methods for their own self-improvement, and in dismantling the mental shackles of those blacks who had acquiesced in the white stereotype of themselves as doomed to political, mental, and moral inferiority.

The erosion of environmentalism as an ethnological doctrine was a slow process that would advance with each succeeding decade in the nineteenth century.[78] Yet some of the earliest black leaders felt compelled to refute the racist notion that their degraded condition was due to their color and natural disposition and that their color hopelessly perpetuated their condition. Absalom Jones and Richard Allen in *A Narrative of the Proceedings of the Colored People, During the Late Awful Calamity in Philadelphia* (1794) and *An Address to those who keep Slaves and Approve the Practice* (1794), for example, contended that blacks were not innately inferior, but were suppressed by repressive environ-

---

nizing *Free People of Colour, in the United States, with their own consent* (Baltimore, 1818), 6, as cited by George M. Fredrickson, *The Black Image in the White Mind* (New York, 1971), 17–18.

78. See Winthrop D. Jordan, *White Over Black: American Attitudes Toward the Negro 1550–1812* (Chapel Hill, North Carolina, 1968), 533–38.

ments. If the minds of black children were cultivated with the same amount of tender care as taken with white children, there would be no inferiority in mental endowments.[79]

John B. Vashon and Lewis Woodson set out to prove empirically that blacks were not branded with the stigma of inferiority. In the early 1830s they founded the "Pittsburg African Education Society" to demonstrate that whites and blacks were intellectually equal given equal educational opportunities. How much could one legitimately expect, asked the outspoken Maria W. Stewart, of slaves who were taught to say "master" before they were taught to say "mother."[80] What could one expect of blacks, wrote Frederick Douglass, Hosea Easton, and David Walker, who, when educated, were taught that they descended originally "from the *tribes* of *Monkeys* or *Orang-Outangs?*" and could be classified, according to one colonizationist author in 1833, as a "distinct race of animals."[81] Given all these impediments, William Hamilton found it amazing that in spite of "all our embarrassments our genius does sometimes burst forth from its incumbrance." Certainly, wrote Henry Highland Garnet, Jefferson's suspicion of black inferiority had been disproven by a host of black geniuses in America and by "a brilliant galaxy in Ancient History." "NO! the noble mind of a Newton," pronounced George Lawrence in

79. See Aptheker, ed., *Documentary History,* 36; and Richard Allen, *The Life Experiences and Gospel Labors of the Right Reverend Richard Allen* (New York, 1960), 70–71.

80. Stewart, "Address, 1833," in Porter, ed., *Early Negro Writing,* 131.

81. See also "Euthymas' to *Liberator,* 27 August 1831, in Woodson, ed., *Mind of Negro,* 233; and *Productions of Mrs. Maria W. Stewart,* 21, for the express denial that blacks were a species of monkeys and the position that blacks have equal intellects to whites. Easton, *Treatise,* 44; Walker, *Appeal,* 20. William Jay, in his *Inquiry into the Character and Tendency of the American Colonization, and American Anti-Slavery Societies,* 2nd ed. (New York, 1835), 45–46, quotes disparagingly from a book written by an unnamed colonizationist, *Evidences against the views of the Abolitionists, consisting of physical and moral proofs of the natural inferiority of the negroes* (New York, 1833).

1808, "could find room, and to spare, within the tenement of many an injured African."[82]

So despicable were allegations of physical and mental inequalities based on skin to William Hamilton and George Lawrence that they even refused to condescend to refute them. One called such propositions "below our notice" and the other called defenses against racist bigotry "superfluous." Blacks were impaired and degraded, the Philadelphia educator Charles L. Reason contended, not because of color and racial inferiority, but because of the egregious system of slavery and oppression. Douglass, in his inimitable way, summed it all up: "Wherein does the white man differ from the black? Why, one is white and the other black. Well, what of that?" Both are equal in all things.[83] Afro-American intellectual history is, to a heroic degree, the history of how black Americans fought imprisonment by the definitions of the larger American society.

Before the advent of abolitionism, white Americans, for the most part, were reluctant to openly express their applied assumptions of black inferiority in terms of white supremacy and permanent black inferiority. But as abolitionists backed the theoretical affirmation of human equality up against the wall of consistency, thereby forcing the open espousal of black inequality, some blacks likewise prodded the abolitionists to be consistent with their own rhetoric, denying that black people were white people's inferior.

The black Presbyterian minister Theodore S. Wright, for example, entreated white abolitionists to "annihilate in their own bosom the cord of caste. We must be consistent—recognize the colored man in every respect as a man and brother,"

82. William Hamilton, *An Address to the New York African Society, for Mutual Relief, delivered in the Universalist Church, January 2, 1809* (New York, 1809), in Aptheker, ed., *Documents,* 52–53; Garnet, *Past and Present Condition,* 181–82; Lawrence, *Oration on Abolition of Slave Trade,* in Aptheker, ed., *Documents,* 59.

83. *Ibid.,* 53, 58; *North Star,* 13 June 1850, in Foner, ed., *Douglass,* II: 130.

whether it be in "the church, the stage, the steamboat, the public house, in all places."[84] After the Buffalo convention had narrowly refused to endorse Henry Highland Garnet's 1843 address urging physical violence in the overthrow of slavery, Garnet was in no mood for the patronizing insinuations of one Garrisonian who remarked that Garnet had succumbed to the influence of bad advisers. "If it has come to this," Garnet retorted, "that I must think as you do, because you are an abolitionist, or be exterminated by your thunder, then I do not hesitate to say that your abolitionism is abject slavery."[85] While lauding the efforts of the abolitionists, Samuel R. Ward lamented, in a letter to the editor of the pro-Garrison *National Anti-Slavery Standard,* that far too many abolitionists "best love the colored man at a distance," duplicating in their own hearts the prejudices of American society.[86] In fact, part of the reason for establishing independent black newspapers, conventions, activities, and structures, according to Ward and to the editors of *Freedom's Journal* and the *Colored American,* was the presumption of white abolitionists, which in itself exhibited the persistence of prejudice, that abolitionists could speak for blacks without listening to blacks.[87] Galled by the white emotional antipathy within the abolitionist movement to the idea that blacks and

84. *Colored American,* 4 October 1837. In the same year, a white abolitionist, Harvey Newcomb, wrote that abolitionists should strive to slay not only slavery but also caste, a prejudice which Newcomb charged stalked even the hearts of the professed abolitionists. (See *"Negro Pew,"* 10.)

85. *Liberator,* 3 December 1843. Prominent black abolitionists who at this time opposed Garnet's speech included Charles Lenox Remond, Frederick Douglass, William Cooper Nell, Robert Purvis, and William Whipper.

86. Litwack, *North of Slavery,* 237.

87. *Colored American,* 2 November 1839. The first editorial of *Freedom's Journal,* 16 March 1827, expressed the hope that as "our friends" listened to what blacks had to say about themselves and what blacks were doing for themselves, they might be prompted to stop "actually living in the practice of prejudice, while they abjure it in theory, and feel it not in their hearts."

whites were peers, by the 1850s many blacks despaired of attaining leadership parity with whites. Thrown on their own resources, blacks increased in self-reliance and self-esteem.

Wherever "the cord of caste" abounded, it had to be severed, and the document which issued from the 1847 black national convention held in Troy, New York, proclaimed that "the best means of destroying caste is the mental, moral, and industrial improvement of our people."[88] Blacks believed that the source of white prejudice either had to be their color or their blighted condition. If they had opted for the color, prejudice would have been a white problem (since blacks could not change the color of their skin)—but a problem which most likely would have been solved only by colonization. If they opted for condition (as all of them did), prejudice became a black problem—but a problem which was caused not by deficiencies within themselves but by the debasement of a white, oppressive environment. Since blacks believed that racial prejudice arose from condition, the question became how to ameliorate the condition and thus eliminate the prejudice of whites. As Frederick Cooper has shown, the history of black Americans in the second quarter of the nineteenth century is the history of black preoccupation with the answer they found to this question—self-improvement.[89] Perhaps nowhere else did blacks reflect their widespread adoption of American evangelical and reform attitudes more than in their vigorous attempts, through hard work, diligence, piety, agrarianism, education, and massive moral uplift (such as, temperance and Sabbatarianism), to storm the bastille of prejudice and assert their manhood and equality with white Americans.[90]

88. *Proceedings of the National Convention of Colored People, and Their Friends, held in Troy, New York on 6th, 7th, 8th, and 9th October, 1847* (Troy, New York, 1847), 31.

89. Frederick Cooper, "Elevating the Race: The Social Thought of Black Leaders, 1827–1850," *American Quarterly,* XXIV (December 1972): 604–25.

90. *The State Convention of the Colored Citizens of Ohio, con-*

Notably absent from these paths to self-improvement en route to recognized equality was the single-minded pursuit of wealth and material aggrandizement. To be sure, there were a few blacks who energetically pursued the American dream of material acquisition and affluence, even while denouncing it. In a speech commemorating Crispus Attucks and the Boston Massacre, Dr. John S. Rock emphasized that "in this country, where money is the great sympathetic nerve which ramifies society, and has a ganglia in every man's pocket, a man is respected in proportion to his success in business." Since Rock despaired of any way to beat American materialism, he decided to join it. The solution to the problem of racial inequality was thus for educated black men to seek power and wealth, whereupon blacks could live and work with whites as among peers. Similarly, Samuel Ringgold Ward, known as the "black Daniel Webster," condemned whites for their overweening concern with the "acquisition of money and pursuit of pleasure," at the same time he advised his readers that "black men must seek wealth."[91] Most black leaders, however, advocated a different view. If prejudice was born of slavery and oppression, what was oppression and slavery born of? The universal answer to this question was greed.

The mulatto historian John W. Cromwell began his book on *The Negro in American History* (1914) with the declaration that "the discovery and colonization of America was primarily for greed, and this dominant principle was illustrated in different stages of the growth and development of the country." Cromwell expressed an interpretation of American history which was common among blacks for over a

---

vented at Columbus, January 10–13, 1849 (Oberlin, Ohio, 1849) made it clear that in seeking their political, moral, and social elevation, blacks were not begging whites for assistance, but were demanding "equal privileges, *not* because we would consider it a condescension on your part to grant them—but because we are *MEN,* and therefore entitled to all the privileges of other men in the same circumstances."

91. John S. Rock to *Liberator,* 12 March 1858; Ward, *Autobiography,* 71, 163.

century. In 1808 Peter Williams preached a sermon on the abolition of the slave trade during which he isolated the source of slavery—"the desire of gain." It was this motivation that allured the first colonists to America, and it was this motive that allowed rights to be violated and black peoples to be enslaved. According to Hosea Easton, "the love of money is the root of all evil," especially the evil of slavery. Slavery did not emerge from the white man's response to the inferior condition of the African, wrote J. W. C. Pennington, but from the insatiable greed of the white man who lived by "the chattel principle, the property principle, the bill of sale principle." Henry Highland Garnet purported that avarice and cupidity, "the besetting sins of the Anglo-Saxon race," numbed white Americans to the humanity and equality of blacks and chained blacks to a state of servility. Greed was the source of American slavery and the sickness of American society.[92]

To many black Americans, the adoption of the values that had spawned slavery and thus racial prejudice—avarice and acquisitiveness—offered no solution to the problem of black elevation and integration into American society as equals. On the contrary, they were seen as impediments to the struggle for self-improvement, and caveats were issued against the undertow of materialistic values. Alexander Crummell, who founded the Negro Academy in March 1897, lectured to his people on the aims of the academy and on the pitfalls of believing that progress for blacks in America depended on the acquisition of material items such as "property," "money," "positions," or status. Rather, the true destiny of black Ameri-

---

92. Cromwell, *Negro in American History*, 1; Peter Williams, *An Oration on the Abolition of the Slave Trade; Delivered in the African Church, in the city of New York, January 1, 1808.* (New York, 1808), in Porter, ed., *Early Negro Writing*, 346; Easton, *Treatise*, 43; James W. C. Pennington, *A Text Book of the Origin and History of the Colored People* (Hartford, Connecticut, 1841), chap. V, 39 ff.; Pennington, *Fugitive Blacksmith*, iv; Garnet, *Past and Present Condition*, 181. See also Walker, *Appeal*, 27–28, 47–48, 53.

cans lay with participation and involvement in transcendent spiritual ideals and goals.[93]

In his famous pamphlet "The Conservation of Races," written in 1897 for the same institution, Du Bois reinforced Crummell's indictment of crass materialism and argued that blacks had special "soul" traits to offer the "money-making plutocracy" in the United States. In fact, at least a part of Du Bois's attack on Booker T. Washington's industrial education scheme to elevate American blacks should be seen in the context of Du Bois's conviction that industrial arts took the white American preoccupation with money and fashioned it into a pattern for blacks. The line that demarcated Du Bois's Talented Tenth from Washington's Tuskegee Tradesman was the line that distinguished the ascendancy of intellectual and spiritual versus material values. In *The Souls of Black Folk,* Du Bois asked whether or not "the industrial school is the final and sufficient answer in the training of the Negro race? . . . Is not life more than meat, and the body more than raiment?" As Du Bois would later pose it, the difference between a liberal arts and an industrial-school education was the difference between the present white American "ideal of Wealth" and the proper black American "ideal of Poverty".[94]

Black leaders responded to the grasping, exploitative nature of their oppressors not only by issuing jeremiads to their people to be true to their color in the struggle for advancement and to resist in their modes and values of life the allures of the American moloch of mammonism. Blacks also exhibited a subtle sense of self-glorification and moral superiority in countering the charges of inferiority and ignobility.[95]

93. This is referred to in Cromwell, *Negro in American History,* 134–35. For a contrasting interpretation of black attitudes towards materialism, see Pease and Pease, *They Who Would Be Free,* 124.

94. Du Bois, "Conservation of Races," in Lester, ed., *Seventh Son,* I: 181; Du Bois, *The Souls of Black Folk* (New York, 1970; originally published Chicago, 1903), 69, 77–78; Lester, ed., *Seventh Son,* I: 574.

95. This theme has been noticed by Sterling Stuckey, "Through the Prism of Folklore: The Black Ethos in Slavery," in Ann J. Lane, ed., *The Debate Over Slavery: Stanley Elkins and His Critics* (Urbana, Illi-

Throughout the poetry, petitions, spirituals, folktales, short stories, fugitive slave narratives, and novels produced by Afro-Americans in the nineteenth century, one can find the recurring theme of the moral superiority of blacks vis-à-vis whites.

Absalom Jones and Richard Allen informed whites that the black man, even in the most wretched state of slavery, was still a man with intellect and feelings, although they taunted whites with the fact that this intellect and feeling might not harbor "the same degree of keen resentment and revenge, that you who have been and are our great oppressors, would manifest if reduced to the pitiable condition of a slave." According to the black preacher G. W. Offley, the acute black sense of the injustice of slavery rightly inhibited the overbearing sense of moral guilt both for their degradation and for their acting out aggressions against whites through various forms of day-to-day resistance.[96] The oppressors had to bear the guilt of depravity, not the oppressed.

In 1837, the *Colored American* and the American Moral Reform Society proudly asserted that they pitied the oppressors more than they envied them, for blacks would rather suffer injustice than administer it. "You may antagonize us," the wealthy Byberry landowner Robert Purvis told his audience, "but we do not antagonize you. You may hate us, but we do not hate you." The tragedy of white oppression, according to David Ruggles, was that after all the torture, starvation, cruelty, and murder that whites had inflicted upon blacks,

---

nois, 1971), 262; and Herbert Aptheker, "Afro-American Superiority: A Neglected Theme in the Literature," *Phylon,* XXXI (Winter 1970): 336–42 (although it is hard to see how some of Aptheker's examples apply to his thesis).

96. *A Narrative of the Proceedings of the Black People, during the late awful calamity* (Philadelphia, 1794), in Aptheker, ed., *Documentary,* 36; G. W. Offley, *A Narrative of the Life and Labors of the Reverend G. W. Offley, A Colored Man, and Local Preacher* (Hartford, Connecticut, 1860) in *Five Black Lives* (Middletown, Connecticut, 1971), 136.

whites could become so morally blind as to claim that they have "virtuous 'characters' and we are *brutes*!" With this in mind, Samuel Ringgold Ward deemed it much too "degrading" even to argue the equality of whites and blacks. His "private opinion" was "that to say the Negro is equal morally to the white man, is to say but very little."[97]

For at least three black Americans in pre-Civil War America, blacks had a legitimate right to question whether whites were physically and morally equal to blacks at all. David Walker's "Appeal" to the black citizens of the world, which is permeated by a sense of moral superiority to whites even when blacks are "half enlightened and ignorant," advanced Walker's "suspicion" that whites are not "*as good by nature* as we." Martin R. Delany used the white colonization belief that blacks are physically more suited to warmer climates than whites to show how even "according to our oppressors' own showing, we are a *superior race*," since blacks can adapt to all environments while whites only to favorable ones. In responding to Theodore Parker's assertion that if the blacks had struck a violent blow against slavery themselves, the white stigma of black cowardice would have been averted, John S. Rock jeered that Anglo-Saxon courage must be minimal if Parker expected two and one-half million blacks to overpower from ten to fifteen million whites. Rock had little doubt that in an equal fight the physically fit black man would emerge the victor. Ironically, the white enslavement of blacks had rendered blacks physically and morally superior to whites, since the shadow of slavery made whites morally sick and physically soft.[98]

97. *Colored American*, 15 April 1837; *Minutes American Moral Reform Society* (1837), 202 in Porter, ed., *Early Negro Writing*. The first quote is taken from a speech by Robert Purvis, cited by Brown, *Black Man*, 258–59. For Ruggles, see his *"Extinguisher" Extinguished*, 12; Ward, *Autobiography*, 63.

98. Walker, *Appeal*, 27–29, 35–36; Delany, *Condition, Elevation, Emigration*, 94; *Liberator*, 12 March 1858. In 1854 Delany wrote that "we barely acknowledge the whites as equals—perhaps not in every

Just as slavery did violence to Judeo-Christian morality, so it wrecked havoc with Judeo-Christian spirituality, and many black Christians asserted a superiority of spiritual attributes over whites, which in some cases led blacks to profess a superior depth of theological insight.[99] For the most part, such professions were framed within the backdrop of the slave experience, which supposedly heightened the black felt-need of God as it hardened the hearts of whites to the movings of the Spirit.

Yet there are scattered indications that some blacks interpreted moral and spiritual superiority more in terms of racial characteristics than of environmental conditioning. Martin Delany, for example, wrote that "the colored races are highly susceptible of religion; it is a constituent principle of their nature, and an excellent trait in their character."[100] In a letter to Frederick Douglass, the black college professor William G. Allen of Central College in McGrawville, New York, defended Horace Mann from the bitter attacks of New Bedford, Massachusetts blacks who castigated Mann's allegation that the black race, although intellectually inferior to the Caucasian, was spiritually superior to all races in sentiment and affection. Allen implied that this allegation should not be denied but should be embraced as a source of pride, for " 'the heart is the King of the head.' "[101]

---

particular," prompting Frederick Douglass to declare that Delany "has gone about the same length in favor of blacks, as the whites have in favor of the doctrine of white superiority. He stands up so straight that he leans back a little." (See Ullman, *Delany,* 169; *Douglass' Monthly,* August 1862.)

99. This has been documented by Timothy Smith, "Slavery and Theology: The Emergence of Black Christian Consciousness in Nineteenth-Century America," *Church History,* 41 (December 1972): 498, n. 6, 500–501.

100. Delany, *Condition, Elevation, Emigration,* 50.

101. See Woodson, ed., *Mind of Negro,* 282. See also remarks of Sarah Grimke, Thomas Hope, and Dr. Channing on the meekness and affection of black in "Moral Character of Africans" in the *Colored American,* 8 April 1837.

The black Boston minister Hosea Easton, however, developed most fully the concept of racial characteristics in *A Treatise on the Intellectual Character, and Civil and Political Condition of the Colored People of the United States.* Although Easton began by explicitly denying the existence of biological or hereditary "constitutional differences" between the races, he proceeded to logically somersault into an historical account of the differing "traits" of African, European, and American "national characteristics." In contrast to the trail of blood, barbarism, belligerence, and avarice left by the Anglo-Saxon throughout history, Easton outlined the scientific and cultural achievements of the African or Egyptian race which had contributed to history nearly "everything conducive to the happiness of mankind." Without a doubt, stated Easton, history had proven the superior and greater race to be the descendants of Ham, the African race, over the descendants of Japhet, the European and American race.[102]

Before accepting the standard biblical explanation of the origin of races, blacks like Easton first had to refute the notion that the geneological tree of Ham was cursed. Samuel Ringgold Ward endeavored to disprove the pro-slavery justification of the "curse of Ham" on biblical grounds. The Bible's first mention of slavery, Ward observed, was the selling of the Israelite Joseph to the Hamitic Egyptians. Elaborating further from I Chronicles 4:40, where the land of the Assyrians is referred to as "wide, and quiet, and peaceable; for they of Ham had dwelt there of old," Ward acknowledged that "I set a very high value upon this piece of sacred testimony," for the Bible recognized that "Negroes exhibit most prominently those characteristics which accord with quietness and peaceableness." Clearly blacks constituted, Ward conjectured, "in feeling, the most *religious* people in the world." For this reason, if none other, their progress was assured.

102. Easton, *Treatise,* 5–6, 18–19.

Whites are "degenerating" in a spirtual slumberland of affluence, complacence, and indulgence. Blacks on the other hand are becoming

> less lethargic, and more energetic; until the latter, for all practical purposes, will exhibit, and wield too, more of the real American character, its manliness, its enterprise, its love of liberty, than the former. . . . Thus will it be, in my opinion, as between the blacks and the whites in America. They are now in the relation of teacher and taught, in the matter of liberty and progress; they will reverse positions ere the struggle be over, unless unforeseen changes occur.[103]

Ward's characterization of the black "religious disposition" and "natural mildness of temper" was in no way apologetic.[104] The "black nationalist" James Theodore Holly, however, did use these avowed traits for an apologetic purpose in a political context. Holly's 1857 *Vindication of the Capacity of the Negro Race for Self-Government, and Civilized Progress* . . . cited the "calm indifference" of blacks amid the first rumblings of revolt in Haiti not as proof of cowardice or ignorance of the blessings of liberty. Rather, it was proof of the strong faith blacks had in the workings of divine providence in history. "And let no one dare to rob them of this glorious trait of character," Holly warned, for it illustrated "the conservative characteristics of the negro race, that demonstrate their capacity for self-government." In the hands of many whites, the lineage of Ham and the legacy of forbearance justified oppression of blacks. In the hands of blacks like Easton, Ward, and Holly, the same lineage and legacy became a source of race pride which, through Holly's eyes, "ought to silence all pro-slavery caluminators of my race at once, and forever, by its powerful and undying reputation of their slanders."[105] Nevertheless, the concept of bred or inbred national characteristics, the very essence of cultural nationalism, remained only as a faint undercurrent in Afro-Ameri-

103. Ward, *Autobiography,* 186–87, 71–72.
104. *Ibid.,* 259.
105. Holly's essay is reproduced in Bell, ed., *Black Separatism and the Caribbean 1860,* 9, 27 ff., 31.

can thought during the first half of the nineteenth century. Although, as we have seen, many blacks claimed as a part of their heritage of slavery a moral and spiritual superiority to their white oppressors, it was a superiority of practice in relation to the professions of white Americans. Likewise, when most blacks ferreted out avarice as the animating power behind slavery, they did not feature it as a constituent trait of the Anglo-Saxon people.

In short, the pluralistic perception of distinct ethnic "gifts," whether acquired through heredity or a common heritage, was usually lacking, as was the assumption that the possessors of those "gifts" had a special mission to instruct those ethnics who suffered gaps. Although the rudiments of these ideas seemed present in the thought of John Swett Rock, Samuel Ringgold Ward, and Martin R. Delany during the 1850s, it was not until the theologian Alexander Crummell, the poet Leslie Pinckney Hill, the African linguist Edward Wilmot Blyden, and the sociologist W. E. B. Du Bois that they burst forth as a powerful and dominant theme among a segment of the black intelligentsia.

III

The celebration of Anglo-Saxon superiority in love of liberty, individualism, inventiveness, and aggressiveness was a common theme which achieved "scientific" status in the writings of such white historians as George Bancroft, John Lothrop Motley, William H. Prescott, and Francis Parkman.[106] It also achieved doctrinal status among anti-slavery circles. The tragic witness of slavery, however, attested to moral and spiritual inadequacies in the Anglo-Saxon heritage.

106. See Thomas F. Gossett, *Race: The History of an Idea in America* (Dallas, 1963), 89–96; and Edward N. Saveth, *American Historians and European Immigrants, 1875–1925* (New York, 1948), 103 ff. Saveth's study of the attitudes of American historians and social scientists to immigrants demonstrates that, with few exceptions, historians subscribed to the Teutonic or Anglo-Saxon myth until 1925, when Marcus L. Hansen introduced a more scientific view.

By the 1840s, white anti-slavery antagonists began to attribute to blacks in an idealized fashion those precise qualities deficient in the Anglo-Saxon race, a conception which found its classic expression in Harriet Beecher Stowe's *Uncle Tom's Cabin*. George M. Frederickson has brilliantly analyzed this phenomenon, which he calls "romantic racism," as a composite, sentimental stereotype of blacks as childlike, affectionate, docile, patient, loyal, and meek, which, in the words of C. Vann Woodward, involved a tacit or express denial that blacks had the "qualities essential to survival."[107]

Yet the point of romantic racism, as used by Harriet Beecher Stowe and others, was just the reverse. The black qualities were those essential to survival. The meek, not the proud, would be the ones who inherited the earth. Likewise, the blacks who shared this "romantic racist" image of themselves did not deny their ability to survive the competition with Anglo-Saxons because of their "childlike" and "feminine" virtues. Rather, "romantic racialism" endorsed the claims of the Methodist Bishop Gilbert Haven when, during the Civil War, he wrote that blacks were the superior race— "the choice blood of America"—because their submission and humility stood in the vanguard of progressive Christian virtues.[108]

One of the first uses of "romantic racialism" by a white anti-slavery writer occurred in William Ellery Channing's celebrated essay on slavery (1835). On August 15, 1883, Alexander Crummell spoke before the Freedmen's Aid Society of the Methodist Episcopal Church on the topic of "The Black Woman of the South: Her Neglects and Her Needs." Besides being a remarkable prolepsis of E. Franklin Frazier's sociological study of the black family structure in *The Negro Fam-*

107. Fredrickson, *Black Image in White Mind,* 97–129; C. Vann Woodward, "Our Own *Heerenvolk,*" *Saturday Review of Books* (12 August 1971), 11.

108. Gilbert Haven, *National Sermons* (Boston, 1869), 358, as cited by Fredrickson, *Black Image in White Mind,* 102.

ily (1939), Crummell's essay quoted the "wise, observing, tenderhearted" Channing who had written that blacks are "one of the best races of the human family. The Negro is among the mildest, gentlest of men." Harboring an "affectionate, easily touched" disposition, the black man is "more open to religious improvement than the white man," who excelled in "courage, enterprise, and invention." "The African carries with him much more than *we*," Crummell quoted Channing as saying, "the genius of a meek, long suffering, loving virtue!" Crummell applauded these words as music to his ears and encouraged his audience to listen with pride to such serenading of illustrious black characteristics.[109]

In an 1852 sermon on "Hope for Africa," Crummell reiterated his belief in the lofty character of blacks, heralding them as "remarkably docile, affectionate, easily attached, and when attached, ardently devoted—a race with the strongest religious feelings, sentiments and emotion." In short, Crummell wrote, "God has given this race a *strong moral character*" and a nature which is "the highest *natural* type of Christian requirement." Through the exposure to Anglo-Saxon Christianity and civilization in the New World, blacks had acquired Anglo-Saxon strengths while incorporating them into what was uniquely black—a strong moral, religious, and affective sense.[110] In all those ideals towards which the world was advancing, the blacks were leaders and would instruct the whites.

109. Crummell, *Africa and America,* 70–71. See also the chapter on "Negro Idiosyncrasies" in George Washington William's *History of the Negro Troops in the War of the Rebellion* (New York, 1888), especially p. 169. Williams contends that "the Negro slave was a remarkable personage," due to his "powerful physique, his celerity and poetry of movement, his sentiment and love of music, his firm attachment to friends, his deep longing for freedom, his splendid courage and power of endurance, his patience in suffering and hope in despair, his trust in God and instinct for the right, his cunning aptitude and perfect obedience." The similarities between Crummell's essay and Frazier's book have been delineated by Moses, "Civilizing Missionary," 250–51.

110. Crummell, *Future of Africa,* 320–21.

Such ideas resounded through the writings of Edward Blyden, W. E. B. Du Bois, and Kelly Miller in the late nineteenth and the early twentieth centuries. Blyden believed that the materialistic race of Anglo-Saxons was offset by the ministerial race of Africans.

The African is a spiritual and ministerial race. The European is an imperial and conquering race. He is by calling the statesman, the soldier, the sailor, the policeman of humanity. The Negro is the protege of the child, the attendant, the servant, if you like, of this dominant race.[111]

The history of intense suffering had nourished the spiritual, ministerial side of the blacks and equipped them to be the spiritual leaders of the world.[112] According to Blyden's philosophy of history, the time of conquering and materialism had past. The time of ministering had arrived. God had mapped out for the world a route to progress surpassing that of conquest—that of service. For this task "God hath chosen the weak things of this world," and Blyden anticipated "a day coming when a little child shall lead."[113]

Du Bois throughout his life challenged blacks to take pride in the fact that their strength came in weakness. In *The Gift of Black Folk* (1903) Du Bois wrote that "the black man has brought to America a sense of meekness and humility," a nature that in its honesty, "its hesitancy and heart searching, its submission to authority and its deep sympathy with the wishes of the other man" will one day serve as a "despised corrective" to the relentless Anglo-Saxon determination to conquer.[114] God has given black folk special gifts:

111. Edith Holden, *Blyden of Liberia* (New York, 1966), 699. Crummell felt that the Anglo-Saxons, the most domineering of all races, had such a drive to dominate that they even could dominate their racist prejudices, that is, "when chastened and subdued by Christianity." (See *Future of Africa,* 24.)
112. Lynch, *Blyden,* 64.
113. Holden, *Blyden,* 698, 700.
114. W. E. B. Du Bois, *The Gift of Black Folk: The Negroes in the Making of America* (Boston, 1924), 339.

courage, laughter, "gaity and exotic charm," which expresses itself in the gift of "a subtle sense of song" and which has given to America "its only American music, its only American fairy tales, its only touch of pathos and humor." But the greatest of all gifts of the black man to America has been his "gift of the spirit," which Du Bois, with acknowledged difficulty, defined as "an intense sensitiveness to spiritual values" or again as a "certain spiritual joyousness, a sensuous tropical love of life, in vivid contrast to the cool and cautious New England Reason."[115] As Du Bois would later phrase it with greater sophistication, the white expression of culture is in the wealth and power of the modern industrial state; the black expression of culture is in spirit, in laughter, in the exaltation of "the Lynched above the Lyncher, and the Worker above the Owner and the Crucified above Imperial Rome." The aggressive, materialistic, and domineering qualities of the "haughty Caucasian," Kelly Miller boasted, were no match for the black man's natural "meekness" and aptitude for Christianity. Is there no white man who believes, Du Bois quizzed, "that the meek shall inherit the earth?"[116]

It was within this context that blacks came to develop a messianic attitude about the ethos of black American culture and heritage. Of course, black messianism was not new to the late nineteenth century. In 1808, Absalom Jones conjectured that at some time a black "Joseph" would emerge to lead his people in the redemption of Africa; in 1809 the black arch-federalist Joseph Sidney awaited some black "Wilberforce" who would champion African freedom and salvation; in 1829 David Walker believed that God would raise up another Han-

115. Du Bois, "Conservation of Races," in Lester, ed., *Seventh Son,* I: 183: *Gift of Black Folk,* 287, 320.
116. W. E. B. Du Bois, *Dusk of Dawn,* 139; Kelly Miller, *Race Adjustment: Essays on the Negro in America* (New York and Washington, 1908), 144–51; Du Bois, *Gift of Black Folk,* 339. Alain Locke, in "Negro Contributions to America," *World Tomorrow,* XII (June 1929), believed that the black man was destined for "a special, creative role in American life as a reagent, and as a spiritual leaven."

nibal who would liberate blacks from enslavement and wretchedness; in the same year the author of "The Ethiopian Manifesto" promised the advent of another "John the Baptist" who would free blacks from bondage and "call together the black people as a nation in themselves"; and generally, throughout the nineteenth century, black Americans believed that they had a special obligation to share the blessings of Christianity and civilization with their African forebears.[117] But in the hands of Crummell, Du Bois, Blyden, and others, the sense of American black vocation was transformed into a more global, more millennialist messianism. Leslie Pinckney Hill, in his postbellum poem "God Sends the Negro on a Special Errand," pleaded with American blacks to wake up to their millennial mission. Just as American progress had depended on the black contribution of a spiritual-oriented culture, so the path of the world's progress would be led by American blacks with their gifts of the spirit of religion and the spirit of true brotherhood.[118]

Blyden elaborated the messianic role of black Americans in an essay appropriately entitled "The Call of Providence to the Descendants of Africa in America." To Blyden's regret God had not provided a black Moses to command an end to the American exile and an exodus to the promised land of Africa. Nevertheless, God's destiny for black Americans was graphically revealed in his "providences." Blacks had been brought to America for a "training fitting them for the work of civilizing and evangelizing Africa." They had been forcibly ostracized from America as aliens and strangers, thereby

117. Jones, *Thanksgiving Sermon,* in Porter, ed., *Early Negro Writing,* 359, 340; Joseph Sidney, *An Oration Commemorative of the Abolition of the Slave Trade in these United States; Delivered Before the Wilberforce Philanthropic Association, in the City of New York, on the Second of January, 1809* (New York, 1809); Walker, *Appeal,* 30; *The Ethiopian Manifesto, issued in defense of the Black Man's Rights in the scale of Universal Freedom* (New York, 1829), reprinted in Sterling Stuckey, *The Ideological Origins of Black Nationalism* (Boston, 1972), 36–37.

118. Kenny J. Williams, *They Also Spoke: An Essay on Negro Literature in America, 1787–1930* (Nashville, 1970), 76.

preserving "African peculiarities" and producing an "anguish of spirit" which drove them to search for an asylum from deprivation and discrimination. Black mission, Blyden wrote, was revealed in black history: God had called "the black men of this country" to disperse "the appalling cloud of ignorance and superstition which overspreads the land, and to rear on those shores an asylum of liberty," an African nation which "will furnish a development of civilization which the world has never yet witnessed. Its great peculiarity will be its moral element."[119]

Blyden's black messianic ideology had at least a conceptual affinity with the views of Emanuel Swedenborg, the eighteenth-century Swedish mystic. Swedenborg's thesis that Africans promised the greatest potential for religious perfection greatly intrigued Blyden, and the Swedenborgian James Garth Wilkinson dedicated his book on *The African and the True Christian Religion* (1892) to Blyden. The "African nationality" which Blyden envisioned, therefore, would not simply be a dark mirror of American nationality. It would be "an unfolding of a new bud, an evolution in the development of a new side of God's character and a new phase of humanity." Instead of the coarseness of the individualistic, competitive, combative, materialistic, scientific European character, black Americans would create in Africa a personality which would prize the "softer aspects of human nature": cheerfulness, sympathy, spirituality, willingness to serve, and an aesthetic sense. As the "spiritual conservatory" of the world, black Americans in Africa would excite a universal moral and

119. See Blyden's "Call of Providence to the Descendants of Africa in America" in Brotz, ed., *Negro Social and Political Thought*, 112–22. By 1900, Blyden would modify his views by asserting that this mission of blacks could be accomplished by a "remnant" of American blacks, not by a complete exodus. (See Lynch, *Blyden*, 79–80.) Also see T. Thomas Fortune's comment in "The Nationalization of Africa" that an African civilization based on the English language, English politics, and Christianity would grow to "eclipse all others that now are" or that have been. (See Hill and Kilson, ed., *Africa*, 359.)

spiritual revolution by projecting inherent attributes into a distinctive "African personality," exemplifying in an "African nationality," the essence of Christian teaching to rapacious European nations bent on their own physical and moral destruction through the "idolatrous" drift of material and scientific progress.[120]

Although the early Du Bois disagreed with Blyden that Africa was the only home for blacks, he did put his stamp of approval on this ideology which envisioned American black aliens as transformers and redeemers of the world's destiny through the contribution of black "racial gifts." As the "advance guard of the Negro people—the Eight Million people of Negro blood in the United States of America," Du Bois believed that black Americans would contribute to the world through economic, political, cultural, and moral solidarity those spiritual, moral, and aesthetic gifts that would "help to guide the world nearer and nearer that perfection of human life for which we all long, that 'one far off Divine event.' "[121] Black Americans had a messianic role to use their "gifts" in the salvation of mankind from destruction and in the inauguration of that millennial kingdom where "the meek shall inherit the earth."

120. Blyden, "The African Problem and The Method of its Solution," in Brotz, ed., *Negro Social and Political Thought,* 137–38; and Lynch, *Blyden,* 61–63. Lynch makes the connection between Swedenborgianism and Blyden on p. 82.

121. See Du Bois's black messianic document, "Conservation of Races," 181, 180. Vincent Harding has argued that Du Bois, who "never referred to himself as a 'Negro Nationalist,' " can best be seen when his hopes and aspirations are placed under the rubric of "Black Messianism." (See Harding's "A Black Messianic Visionary," in Rayford W. Logan, ed., *W. E. B. Du Bois: A Profile* [New York, 1971], 274–93.)

6

The Goals of Black Separatism

The Advocate will be like a chain, binding you together as ONE. Its columns will always be the organ of your wishes and feelings, and the proper medium for laying your claim before the Public. Only one plan can give SUCCESS to the Advocate, and place it upon a firm and lasting basis. And that is a UNION of action among you all as a body. Our Enemies are United! *'UNION' is their Watchword. And nothing do they dread as much as a 'destruction of the UNION!' Let us then learn OUR DUTY from them, if our own experience and observation fail to instruct us.*

THE WEEKLY ADVOCATE

ACCORDING TO THE correspondent to the *Colored American* who called himself "Sidney," the "very respectable portion of our people" who shared the anti-separatist views of William Whipper of Columbus, Ohio, were introducing a "new theory" into the creed and tactics of the black abolitionist movement. Sidney contended that separate and systematic actions by blacks for their own advancement were part of an historical heirloom passed on by the black American tradition. Those who disputed "separate institutions" and denied the necessity of self-help and self-elevation would have blacks "leave the path of our sires."[1]

In a sense Sidney was right, though he did greater justice

1. *Colored American,* 13 February, 6 March 1841.

to black history than he did to William Whipper. Although accused of self-interest in separating to promote their psychological and physical well-being, blacks early came to realize that they had to rely on themselves for their moral, social, and religious elevation. Ever since the American Revolution, independent black mutual-aid societies and congregations had been organized, the latter remaining under the jurisdictional aegis of white denominations until 1816, when the African Methodist Episcopal Church attained legal independence. Tired of submitting to "colonization in the house of God," several blacks, led by Richard Allen and Daniel Coker, decided to unite as a "band of brethren" and, as Daniel Coker preached, to "sit down under our own vine to worship, and none shall make us afraid."[2]

Any analysis of the black image of America must reckon with what Sidney called a tradition of separatism amongst black Americans, a tradition which served to gather black "bands of brethren" under separate "vines" for worship, work, and play. Ostensibly, black separatism seems to undercut an image of America where all ethnic groups are integrated into American institutions and American life. In reality, however, black separatism undergirded such an image. Blacks, typified by those who attended the 1848 national convention, justified their separation not to avoid integration or to preserve the "color line" but to achieve integration and to smash the color barrier. Blacks should neither join an institution because it was black nor join an institution because it was white, the convention stated. Yet as long as blacks were denied their rights and equality, the convention took a firm stand behind the necessity of striving for the "ideal of

2. Jeremiah Asher, *Autobiography,* 40; [Daniel Coker], *Sermon Delivered Extempore in the African Bethel Church in the City of Baltimore,* reproduced in Aptheker, ed., *Documentary History,* 68. Asher relates how even after black members in the Connecticut Baptist Church of which he was a member protested successfully against the "colonization" of "colored pews" and won the right to sit anywhere they pleased, they still felt that the insult necessitated their worshipping separately.

human brotherhood" by the seemingly contradictory means of "institutions of a complexional character." The convention advised blacks, however, to integrate themselves into white societies and institutions "just so fast as our rights are secured to us."[3] Black separatism was a provisional prerequisite for achieving full stature as an American citizen. And black solidarity was a prerequisite for black separatism.

Racial unity and racial solidarity was the avowed raison d'être for the black press among antebellum abolitionists. Yet at this time, black unity and solidarity were not ends in themselves, but means to the ends of emancipation, elevation, and equality. "Our *cause* . . . demands our own advocacy," proclaimed one newspaper, and Frederick Douglass dedicated the *North Star* to his "fellow countrymen" and to the recollection of the reality that "we are one, that our cause is one, and that we must help each other if we could succeed. . . . What you suffer, we suffer; what you endure, we endure. We are indissolubly united, and must fall or flourish together."[4]

Four years before William Lloyd Garrison began publishing the *Liberator,* the initial issue of the first black newspaper, *Freedom's Journal,* came from the press in New York City with the declaration that "we wish to speak our own cause. Too long have others spoken for us."[5] Ten years later another black newspaper, the *Weekly Advocate,* was launched in an attempt to provide "native-born Colored AMERICANS" with an advocate, and it spoke in no uncertain terms about what it would advocate—black unity of action directed to-

3. From "Address to the Colored People of the United States" in *Report of the Proceedings of the Colored National Convention . . . 1848* (Rochester, New York, 1848), in Bracey, Jr., Meier, and Rudwick, ed., *Black Nationalism,* 55.

4. Thomas Hamilton, editor of the *Weekly Anglo-African,* 23 July 1859; *North Star,* 3 December 1847.

5. *Freedom's Journal,* 16 March 1827. In the light of this profession, it is hard to see how Frederick Cooper can contend that "*Freedom's Journal* can be better understood as a journal designed to serve a developing black community than as a paper of protest." The paper appears to have been both. (Frederick Cooper, "Elevating the Race," 607.)

wards immediate, universal emancipation, towards social and
civil equality, and towards the political and moral elevation
of black Americans. It was the view of this paper (which
changed its name to the *Colored American*) and the view of
the black press in general that black Americans should seek
self-reliance, self-exertion, and self-improvement not as individuals, but collectively "as a people."[6] Thus racial unity
held pride of place in the pages of the black press as the
means for elevation of blacks.

The dispute among blacks which dominated the letters
written to the *Colored American* revolved not around the desirability of racial unity in quest of emancipation, elevation,
and equality. Chained together by a common history of suffering, blacks sensed "what they should do" and "for whom"
they should do it. The point of disagreement arose over the
"how" question—the "mode of operation for the elevation
of our people."[7] Even William Whipper, the most strident foe
of exclusive action by blacks, participated in the black convention movement of the 1830s and hoped to unite blacks in
the struggle for self-improvement by helping to found with
James Forten and David Ruggles an organization that was
eventually to become the American Moral Reform Society.
Dr. James McCune Smith, who took a firm stand against separate conventions because he opposed "action based upon
complexional distinction," hastened to add that "I am not at
all opposed to all action on the part of the colored people."[8]
Regardless of their alignment on the issue of separatism, blacks
condemned disunity as a bane to their progress and called for
a tightening of the bonds of racial unity.[9] The main ques-

6. *Weekly Advocate,* 14, 21 January, 4 February 1837; *Colored
American,* 27 January 1838. The *Weekly Advocate,* in its second issue,
called for a directory of black individuals, ministers, churches, societies,
and lodges to aid in disseminating information about concrete activities
open to blacks in the struggle for self-improvement and in the battle
against slavery. (*Weekly Advocate,* 21 January 1837.)
7. *Colored American,* 13 February 1841.
8. *Ibid.,* 12 August 1841.
9. For the importance accorded to black unity, see Steward, *Twenty-
Two Years a Slave,* 332; Walker, *Appeal,* 30.

tion was whether racial unity should be exclusive or inclusive of white endeavors for the amelioration of the condition of blacks. As David Nickens, in his fifth of July oration put it, the issue is not what can be done for blacks, but what can blacks do of themselves, for themselves, and by themselves.[10]

Thus the controversy swirled not around whether blacks should emphasize self-improvement or abolition. The two were inextricably connected, as the revived National Negro Convention, meeting in 1853, made clear by saying that "in *our* elevation lies the freedom of our enslaved brethren."[11] There seems not to have been a single black abolitionist who did not merge his crusade to end slavery and prejudice with the complementary crusade for moral reform and self-improvement. Indeed, emancipation and elevation were often seen as opposite sides of the same coin. Even in the late ninteenth century the theme lingered in the thought of W. E. B. Du Bois, who believed that "the first and greatest step toward the settlement of the present friction between the races—commonly called the Negro problem—lies in the correction of the immorality, crime, and laziness among the Negroes themselves, which still remains a heritage from slavery."[12] What varied was the degree to which self-improvement

10. David Nickens, "Address to the People of Color in Chillicothe, July 20, 1832," in *Liberator,* 11 August 1832, in Bracey, Jr., Meier, and Rudwick, ed., *Black Nationalism,* 34–37.

11. Quoted in Gerald Sorin, *Abolitionism: A New Perspective* (New York, 1972), 111. Martin L. Delany wrote that "to elevate the free colored people of America, any where upon this continent" facilitated "the speedy redemption of the slaves." (See *Condition, Elevation, Emigration* in Brotz, ed., *Negro Social and Political Thought,* 96.)

12. W. E. B. Du Bois, "Conservation of Races," in Lester, ed., *Seventh Son* I: 186. Frederick Cooper makes the distinction between abolitionism and self-improvement. It may be that whereas all black abolitionists were involved in self-improvement, not all blacks involved in self-improvement were abolitionists. Such a conclusion, however, needs to be based on more evidence than simply the greater proliferation of self-improvement societies over abolition societies. Furthermore, Cooper fails to realize that self-improvement, when seen in the context of the black experience, might be itself a decidedly abolitionist activity. To say that "Black leaders were mainly interested in neither protest nor nationalism" but self-improvement fails to take into account that self-

was seen as the exclusive vehicle for social reform. The first half of the nineteenth century witnessed the increasing politicization of the abolitionist movement, as black leaders supplemented their drive for self-improvement with a developing political consciousness and political cohesion.[13]

---

improvement itself could be a form of protest (Cooper, "Elevating the Race," 605, 619). The expatriate black American, Samuel Ringgold Ward, criticized the notion that abolitionist activity could be confined to the more glamorous arena of lecturing, conventions, and writing. "Antislavery labour" also encompassed "the cultivation of all the upward tendencies of the coloured man." (See Ward's *Autobiography*, 29, 32.)

13. The betrayal and ostracizement of blacks by political parties, which prompted T. Thomas Fortune to declare "I have no faith in parties" (*Black and White*, 131), and which Paul Laurence Dunbar portrayed in his short story "A Mess of Pottage" (in *The Strength of Gideon and Other Stories* [New York, 1900]), symbolized the recalcitrance with which blacks became involved in political activity. Before the organization of the Liberty Party in 1840, blacks exhibited an anti-party and anti-politics bias. Instead of political agitation, they channelled moral agitation (in conjunction with white allies) towards redirecting the weathervane of public opinion against slavery and prejudice. David Ruggles believed that if women, with their superior moral sense and "resistless influence," had attempted to arouse and mobilize public opinion against slavery, "long ere now the term 'American Slavery' would have been used only to express a dead monster, loathed amid universal execration" (*The Abrogation of the Seventh Commandment by the American Churches* [New York, 1835], in Porter, ed., *Early Negro Writing*, 478); see also J. M. Langston's belief that women held the power of determining how their husbands voted in *Virginia Plantation*, 458; and the black feminist Maria W. Stewart's assertion that upon the shoulders of women "almost entirely depends whether the rising generation shall be anything more than we have been or not. O woman, woman! your example is powerful, your influence great; it extends over your husbands and over your children, and throughout the circle of your acquaintance" (in her "Address Before Afric-American Female Intelligence Society of Boston" in *Productions of Mrs. Maria W. Stewart*, 62). The dispute between black moral suasionists and black political activists, precipitated by the emergence of the Liberty Party, was most blatant in the August 1843 national convention held in Buffalo. Ministers Henry Highland Garnet, William C. Munro, J. N. Gloucester, Theodore S. Wright, and Charles B. Ray supported a resolution to affiliate with the Liberty ticket. The resolution passed—but not without seven dissenting votes, including those of Frederick Douglass, Charles Lenox Remond, and William Wells Brown. David Ruggles, William Whipper, William C. Nell, and James

Likewise, the issue revolved not around whether blacks should act in concert with other blacks to effect their liberation. There is no evidence to refute the thesis that blacks espoused racial solidarity in their pursuit of self-improvement, moral reform, and the abolition of slavery, all of which were considered avenues to integration in American life. Racial solidarity and group consciousness were shibboleths common to all camps of black thinking throughout the nineteenth century.

Nor was the issue, as many historians have posed it,

McCune Smith also opposed riding partisan politics to equality as too corrupt a vehicle. (See Bell, "National Negro Conventions," 249 ff.) Gradually, however, the holdouts did acquiesce in political abolitionist activities. In 1845 Charles Lenox Remond wrote that "the sin of our country is in having too much politics, and too little humanity. The reform wanted is not in our politics but in our hearts." (See "The New Age of Anti-Slavery" in Friends of Freedom, *The Liberty Bell* [Boston, 1844], 189.) But by 1848, Remond had joined Douglass in participating in the Free Soil Party convention. Likewise, in 1850, William C. Nell ran for the Massachusetts State Legislature on the Free Soil Party platform. (See Robert P. Smith, "William Cooper Nell: Crusading Black Abolitionist," *Journal of Negro History,* LV [July 1970]: 188.) Nevertheless, the first black newspaper's caveat issued against blacks becoming "the tools of party" lingered throughout the nineteenth century (*Freedom's Journal,* 16 March 1827). The *Colored American* repeatedly stated that the abolitionist cause of liberty should preempt party loyalty, yet in October 1840 it endorsed James G. Birney and the Liberty Party. (See *Colored American,* 2 September 1837; 12 September, 3 October 1840.) The *Weekly Anglo-African* announced in 1859 that it was concerned with principles, not with parties, which were "mere scaffolding to the building"; by March 1860 the newspaper had abandoned party action in favor of relying "on ourselves, the righteousness of our cause, and the sense of justice among Americans" (*Weekly Anglo-African,* 15 October 1859; 17 March 1860). Politics, William Wells Brown charged, had transformed Millard Fillmore from a legal counsel offering free services to a fugitive slave into a president who signed the Fugitive Slave Bill of 1850 (*Liberator,* 27 October 1854). And in 1890, the Reverend A. B. Gibson of Milledgeville, Georgia, confessed that he despaired of political parties: "The Negro's back is sleek where they have rode him so much." (See *Christian Recorder,* 26 June 1890, cited by Herbert Aptheker, "Consciousness of Negro Nationality to 1900," in *Toward Negro Freedom* [New York, 1956], 110.)

"whether or not the Negro should seek entry into white American life."[14] Nearly every action taken by blacks, whether separatist or integrationist, was directed toward the aspiration of national assimilation. Black newspapers, for example, did not transmit a distinct Afro-American culture. Rather, they transmitted an American middle-class culture. In sum, the rift within the ranks of black leadership, which reached its greatest expanse in the late 1830s and early 1840s, occurred not over whether blacks should strive for inclusion into American society or should act in unity for their emancipation and elevation but whether this united action should be separated from the actions of whites.

I

Black nationalism in the three decades prior to the Civil War has most often been equated with the black desire and drive for autonomy.[15] It is important, however, to consult black "separationists" for their explanation of why they felt the need to come out from whites and what they hoped to gain in autonomy. The separationist Sidney, for one, felt no need to

14. See, for example, Joanne Grant, ed., *Black Protest: History, Documents, and Analysis 1619 to the Present* (Greenwich, Connecticut, 1968), 68. Even arch-accommodationist Booker T. Washington considered "race pride and race consciousness" of blackness, black history, and black music—"I would rather hear the jubilee or plantation songs of my race than the finest chorus from the work of Handel or any other of the greatest composers that I have heard"—indispensable imperatives "to bring out and develop the best that is in them." (Booker T. Washington, *The Story of the Negro: The Rise of the Race from Slavery* [New York, 1909], Vol. I, extracts reproduced in Harlan, ed., *Washington Papers,* I: 404–5.)

15. Sterling Stuckey, in *Ideological Origins of Black Nationalism,* 1, n. 1., argues that "the originators of the ideology that we refer to as black nationalism emphasized the need for black people to rely primarily on themselves in vital areas of life." Stuckey leaps further by stating that "this attitude probably owed more to African traditions of group hegemony (which persisted in some forms during slavery) than to any models from European thought or experience." While Stuckey pits "nationalist" against "integrationist" movements (19), he does admit that it is too "simplistic" to see them as entirely mutually exclusive (26–27).

justify racial solidarity, but he did feel compelled to explain the necessity for racial autonomy. One reason he gave for the desirability of blacks "coming forth as colored Americans, and pleading for our rights" was that independent black exertion was needed to refute the reproach of inferiority and servility. White abolitionists "are our allies," he asseverated, but "OURS is the battle," for foreign aid "neither brings forth our latent energies, nor can be imputed to us." Similarly, four years earlier "Augustine" based his defense of separatism on the grounds that black advancement was dependent on a "moral revolution" stimulated by *national feeling, intensity of interest, confidence, energy,* [and] *self-respect,"* qualities blacks had to develop for themselves. Speaking about Jefferson's disparaging remarks about blacks in his *Notes on Virginia,* David Walker argued that it was not enough that "our white friends" have refuted the charges, for "they are *whites* —we are *blacks."* If blacks do not band together and vigorously assert their manhood, Walker believed that their dependency on whites would only endorse Jefferson's suspicions. Maria W. Stewart challenged blacks, in an 1833 address, not simply to allow whites to do the job, but "to strive to raise ourselves" and prove their mental and moral endowments which suited them for inclusion into American life.[16]

Philip A. Bell exhibited this independent spirit in the *Weekly Advocate,* when he contended that whites may make "OUR CAUSE" their cause all they want, but their efforts will be unavailing "without our thinking and acting, as a body, for ourselves."[17] The rationale for autonomous action given by a group of young New York blacks was that if blacks speak with "our white friends" for black equality, the words will only be considered an "echo" of white voices,

16. *Colored American,* 20 February, 6 March 1841; 30 December 1837; 10 February 1838; Walker, *Appeal,* 25, 26; Maria W. Stewart, "Address [in] African Masonic Hall 1833," in Porter, ed., *Early Negro Writing,* 134.
17. *Weekly Advocate,* 21 January 1837.

thereby vitiating the assertion of equality. Guest editor A of the *Colored American* made this same point when he remarked that blacks who united their efforts with whites would be heard as playing "second fiddle" to whites, an unbecoming part for those who were claiming full recognition and equal participation in America. Even in a religious sphere, wrote the African Methodist Episcopal bishop and church historian Daniel A. Payne, separation from whites was necessary, for it forced blacks to "tax our own mental powers both for government and support," it proved black manhood, and it refuted the "slander" that blacks were "incapable of self-government and self-support." All of this blacks would have sacrificed, Payne believed, if they had remained the "ecclesiastical vassals" of white churches.[18]

Even some blacks who were originally Garrisonians capitulated to support independent black endeavors based on this felt need for proving their own manhood and citizenship. Frederick Douglass, in an address celebrating West Indian Emancipation in August 1857, raised to the level of a "philosophy of reform" the dictum that "if there is no struggle there is no progress." And there certainly was no struggle involved in allowing "our white friends to do all the work, while we merely hold their coats."[19] William Wells Brown encouraged blacks to "make equality" themselves, since "no society, no government, can make this equality." The main support whites could give to the black man was to "take their heels off his neck, and let him have a chance to rise by his

18. *National Anti-Slavery Standard,* 16 July 1840, as cited by Howard H. Bell, "Expressions of Negro Militancy in the North, 1840–1860," *Journal of Negro History,* XLV (January 1960): 11; *Colored American,* 27 June 1840; Daniel A. Payne, *History of the African Methodist Episcopal Church* (Nashville, 1891), 9–10.
19. Foner, ed., *Douglass* II: 437. While Douglass differed from Samuel Ringgold Ward in espousing that all efforts for self-improvement should be done at home in America, they were at one in their conviction, in Douglass's words, "that our elevation as a race, is almost wholly dependent upon our own exertions." (See *Frederick Douglass' Paper,* 13 April 1855, in Foner, ed., *Douglass,* II: 359–62.)

own efforts."[20] Black leaders before the Civil War justified distinct black organizations, not out of a desire to cultivate black uniqueness in uncontaminated surroundings, but out of a desire to disprove inferiority and prove that the black man was fit to be a free man in America. The Peases have shown, furthermore, that overt nationalist manifestations such as organized black communities of, for, and by blacks cannot easily be identified with a black nationalism which rejected white America, for they were primarily designed to train "the Negro to live in white society," and as such "were but way stations, training grounds for Negroes headed toward eventual assimilation into American Society."[21]

The Jeffersonian ideal of agrarianism exemplifies one way in which American ideologies were adopted and adapted by blacks into a separationist program that would secure the inclusion of blacks in American society. A recurring theme in the editorials of Samuel E. Cornish was the importance of agricultural pursuits for blacks because of the independence inherent in the agrarian environment over against the dependency of city life. Samuel Cornish entitled one editorial "Go to the Country, Brethren," and he extolled the virtues of getting close to the land and the value of agriculture for black elevation and power. The influence which blacks were denied in congested cities could be gained through the independent life of farming, and Cornish prefaced a letter from the ardent black advocate of agrarianism, Augustus Wattles, with the declaration that "farming is the policy for colored Americans. Get land, brethren."[22]

20. Brown, *Black Man,* 47–48.
21. Pease and Pease, *Black Utopia,* 20, 160, 162.
22. *Rights of All,* 29 May 1829; *Colored American,* 30 June 1838; 15 April 1837; 15 January 1838. Cornish and Augustine agreed that blacks should leave the city and settle in the country. They quarreled, however, over whether blacks should "mix" and "scatter" with the whites once they got there, as Cornish advocated, or whether they should build their own churches, schools, and societies, as Augustine recommended. (See *Colored American,* 28 July 1838.)

Augustus Wattles (who had attended Oneida Institute, entered Lane Seminary in 1833, and left the next year to supervise a school for blacks in Cincinnati) could tolerate the big city for only two years. With appropriate evangelical conviction, Wattles condemned the city as a hotbed of wickedness which "contaminated" blacks and impeded their improvement. In 1836 he founded the Carthagena settlement in Mercer County, Ohio, and admonished blacks to repair as quickly as possible to the countryside and seek the independence which accrues to the farmer.[23] Henry Highland Garnet also stressed the impact of black ownership of land and the subsequent advantages of controlling one's life through farming.[24] And one of the reasons why William Wells Brown in 1859 came down with what he called the "Haitian Emigration fever" was because he believed that the best way for blacks to assert their influence was through prosperous farming and land ownership, mediums which Haiti promised and the United States prohibited. In Brown's mind the time was long overdue for blacks to "become possessors of the soil, to leave the large cities, take to farming, and make themselves independent."[25]

Whenever blacks congregated in local meetings or in state and national conventions, resolutions were perpetually adopted which singled out the importance of the agricultural vocation to the elevation of blacks. The first national black convention which met in Philadelphia recommended agriculture as a means of gaining respect and independence. The vice-president of the convention, Austin Steward, digressed to acclaim the dignity of the agrarian life-style as opposed to

23. William H. Pease and Jane H. Pease, "Organized Negro Communities: A North American Experiment," *Journal of Negro History,* XLVII (July 1962): 66–67. In *Black Utopia,* 20, 166, n. 29, the Peases have shown that (with the possible exception of Edward Philbrick's venture at Port Royal) all black utopian communities were founded in the belief that blacks could best be elevated by the "training device" of agriculture.
24. Garnet, *Memorial Discourse,* 39.
25. Farrison, *Brown,* 335, 309.

the crushing effects of crowded cities, where blacks occupied mostly servile positions and "allow themselves to be made 'hewers of wood and drawers of water.'" Prejudice often permeated the pure air of the countryside, Steward admitted, but at least there "a farmer can live less dependent on his oppressors."[26] When the convention movement resumed in 1843 (after an eight year interlude) a committee, chaired by Charles B. Ray, reported on the merits of choosing a career in agriculture, where one could attain an independence which led to "respectability," a quality hard to attain elsewhere.[27] Garnet's report on the "Best Means for the Promotion of the Enfranchisement of Our People" to the New York convention of 1844 accented the dissemination of knowledge, education, trades, and the migration from cities where blacks were entrapped in menial jobs.[28] The resolution of a black convention at Sandwich, Ontario, proposed to organize an agricultural benevolent association because farming is "the most certain road to independence and self-elevation."[29]

The philanthropist Gerrit Smith opened this road when, in 1847, he offered 140,000 acres of land to some 3,000 blacks, in effect making many of them eligible for the suffrage. Addressing these 3,000 landowners, Theodore Wright, Charles B. Ray, and James McCune Smith reminded them that "there is no life like that of the farmer, for overcoming the mere prejudice against color." By possessing land and working in the fields blacks will be participating in a labor which is "the

26. Steward, *Twenty-Two Years a Slave,* 166–67.
27. *Minutes of the National Convention of Colored Citizens, Buffalo, 1843,* 30–36.
28. *Minutes of the Fifth Annual Convention of the Colored Citizens of the State of New York, Schenectady, 1844* (Troy, New York, 1844), 14–17.
29. *Voice of the Fugitive,* 1 January 1851, cited by Pease and Pease, "Organized Negro Communities," 27. Samuel Ringgold Ward reminisced that "had I clung to the use of the hoe, instead of aspiring to a love of books, I might by this time have been somebody" (and could have labored for the betterment of his race through wealth rather than writing). (Ward, *Autobiography,* 20.)

common destiny of the American people."[30] Paul Laurence Dunbar's book of social criticism, *The Sport of the Gods* (1902), which denounced the allures of city life, stood at the end of a long agrarian tradition among black Americans who praised farming as the chance to prove their manhood and independence.

II

The second reason Sidney gave in 1841 for the need of independent black positions was that "the oppressed are ever their best representatives." Rationalizations about slavery could best be banished by the injection of a black perspective. Many blacks came to this conclusion partly out of a conviction that they had suffered what only black experience, not white eloquence, could express. Maria Weston Chapman was informed of this fact by two free black women whom the Boston Female Anti-Slavery Society had helped rescue from being shipped back to Baltimore as slaves in July 1836. When Mrs. Chapman asked the women for their impressions of some descriptions of slavery in anti-slavery publications, one of the women reminded Chapman that "it is impossible to put such dreadful sufferings properly into print."[31]

Similar problems of entering into the black mental world plagued other white abolitionist publications, according to black abolitionists. In the winter of 1860 Robert Purvis cautioned a white author about the writing of Afro-American history with these words: "I have often heard that it takes a woman to understand a woman's wrongs; so I say it takes a man of African blood to understand the contempt which is cherished by a certain class against people of African blood." As the white historian Richard Hildreth remarked, "It is im-

30. *Proceedings of the National Convention of Colored People and their Friends, Troy, 1847* (Troy, New York, 1847), 25–30, 31; Wright, Ray, and Smith, *Address,* 10.
31. The story of the *Chickasaw* rescue can be found in Alma Lutz, *Crusade for Freedom,* 74–75.

possible to convince men of the iniquity of slavery, except by making them feel it." Many blacks believed that only those who had experienced slavery could adequately make whites feel it.[32]

Despite paternalistic pushes towards dependency by white abolitionists and proscriptive laws, blacks stoked white fears and hostility by insisting on institutional independence. Blacks increasingly came to realize that they had to represent themselves and take the initiative themselves, partly in response to the domineering and discriminatory policies of white organizations. It is true that abolitionists desired black representation in their societies, as the presence of James McCrummell, James Barbadoes, and Robert Purvis at the founding convention of the American Anti-Slavery Society makes clear. But such representation was mostly window-dressing. Black leaders widely participated as orators and attenders at anti-slavery conventions and meetings, but they were deprived of crucial administrative, policy-making roles, especially at a national level. The seventy-four-member Board of Managers of the American Anti-Slavery Society boasted five black constituents, but the Board was powerless and largely honorific. Furthermore, in 1834 the American Anti-Slavery Society renounced social mingling of races and opposed giving blacks any more equality than their elevation allowed.

The domineering disposition of white abolitionists followed closely behind their discriminatory policies. In August 1841 James W. C. Pennington, the black Congregational minister from Hartford, Connecticut, founded the Union Missionary Society, which aimed at the establishment of anti-slavery missions at home and abroad. Originally most of the society's directors were black clergymen, but when LaRoy Sutherland, Simeon S. Jocelyn, and Lewis Tappan merged their "Ami-

---

32. *Colored American,* 6 March 1841. See Robert Purvis to editor of the *National Anti-Slavery Standard,* 4 December 1860, quoted in Purvis, *Speeches and Letters,* 5. Richard Hildreth, "Complaint and Reproach," in Friends of Freedom, *Liberty Bell,* 57.

stad" committee in May 1842 with the society, some of the
black directors were dismissed, the whites took control, and
within no time the blacks held only minor and honorary
positions. Whites took charge of what had begun in 1841 as
a black-controlled Union Missionary Society and enlarged it
by 1846 into a white-controlled American Missionary Association.[33]

It was a sad commentary on the abolitionist movement,
Martin Delany remarked, to see the way in which black
abolitionists, once they began fighting alongside white abolitionists, found themselves occupying the same "mere second-
ary, underling position" within the abolitionist movement as
they did within the pro-slavery community.[34] White abolitionists who were more anti-slavery than anti-prejudice worked
in a North which was more Union-loving than slavery-hating.
And after the emergence of the "anti-slavery" Republican
party, it became obvious that many whites were both anti-
slavery and anti-slaves. "Opposing slavery and hating its
victims," Douglass commented, "has come to be a very common
form of abolitionism."[35]

The tempo of black abolitionist demands for independent
organizations kept apace with the dissatisfaction over the
way the abolitionist movement sacrificed its correlative goals
of racial justice and equal rights for the single goal of legal
emancipation. Although abolitionist patterns of action were
not fissured neatly along racial lines, black abolitionists upheld a vision of society which too many white abolitionists
did not—a society based not just on the abolition of slavery

33. The story can be found in Wyatt-Brown, *Lewis Tappan,* 292–93.
See also Jane H. Pease and William H. Pease, "Black Power: The Debate
in 1840," *Phylon,* XVI (Spring 1969): 19–20.
34. Delany, *Condition, Elevation, Emigration,* in Brotz, ed., *Negro
Social and Political Thought,* 45. For the problem of prejudice among
white abolitionists, see Pease and Pease, *They Who Would Be Free,* 82–93.
35. *Douglass' Monthly,* November 1860. For Henry Highland Garnet's disaffection with white abolitionists, see his 1859 speech in Boston,
in Sterling Stuckey's *Ideological Origins of Black Nationalism,* 184–85.

but on the annihilation of race prejudice and the affirmation of equal rights and equal justice.[36] Accusatory black auxiliaries reminded the abolitionist crusade that it should embrace goals higher than those just of anti-slavery.

In advocating "complexionally distinctive organizations," Sidney contended that the motivation was not simply "devotion to color." The anomalous situation of blacks in American society dictated an autonomous position. Just as prejudice was born not of color but of oppression, so autonomous black institutions to annihilate that prejudice were born of oppression, not of color.

Whenever a people are oppressed, peculiarly (not complexionally), distinctive organization or action, is required on the part of the oppressed, to destroy that oppression. The colored people of this country are oppressed; therefore the colored people are required to act in accordance with this fundamental principle.[37]

Black separatism was prompted not because blacks were black, but because blacks were an oppressed, "aggrieved people" suffering from a multiplicity of wrongs.

Augustine had anticipated this defense of racial autonomy when he had written to the *Colored American,* four years earlier, that blacks should not organize themselves on the basis of color but on the basis of their oppressed condition. As a "distinct class" in America, blacks had the responsibility of establishing "a separate set of means for our elevation" and an "ORGANIZED and *systematic* effort" for "our moral elevation." After calling for a national convention of black Americans which, it was hoped, would effect "a moral revolution" among black Americans, Augustine disclaimed the idea that black exclusiveness was intended to perpetuate the distinctness of blacks. "No man on earth can more cordially abhor the spirit of caste than I do," he observed. "And I treat it, not for the purpose of its continuance, but for the

36. See *National Anti-Slavery Standard,* 2 July 1840; and Sorin, *Abolitionism,* 106.
37. Sidney to *Colored American,* 13 March 1841.

purpose of its speedy abolition."[38] Black separatism was a vehicle for integration, not a vehicle for exclusive nationalist identity. The isolation of blacks from whites was the means some blacks adopted to put an end to the isolation of blacks from the mainstream of American life.

Blacks who defended complexional projects entertained a strong sense of the provisional, tactical nature of separate institutions. William Hamilton, chairman of the 1834 national convention and president of the conventional board, explained that "under present circumstances" blacks "should combine, and closely attend to their own particular interest." Hamilton believed specifically that "as long as the Colonization Society exists, will a convention of colored people be highly necessary."[39] Responding to "A Friend" suggesting that blacks establish their own schools, the *Colored American* opposed in principle "separate institutions for our people" but in practice supported such efforts.[40]

The architects of the Albany National Convention, held in August 1840, were Henry Highland Garnet, his cousin Samuel Ringgold Ward, Charles B. Ray, Alexander Crummell, and Theodore Wright. The *Colored American,* however, first proposed it and justified its being run exclusively by blacks. "While we believe that, being of the American nation, we ought to identify with the American people, and with American interests," the paper editorialized, "yet there are and will be, special interests for us to attend to, so long as American caste exists, and we have not equal rights, in common with the American people. When such shall be our condition, there will be no longer special interests to attend to."[41] The "Address of the New York State Convention of Colored Citizens

38. *Colored American,* 2, 30 December 1837; 10 February 1838.
39. *Minutes of the Fourth Annual Convention for the Improvement of the Free People of Colour,* 7.
40. *Colored American,* 23 May 1840. Cf. the opposition to separate school systems by T. Thomas Fortune in his *Black and White,* 69–71.
41. *Colored American,* 2 May 1840. Charles B. Ray was editor at this time.

to the People of New York," written largely by Garnet, defended separate schools, churches, and artistic societies because blacks were denied full equality in American society. Not until blacks were recognized as in every respect equal to whites, Garnet posited, would blacks stop holding separate conventions.[42]

To one of the most strident supporters of black autonomy, Samuel Ringgold Ward, there came a time when separation had proven its point and should be abandoned. "Experiments have been made," observed Ward, "they have proved triumphantly successful: now we need no more of them."[43] Frederick Douglass was not so optimistic. In Douglass's dedicatory address at the inauguration of the Baltimore Douglass Institute in October 1865, Douglass confessed that he had once "flattered" himself in thinking that blacks did not have to act representatively as a "separate class" any longer but could integrate themselves into all facets of American life. Douglass went on to state that continued oppression justified continued black conventions, associations, and institutions of all kinds.[44]

Even as late as 1883, Douglass argued that as long as the nation abnegated its true heritage and discriminated against blacks, it would be necessary to countenance "the color line," to hold black conventions, and to "keep up this odious distinction between citizens of a common country."[45] Antebellum

42. *Ibid.,* 19 December 1840. See also Henry Highland Garnet's 1859 speech in Boston, where he argues that blacks must not confine themselves to rhetoric about "universal rights and universal liberty." Instead, they must coalesce around the banner of black rights and black liberty, anticipating the day when "we should lay aside all distinctive labors, and come together as men and women, members of the great American family." (Reproduced in Sterling Stuckey, *Ideological Origins of Black Nationalism,* 177–78.)

43. Ward, *Autobiography,* 150.

44. Foner, ed., *Douglass,* IV: 178–79.

45. See Douglass's "Address to the People of the United States," delivered at a black convention in Louisville, Kentucky, September 24, 1883, in Foner, ed., *Douglass,* IV: 375–78, 380. T. McCants Stewart applied the same reasoning to the political situation. After beginning his 1891 address endorsing the Democratic ticket with an optimistic assess-

opposition to separate, "complexional" institutions, which occurred primarily among blacks who held the moral suasionist position of the Garrisonians, was based not on any paternalistic dependency on whites or a lack of self-confidence and racial pride, but on a conviction that in separating themselves from whites, blacks were defeating their purpose in changing public opinion by imitating the prejudiced public opinion that existed in American society. James W. C. Pennington contended that one ramification of American prejudice was a "refined heathenism" which desecrated sacred institutions. "Who has authorized," he queried, "the division of the church of God into *white* and *black* divisions?"[46] The indefatigable optimist William C. Nell, the first black man appointed to a federal post (postal clerk), crusaded almost as hard against separationist tendencies within the black community as he did against slavery. He helped to dismantle what his father had helped to build in 1826, the Massachusetts General Colored Association. He admonished blacks to seek admission into white colleges, and at the August 1843 convention he fought separate conventions, which to him implied that blacks were not " 'part and parcel of the general community.' "[47]

Yet both Nell and Douglass, as well as other moral suasionists such as James McCune Smith, David Ruggles, William Whipper, and Robert Purvis, condemned separate-complex-

---

ment of the future ("The time will come when it will not be necessary for Afro-Americans to hold special political meetings") Stewart proceeded to analyze for his black audience the political interests peculiar to blacks which necessitated an independent black political position. (T. McCants Stewart, *The Afro-American in Politics: An Address Delivered By T. McCants Stewart, Esq., At a Meeting of Colored Citizens ratifying the Democratic Ticket, at Everett Hall, Tuesday Evening, October 27th, 1891, with the Opening Address by Mr. Charles H. Lansing, Jr.* [Brooklyn, New York, 1891], 5.) Stewart, opposed to the black bloc vote of debt for the Republicans, argued for splitting the black vote between the two major political parties.

46. Pennington, *Text Book*, 80, 85.

47. See *North Star*, 3 December 1847; Nell, *Colored Patriots*, 359; and Smith, "Nell," 183, 184, 187.

ioned institutions at the same time they participated in the black convention movement.[48] Frederick Douglass, whose inconsistent behavior was most vulnerable, found himself taken to task in the *North Star* for his contradictory attitudes towards separatist institutions. Douglass wrote a series of articles on "Colored Churches" in which he tagged them prejoratively "glorified Negro pews." He advised black Christian congregations to disband and demand equality within white denominations. A black pastor questioned Douglass's conception of the church as an agency of integration, pointing out that Douglass himself should "set the first example, by dismissing his colored coeditors in his printing establishment, and knocking loudly at the door of the 'white' printer, demanding to be admitted to 'equal' editorship."[49] Black integrationists like Douglass found it virtually impossible to resist the undertow of separatism amid the maelstrom of American prejudice.

Black separatists won the debate which raged in the early 1840s over the issue of separate black conventions. It was the intruding alienation of the 1850s, however, that most united black spokesmen behind autonomous black endeavors. Yet even then some were still cautious and apologetic in their separation. The Fugitive Slave Act, the revitalization of the American Colonization Society, and the Dred Scot decision fostered black restiveness about the seemingly unbreakable strangehold of white supremacy and prodded estranged blacks to become increasingly independent of whites. Widely disparate in their views on the other subjects, Samuel Ringgold Ward, Frederick Douglass, and Martin Delany agreed in the 1850s that "our elevation must be the result of self-efforts, and, the work of our *own* hands," and

48. Less than a month after James McCune Smith, Robert Purvis, William Whipper, and David Ruggles came out opposed to complexioned action (*Colored American,* 15 August 1840; *National Anti-Slavery Standard,* 10 September 1840) Purvis, Whipper, and Ruggles inconsistently argued that blacks should latch on to their birthright of citizenship in unmixed conventions (*National Anti-Slavery Standard,* 1 October 1840).

49. *North Star,* 17, 24 March 1848.

that "our elevation as a race, is almost wholly dependent upon our own exertions." Wilberforce University, in its dedication in October 1856, resolved "that the colored man must, for the most part, be the elevator and educator of his own race."[50] When Douglass changed his mind about race organizations and proposed at the July 1853 national convention of blacks at Rochester an all-black improvement society, including a Colored National Council and a Manual Labor School, Nell opposed Douglass vigorously. This threw Douglass into a rage against Nell, Charles Lenox Remond, and Robert Purvis, three blacks who remained loyal Garrisonians.[51] By 1859, however, Nell joined William Wells Brown in organizing a convention to consider "the Moral, Social, and Political Elevation" of blacks. Nevertheless, both Nell and Brown did so reservedly, Nell apologizing at the convention for its exclusive nature but justifying it on the grounds that such conventions helped to shape a sorely diseased public opinion; and Brown confessing that "I am unfavorable to any gathering that shall seem like taking separate action from our white fellow citizens" while admitting that the setbacks of the 1850s necessitated exceptions.[52]

At the height of alienation from American society, blacks like Nell and Brown were still ambivalent about autonomous action and its implication that blacks were pariahs in American life. The radical integrationism of Brown and Nell can not be construed as an indication of their dependency on whites, or of a void of racial esteem. This is demonstrated by the newspaper controversy between Henry Highland Garnet, president of the African Civilization Society, over the issue of "begging." Brown accused Garnet of obsequiously "begging" white Americans for money, and Garnet retaliated by accusing Brown of "begging" the British. In the aftermath of Fort Sumter's fall and Lincoln's call for volunteers, Brown revealed again

    50. Delany, *Condition, Elevation, Emigration,* 54; *Frederick Douglass' Paper,* April 1835, cited by Foner, ed., *Douglass,* II: 359–62. See also Ullman, *Delany,* 291.
    51. Smith, "Nell," 188–89.
    52. *Ibid.,* 193; Farrison, *Brown,* 310–11.

his sensitivity to demeaning overtures when he spoke in Boston on April 23 at a mass black assemblage which had gathered to publicize its thoughts on the war. When the group tendered the services of black men and women in the war effort, Brown interrupted and pleaded with them not to betray their self-respect by "begging" the government for a chance to defend it. Brown, however, was drowned out by shouts of "liar" and "slaveholder."[53]

What united blacks of all persuasions was their insistence that black Americans should not be excluded from the mainstream of American life. Even when blacks branched off from that mainstream, it was mainly to prove their right to be included in it. Separatist ideology served black Americans from Richard Allen to Booker T. Washington and W. E. B. Du Bois, not so much as substance, but as sanction for an integrationist ideal. If black separatism among antebellum black abolitionists can be legitimately classified as a surging black nationalism, it was a black nationalism whch affirmed black Americanism, a black nationalism which sought to display, in the words of the *Colored American,* that "we are strongly American in our character and disposition," and a black nationalism that strove "to claim an equal place among the *American people,* to identify ourselves with American interests, and to exert all of the power and influence we have, to break down the disabilities under which we labor, and look to become a happy people in this extended country."[54] The direction of black nationalism, which manifested itself in black separatism, black solidarity, and black consciousness, was not towards exclusion from America but inclusion into American society. Black leaders were Americans, that they knew, but to secure that status they had to separate themselves from white Americans and assert themselves as black Americans. Black separatism, therefore, was often the means of concretizing an identity as Americans and an image of America which recognized no racial distinctions.

53. Farrison, *Brown*, 310–11, 332.
54. *Colored American,* 9 May 1840.

7

The Role of Blacks in American History

*Drive out the Negro and you
drive out Christ,
American liberty with him.*

FREDERICK DOUGLASS

WILLIAM WELLS BROWN stood pensively as he gazed at the monument immortalizing the names of those who died storming Fort Griswold, Connecticut, in the cause of freedom and equality. For a moment he was overcome with pride at seeing inscribed on the monument the names of two black Americans who died in the battle. But Brown's elation vanished when he noted that the two black soldiers were colonized off by a line separating their names from those of the white soldiers. The monument carved in granite more than the contributions of blacks to the fight for American independence. It also carved for posterity the segregation of blacks from the mainstream of American life. Brown confessed that he had little room for surprise at this, only grief, for such treatment "was in keeping with American historical injustice to its colored heroes."[1]

Monuments were not alone in being guilty of "historical

1. William Wells Brown, "Visit of a Fugitive Slave to the Grave of Wilberforce," in Julia Griffiths, ed., *Autographs for Freedom* (Rochester, 1854), 71.

148

injustice." Historians were equally guilty. James L. Smith noted with regret that "the historians of our country speak so little about the heroic deeds of the colored troops," and William Wells Brown pointed the finger at George Bancroft for being the prime example of a historian who ignored black valor and heroism in America's wars.[2] Black leaders early stressed the symbolic importance of the readiness with which black patriots donned uniforms in the defense of their country and their liberty. Even when the contemporary fashion of military history is taken into consideration, black historiography in the nineteenth century was conspicuously dominated by historics of Afro-American participation in America's war efforts. Black historians attempted to demonstrate that blacks, typified by Toussaint L'Ouverture and Crispus Attucks, were just as devoted to the cause of freedom as whites. They pointed out that the stereotype of black docility and passivity needed dismantling. Blacks in the American military had proven their courage, patriotism, and loyalty and had born proportionately their full share of military service and personal sacrifice in the struggle for independence and freedom.[3]

The Civil War gave added impetus to this pragmatic use of history by black historians in the nineteenth century. The

2. J. L. Smith, *Autobiography*, reprinted in *Five Black Lives*, 217. Brown's remarks are cited by Farrison, *Brown*, 316. It should be noted that Bancroft did record the participation of blacks in the Revolutionary War, though with little elaboration: "They took their place, not in a separate corps, but in the ranks with the white man; and their names may be read on the pension rolls of the country, side by side with those of other soldiers of the Revolution." (Bancroft, *History*, VII: 421.)

3. See Brown, *Black Man, passim;* James McCune Smith, *A Lecture on the Haitian Revolutions; with a Sketch of the Character of Toussaint L'Ouverture. Delivered at the Stuyvesant Institute, for the Benefit of the Colored Orphan Asylum, February 26, 1841* (New York, 1841), 13; William C. Nell, *Services of Colored Americans, in the Wars of 1776 and 1812*, 2nd ed. (Boston, 1852), especially 4. See also James M. Whitfield's poem "America" in *America and Other Poems* (Buffalo, 1853), 10–11. A useful study of the black military experience from the colonial era to the present is Jack D. Foner's *Blacks and the Military in American History: A New Perspective* (New York, 1974).

first two histories of black participation in the "War of the Rebellion" emphasized the fact that blacks had an indispensable hand in securing their own liberation and in providing the means for the salvation of the nation.[4] As the outstanding nineteenth-century black historian George Washington Williams put it, the wartime record of America's black citizens during the Civil War comprised "the proud and priceless heritage of a race," the "glory of a nation," and "the romance of North American history."[5]

I

Just as blacks pointed to their original involvement in the struggle to build an American nation which guaranteed freedom, justice, and equality for all, so they expressed their continuing commitment to the ideals which they had fought to bring to a reality. Maria W. Stewart confessed in 1832 that "the whites have so long and so loudly proclaimed the theme of equal rights and privileges, that our souls have caught the flame also." She proclaimed proudly that "I am a true born American, your blood flows in my veins, and your spirit fills my breast." As an American, then, she would willingly "die by the sword" to achieve for all Americans the inalienable rights and privileges hitherto denied the black minority.[6] Ten years later, Boston blacks reminded Americans of the "last will and testament of the patriots of '76" and reaffirmed their appropriation of the legacy that justified force and even death in the fight for freedom.[7]

Similarly, black leaders of the 1853 national convention in Rochester, New York, boldly addressed all Americans as "fellow-citizens." Nothwithstanding the passage of the 1850

4. William Wells Brown, *The Negro in the American Rebellion: His Heroism and His Fidelity* (Boston, 1867), vii; G. W. Williams, *History of Negro Troops,* xiii, 326–27.
5. Williams, *History of Negro Troops,* xiv.
6. See *Productions of Mrs. Maria W. Stewart,* 53.
7. *Liberator,* 23 December 1842.

Fugitive Slave Act, they felt justified in claiming American citizenship because of "American principles and maxims" which flatly contradicted American laws and practices. Acknowledging that "we cannot announce the discovery of any new principle adapted to ameliorate the condition of mankind," the national black convention stated its intention to stand resolutely on "the great truths of moral and political science" which "have been evolved and enunciated by you. We point to your principles, your wisdom, and to your great example for the full justification of our cause this day."[8] The friction between what blacks perceived as discrepancies between profession and performance ignited incendiary protestations against a prodigal nation which had abandoned its own heritage. The grating between American creed and deed also sparked glowing promises to appropriate that heritage in a crusade to bring to fruition for all Americans those ideals upon which the American nation was founded.

When blacks did consider the use of violence in their struggle for freedom, they usually justified such action on the basis of the precedent set by the Founding Fathers. In 1854 William Wells Brown wrote a lecture on the history of the Santo Domingo Revolution to verify the actual success of a slave revolt in the Caribbean and to predict equal success of a slave revolt in the South. Blacks had fought to their death in defense of American freedom, and blacks would certainly do the same in defense of their own personal liberty and freedom. "The spirit that caused the blacks to take up arms,"

8. *Proceedings of the Colored National Convention, held in Rochester, July 6th, 7th, and 8th, 1853* (Rochester, New York, 1853), as reproduced in Aptheker, ed., *Documentary History,* 344, 348. For later representative sentiments in a similar vein, see Charles Benjamin William Gordon's commencement address to the 1887 graduating class of the Virginia Normal and Collegiate Institute, "The Future Hope of the Negro," in *Select Sermons,* 3rd ed. (Petersburg, Virginia, 1918), 313; and Bishop Reverdy C. Ransom's 1905 query: "Do white men believe that 10,000,000 blacks, after having imbibed the spirit of American institutions . . . will ever accept a place of permanent inferiority?" in Carter G. Woodson, ed., *Negro Orators and Their Orations* (Washington, D.C., 1925), 537.

Brown warned, "and to shed their blood in the American Revolutionary War, is still amongst the slave of the south."[9] This argument was formalized in a resolution made by Brown, subsequently adopted by the 1857 annual New England Anti-Slavery Convention, which stated that if American colonists were justified in rebelling in 1776, American slaves were justified in rebelling in 1857.[10] A similar resolution was passed by blacks in Rochester when they assembled to offer moral support to free black residents of Cincinnati, Ohio, who were being pressured by "black laws" and murderous mobs into leaving the state. After first condemning violence, the resolution proceeded to condone violence in extreme cases. The treason against God and against American principles committed by Cincinnati whites, the resolution read, was just such an extreme case. Sometimes violence was the only way to deal with traitors.[11]

Actually, black insurrectionists needed no such resolutions to remind them of their revolutionary heritage, for Nat Turner symbolically rationalized his revolt by originally setting its date on July 4, 1831.[12] Earlier, one of the leaders of the abortive slave revolt of 1800 led by Gabriel Prosser had told the court that he had only done for blacks what George Washington had done for America. "I ventured my life . . . to obtain the liberty of my countrymen."[13] Finally, prior to his execution in 1860, one of John Brown's black co-conspirators in the raid on Harper's Ferry noted with pride that "as in the

    9. William Wells Brown, *St. Domingo: Its Revolutions and its Patriots. A Lecture Delivered Before the Metropolitan Athenaeum, London, May 16, and at St. Thomas' Church, Philadelphia, December 20, 1854* (Boston, 1855), 32.
    10. Cited by Farrison, *Brown,* 286–87.
    11. Steward, *Twenty-Two Years a Slave,* 173 ff.
    12. The black perception of the Fourth of July, as revealed in what blacks said about it and how they celebrated it (or refused to celebrate it), is an area which needs further research. For a preliminary treatment of the topic, weighted on the side of social history, see Quarles, *Black Abolitionists,* 118–42.
    13. See William Loren Katz, *Eyewitness: The Negro in American History,* revised ed. (New York, 1971), 103.

war of the American Revolution, the first blood shed was a black man's, Crispus Attucks, so at Harper's Ferry, the blood shed by our party, after the arrival of the United States troops, was that of a slave."[14]

The passage of the 1850 Fugitive Slave Act dealt a harsh blow to the hopes of many black leaders. Nagging doubts about the anti-slavery stance of the Constitution spread rapidly. Nevertheless, blacks still retained faith in the unqualified egalitarian principles for which the American Revolution was fought and on which the nation was grounded, principles which were enshrined in the Declaration of Independence.

Blacks clothed themselves in these American ideals when justifying armed resistance and insurrection. Twelve days after the Fugitive Slave Act became law, Martin R. Delany addressed a large biracial crowd: "All the ideas I have of liberty and independence I obtained from reading the History of the Revolutionary Fathers." Prepared to defend the full meaning of such ideas, Delany defied any man, including President Millard Fillmore, to try to capture a fugitive slave in his house without risking his life.[15] In August 1850, a convention of infuriated fugitive slaves met in Cazenovia, New York, to remind their brethren in bonds that the reason which led the American colonists to resort to arms in 1776 were the same as those that summoned the American slave to fight to free himself. This sentiment was expressed more succinctly by Samuel Ringgold Ward when he declared that the Fugitive Slave Act gave black Americans the "right of Revolution."[16] The New York blacks who assembled in an Albany state convention in July 1851 declared that the Fugitive Slave Act violated the Declaration of Independence, the Constitution of the United States, and the divine law. When forced to obey the fundamental law of the land or a conflict-

14. John A. Copeland, *A Voice from Harper's Ferry* (Boston, 1861), as cited by Aptheker, ed., *Documentary History*, 437.
15. Quoted in Thorpe, *Mind of Negro*, 167.
16. *North Star*, 5 September 1850; *Liberator*, 5 April 1850.

ing law, the convention resolved to obey the former.[17] Even the Dred Scott decision, which caused some black leaders like David Ruggles and Robert Purvis to abandon in despair their movement for recognition as American citizens, was peremptorily dismissed as illegal by an Ohio State Convention because it dishonored the Declaration, the Constitution, and "humanity itself."[18] Douglass responded to the Dred Scott decision in a similar fashion: "All I ask of the American people is, that they live up to the Constitution, adopt its principles, inbibe its spirit, and enforce its provisions."[19]

The reaction to John Brown's raid focuses most clearly the black internalization of the revolutionary tradition in America. Speaking of John Brown, William Wells Brown cautioned that no American who took pride in the Revolutionary War for freedom and independence could logically deny the "right of the American bondsman to imitate their high example."[20] To a group of Brooklyn black women, John Brown was more than an example to imitate. He was a representative American, "the greatest it has produced," and an embodiment of "true patriotism." In your act of defiance, they wrote Brown (while imprisoned in Charlestown, Virginia), you have revealed yourself "a Saviour commissioned to redeem us, the American people, from the great National Sin of Slavery."[21] Violent opposition to slavery was seen

17. *Proceedings of the State Convention of Colored People, Held at Albany, New York, on the 22nd, 23rd, and 24th of July, 1851* (Albany, New York, 1851), 29–30.
18. *Proceedings of a Convention of the Colored Man of Ohio, Held in the City of Cincinnati, on the 23rd, 24th, 25th and 26th Days of November, 1858* (Cincinnati, Ohio, 1858), 15–16. Numerous state and local conventions denounced the Fugitive Slave Law for similar reasons. (See Howard H. Bell, "Negro Militancy in the North, 1800–1860," *Journal of Negro History*, XLV [January 1960]: 11–20.)
19. Quoted in Foner, ed., *Douglass*, II: 424.
20. Brown, *Negro in American Rebellion*, 45.
21. James Redpath, *Echoes of Harper's Ferry* (Boston, 1860), 419. Redpath reprints other letters of sympathy to Brown, 387–433. See also Benjamin Quarles, ed., *Blacks on John Brown* (Urbana, Illinois, 1972). Douglass lamented America's amnesia for its "Heroic age," as exempli-

within the context of the true American tradition, and blacks who justified brute force in the fight against slavery did so, not just on humanitarian or religious grounds, but on appeals to a basic bedrock of American ideals which were vouchsafed to all beneficiaries of the American heritage.

II

Given this black appropriation of what Frederick Douglass termed "the just force of admitted American principles"[22] as a referent for action, it is easy to see how blacks tied the success of their struggle against slavery and inequality to the survival of American ideals and to the purification of America's mission in the world. While dedicated colonizers were arguing that the colonization of blacks in Africa would blot out the national sin of slavery and redeem the nation's mission to the world, black abolitionists like Nathaniel Paul were arguing that the holy principles of American abolitionism were the only ones that could "redeem the character of the American people" and reinstate her mission as a beacon of light to the Old World. Paul, an agent of the Wilberforce settlement in Canada and former pastor of an African Baptist Church in Albany, New York, wrote to Garrison in 1834 that America would have to start taking abolitionism seriously, stop supporting slaveholders, and cease from sponsoring colonization before the nation could "raise her flag of liberty, and spread it out unstained and uncontaminated, for the

---

fied in America's failure to aclaim a man "who has imitated the heroes of Lexington, Concord, and Bunker Hill." John Brown (Douglass wrote) "believes the Declaration of Independence to be true, and the Bible to be a guide to human conduct." ("Captain John Brown Not Insane," in *Douglass' Monthly,* December 1859, as cited by Foner, *Douglass,* III: 458–60.) See also the conception of John Brown by the *Weekly Anglo-African* (5 November 1859) as a man with a divine mission: "He was impelled by an unseen hand—a hand notwithstanding, that points the destinies of nations."

22. See Frederick Douglass's 1853 speech at the annual meeting of the American and Foreign Anti-Slavery Society entitled "The Present and Future Prospects of the Negro People," in Foner, ed., *Douglass,* II: 243.

world to look upon and admire."[23] Frederick Douglass, convinced that Providence guided the anti-slavery cause, argued that the only hope for the salvation of the nation and the reclamation of its image as "a blessing to mankind" lay with "the faithful and self-sacrificing labors of the abolitionists."[24]

The glorification of the role of the abolitionists, fed by a sense of America's exalted mission in the world, was taken a step further by William Wells Brown, who believed that the American abolitionists "now occupy a higher and holier position than those who carried on the American Revolution."[25] Throwing all restraint aside, the black historian of emancipation, Joseph T. Wilson, ranked the abolitionist movement, which climaxed in the abolition of slavery, second in historical importance only to Christ's birth.[26]

In a famous lecture before the Female Anti-Slavery Society of Salem, Massachusetts, Brown denounced the effacing of America's image abroad by the capitulation of the American church, benevolent societies, and government to practices totally at odds with the grand democratic principles of the American Revolution. Brown observed that "the profession of the American people is far above the profession of the people of any other country." And yet while America professes

23. *Liberator,* 12 April 1834, as reproduced in Woodson, ed., *Mind of Negro,* 170. For the white colonizationist expectation that with all blacks safely removed from America, America's role in the world as "the great moral and political light-house" would be renewed, see *Nineteenth Annual Report of the American Colonization Society* (Washington, D.C., 1836), 8; also Freeman, *Africa's Redemption,* 260–61, and Staudenraus, *African Colonization,* 20.

24. *Frederick Douglass' Paper,* 19 November 1852, in Foner, ed., *Douglass,* II: 221. See also 359.

25. William Wells Brown, *A Lecture Delivered Before the Female Anti-Slavery Society of Salem, at Lyceum Hall, November 14, 1847* (Boston, 1847), 20.

26. Joseph T. Wilson, *Emancipation: Its Course and Progress, From 1481 B.C. to A.D. 1885, With a Review of President Lincoln's Proclamations, The XIII Amendment, and the Progress of the Freed People Since Emancipation; With a History of The Emancipation Monument* (Hampton, Virginia, 1882), 9.

to embody the essence of Christian principles in all of her institutions, she embraces the practice of slavery which most openly negates American professions of Christianity and mocks the idealism of American institutions.[27] Brown fully understood America's lofty conception of her mission to the world, and he capitalized on it.

The first questions most Americans asked foreigners was "What do you think of America?" Thus one of the most biting arguments against slavery was the two-faced image projected abroad by American oppression and discrimination at home. Black leaders monitored the mutilation of America's image in the world by exploiting the contradiction between principle and practice. How could a people "who profess to be the freest and most enlightened nation under heaven," wrote the anonymous "W. J. W." to the *Liberator,* have passed such foul and wicked legislation as the Fugitive Slave Act?[28] William Wells Brown punctured America's sensitive skin when, speaking of "Our National Character, and How It Is Viewed from a Distance," he inquired, "what will the people of the Old World think? Will they not look upon the American people as hypocrites?" The Old World cannot help but notice, Brown continued, that while other nations are flocking to the shores of America for an asylum, 20,000 blacks have fled into Canada seeking a refuge from the refuge.[29] Because of slavery, Frederick Douglass commented, Americans "have blushed before all Europe." America stands with outstretched Christian arms "to give shelter to a perish-

27. Brown, *Lecture Delivered Before Female Anti-Slavery Society,* 9–11, 15.

28. "W. J. W." to the *Liberator,* 1 November 1850, cited by Woodson, ed., *Mind of Negro,* 248. See also the remarks of Samuel R. Ward to the *Aliened American,* 9 April 1853, in which he warns that America's grand professions will be scorned and scored by the world as long as she continues contradicting these professions.

29. Brown, *Lecture Delivered Before Female Anti-Slavery Society,* 15; also Farrison, *Brown,* 259. The *Colored American,* 2 September 1837, warned that at stake in the conflict between ideals and realities were "our nation's honor" and "national faith."

ing world," Douglass noted, yet she folds her arms when blacks come near. Likewise, America stands with open, democratic doors, bidding welcome to other "nations" like "the Hungarian, the Italian, the Irishman, the Jew and the Gentile," but slams the door in the face of black Americans.[30]

No longer could America be regarded as a harbinger of progress to the world. Pouring salt on the wounds he had opened, Brown stated that the issue was now: "Shall the American people be behind those who are represented as almost living in the dark ages?" According to Brown and Douglass, America's only example to the world was hypocrisy. If she desired to alter her example, purify her character, and recover her original image, America would have to heed the demands of the anti-slavery movement. "But for the blighting influence of slavery," Brown averred, "the United States of America would have a character, would have a reputation, that would outshine the reputation of any other government that is to be found upon God's green earth."[31]

Such an exalted position, of course, only made the national stain of slavery a worse blemish on America's image. What slave-holding Americans embraced as the "essence of Democracy"—slavery—was in the minds of black leaders America's prostitution of democracy and America's downfall. Without the anti-slavery movement, America had no mission and no destiny. With the success of the anti-slavery movement and the annihilation of slavery, inequality, and injustice, Henry Highland Garnet told his congressional listeners, in the first speech delivered by a black American in the national capitol, Americans would be able to "prove to mankind the superiority of our Democratic, Republican Government."[32]

Austin Steward, moreover, believed that once slavery, the main stumbling block in American progress, was de-

30. Foner, ed., *Douglass,* III: 417; II: 243, 244.
31. Brown, *Lecture Delivered Before Female Anti-Slavery Society,* 17, 22.
32. Garnet, *Memorial Discourse,* 89.

stroyed, America would be "no longer a hissing and by-word among the nations; but indeed what she professes to be, 'the land of the free, and the home of the brave'; an asylum for the oppressed of every clime."[33] In similar fashion, the *Colored American* contended that on the success or failure of the abolitionist crusade hinged the "perpetuity of our civil and religious institutions."[34] And it was for this reason that the *Anglo-African* responded editorially to the emancipation of slaves in the nation's capital by rejoicing "less as black men than as part and parcel of the American people, for it is clearly a greater boon to the nation at large than to the class more immediately concerned."[35] Frederick Douglass concurred in this assessment. The abolition of slavery in Washington, D.C., was to his mind "the first step toward a redeemed and regenerated nation."[36]

III

In his introduction to *Narrative of the Life of Frederick Douglass,* Benjamin Quarles observed that Douglass's main contribution to American democracy has been "that of holding a mirror up to it."[37] The same might be said of nearly every black leader in the nineteenth century. If there was one common activity beyond opposing slavery that united all black abolitionists, it was the exposure of the hypocrisy of the American nation. William Wells Brown spoke for most black abolitionists when he denounced "the impious doctrine 'My country right or wrong,' " (although many disagreed with him that the Liberty Party newspapers advocated it).[38] Blacks

33. Steward, *Twenty-Two Years a Slave,* 323, 324.
34. *Colored American,* 12 September 1840. Cf. Woodson, ed., *Mind of Negro,* 298.
35. *Anglo-African,* 19 April 1862, quoted in McPherson, *Negro's Civil War,* 45.
36. Foner, ed., *Douglass,* IV: 367.
37. See Benjamin Quarles, "Introduction," to Frederick Douglass, *Narrative of the Life of Frederick Douglass* (Cambridge, Massachusetts, 1960), xii (originally published Boston, 1845).
38. Cited by Farrison, *Brown,* 103–04.

affirmed the rightness of American ideology at the same time as they rejected the wrongness of those American realities which conflicted with the ideology. America was at war, not with blacks, but with herself, because America was unfaithful to her own ideals. There is little point in searching for patriotism in black Americans, for it pervaded all their writings. But there also is little point in looking for anger, hostility, hatred, and burning sarcasm towards America, "this ideal reduced to reality," as a group of abolitionist black women phrased it.[39] The anger flared at every display of American infidelity. William Wells Brown, for example, wrote his former master, Captain Enoch Price of St. Louis, Missouri, that "I will not yield to you in affection for America, but I hate her institution of slavery."[40] Likewise, H. C. Wright painted a caustic picture of "that gigantic liar and hypocrite, the American Republic, that stands with the Bible and Declaration of Independence in its hands, and its heel planted on the necks of 3,000,000 slaves."[41] Black leaders and black conventions constantly flaunted before Americans the contradictions of American life and warned that no nation at war with itself and at war with divine precepts could long survive.

Through their abolitionist endeavors black leaders sought to reclaim the true heritage of the American nation. But they did more than this. They tested the degree of American commitment to her own professed values. The black experience in America provided the acid test of the success of the American experiment in democratic government and Christian religion. George Bancroft believed that blacks in America tested only the ability of white and black men to live together. "The

39. See the "Address of the Ladies' Anti-Slavery Society of Delaware, Ohio" (to a state convention of forty Ohio blacks who met in Columbus City Hall, January 16–18, 1856), cited by Aptheker, ed., *Documentary History*, 382.

40. Brown to Price, 12 November 1849, in Woodson, ed., *Mind of Negro*, 216.

41. Wright to Douglass, 12 December 1846, in *ibid.*, 451.

real question at issue was, from the first, not one of slavery and freedom generally, but of the relation to each other of the Ethiopian and American races."[42] Frederick Douglass saw the issue differently. To him, race relations were not on trial so much as American civilization, American statesmanship, American refinement, and American Christianity. "Put him in a rail car, in a hotel, in a church, and you can easily tell how far those around him have got from barbarism towards a true Christian civilization."[43] Bancroft was concerned with protecting the ideal American image from corrosive political, social, and economic encroachments—hence the importance to him of the American frontier. Frederick Douglass, as he made clear in an 1886 address on the topic of white and black relations, was concerned with keeping "the soul of the nation" continually "sensitive and responsive to the claims of truth, justice, liberty, and progress"—hence the importance of the black presence in American destiny. As goes the black man, so goes what Douglass termed America's "soul." And as goes America's "soul," so go America's ideals, greatness, and progress.[44] Responding to the Dred Scott decision, Douglass warned that "the white man's liberty has been marked out for the same grave with the black man's."[45] Similarly, William Wells Brown characterized Charles Lenox Remond as a man burning with the conviction that blacks were engaged in a crusade that encompassed the salvation of white Americans as well as black Americans.[46]

This conception of the role of black Americans as the

42. Bancroft, *History*, III: 410.
43. *Douglass' Monthly,* April 1859, as found in Foner, ed., *Douglass,* II: 448. T. Thomas Fortune agreed with Douglass. As editor of the *New York Globe,* Fortune wrote, on 3 January 1883, that the political and social oppression of blacks constituted not a race question but a national question, and this national question must be answered before America could continue functioning. (See Dann, ed., *Black Press,* 102.)
44. Foner, ed., *Douglass,* IV: 425.
45. *Ibid.,* II: 413.
46. Brown, *Black Man,* 254.

index to America's devotion to her ideals reverberated throughout the nineteenth century in the reflections of black Americans. The Ohio lawyer John Mercer Langston ended his address to the twenty-second anniversary celebration of the American Anti-Slavery Society with the declaration that what America does with her black citizens will determine what she will do with herself. "Shall the Declaration of Independence stand? Shall the Constitution of the United States, if it is anti-slavery stand? Shall our free institutions triumph, and our country become the asylum of the oppressed of all climes?"[47]

Alexander Crummel gave this theme fuller treatment in his 1888 essay on "The Race-Problem in America." Implicitly rejecting the fashionable germ theory by asserting that "the democratic idea is neither Anglo-Saxonism, nor Germanism, nor Hibernianism," Crummel argued that democracy is rooted in the Word of God and thus is "the consummate flower of Christianity." Democracy is "God's hand in history." America, whose very "fundamental idea is democracy," must stand or fall on her total adherence to the democratic philosophy, for she has "staked her existence on this principle of democracy." In America's treatment of her black citizens America was on trial, not the black man. Crummell believed that "the Negro has been the test for over two-hundred years" of American democracy. If America failed the black testing of her democracy, "then she must die!" But Crummell was confident that America's destiny was not death or damnation, for democracy prophesied its own fulfillment. "In less than the lifetime of such a man as the great George Bancroft, observe the transformation in the status of the Negro in this land." Democracy demanded the abolition of slavery and got it. Now democracy demands full political equality of blacks. "The only question now remaining among us for the full triumph of Christian democracy is the equality of the Negro." Ameri-

47. Langston, *Virginia Plantation,* 155.

ca's destiny would be hammered out on the touchstone of black equality.[48]

This idea also found surprising expression in W. E. B. Du Bois's doctoral dissertation. In the concluding chapter to *The Suppression of the African Slave Trade to the United States of America 1638–1870,* Du Bois demonstrated the way in which America's democratic principles were tested by the practice of the African slave trade, a theme which pervaded his later work, *The Gift of Black Folk.* Du Bois posited that the black man constituted "the central thread of American history." It was the black American, Du Bois wrote, who "played a peculiar spiritual role in America as a sort of living, breathing test of our ideals and as example of the faith, hope and tolerance of our religion." Black Americans were at the same time the economic spine of the nation's development and the measure of progress of America's religious and political ideals.[49]

IV

By reflecting black realities off the mirror of white ideals, black intellectuals tested America's loyalty to her principles. Just as blacks had demonstrated their American rootage by fighting side by side with whites in defense of their "common country," so they felt that they demonstrated their American commitment by struggling against whites in defense of the country's principles. Whether America would, in Frederick Douglass's words, "have faith in your own principles" and

48. See "The Race Problem in America" in Crummell, *Africa and America,* 51–54. See also Crummell's "Eulogy on the Life and Character of Thomas Clarkson," quoted in Brown, *Black Man,* 166–67, in which he expands the idea of blacks testing American democracy into the idea of all African people providing the "most distinguished test and criterion" of the "true Christianity and civility of the world."

49. The concluding chapter of Du Bois's 1896 dissertation on *Suppression of the African Slave Trade to the United States 1638–1870,* which he entitled "The Essentials in the Struggle," is reproduced in Lester, ed., *Seventh Son,* I: 170–77. See also Du Bois's *Gift of Black Folk,* iv, 135.

actualize the ideal of equality,[50] would determine whether American ideals themselves would survive. The nation would rise or fall on her response to her own principles.

The movement for the abolition of slavery, which blacks viewed as a continuation of the revolution begun in 1776, had exposed the nation's infidelity to vows signed in the Declaration of Independece and sealed by the blood of white and black patriots. American ideals could not be reconciled to American realities. One or the other must go. Yet black abolitionists had failed to extirpate the realities of slavery and inequality by moral and political means. Throughout the 1850s it became increasingly clear that the national judgment predicted in 1829 by Robert Alexander Young's "Ethiopian Manifesto" and David Walker's "Appeal" was imminent. The "day of tribulation and reign of terror," Dr. John S. Rock reminded his Boston audience in January 1862, was not caused by abolitionist agitation. White and black abolitionists had warned of it and explored a variety of alternatives in an endeavor to prevent it.[51] But Americans had turned a deaf ear to their voices. Now a more radical resolution of the national dilemma could not be avoided. A nation which was at war with its ideals must eventually end up at war with itself. Hence the Civil War.

Slavery should have been abolished when the nation was founded. George Bancroft, Samuel Hopkins, and all the black abolitionists were agreed on this. But slavery had not been abolished, and in the words of the black historian George Washington Williams, "once inoculated with the poison of the monster, the government was only able to purify itself in the flames of a great civil war."[52] Slavery had caused the Civil War, a war which Douglass insisted should be more correctly labeled the "Abolition War."[53]

50. Foner, ed., *Douglass,* III: 420.
51. *Liberator,* 14 February 1862.
52. Williams, *History of the Negro Race,* II: vii.
53. Frederick Douglass's 1864 address on "The Mission of the

Until the Civil War, American history, American mission, and American destiny remained incomplete. The full impact of American ideals was stymied by slavery, inequality, and discrimination. Examining the landscape of American history, Joseph T. Wilson asserted that free democracy and slave aristocracy had struggled with endemic tenacity since the discovery of the New World. Although the New England colonists had helped to establish a love of freedom in the New World, "the first great victory of the people" waited upon the events of the American Revolutionary War. Still the victory was incomplete. The Old World slave aristocracy remained in perpetual struggle with the New World free democracy, until the Civil War decided the ultimate victor.[54] George Bancroft put this view succinctly in a letter to Abraham Lincoln in November 1861: "Civil War is the instrument of Divine Providence to root out social slavery." And the very fact that American history demanded that slavery be rooted out "proved true" the "doctrine of liberty."[55] The

---

War," in Foner, ed., *Douglass*, III: 391. For further examples of Dr. John S. Rock's contention that "slavery is the cause of war itself," see *Liberator*, 14 February 1862; William Wells Brown in the *Anglo-African*, 6 February 1864, cited by Farrison, *Brown*, 386; and Foner, ed., *Douglass*, III: 388.

54. Wilson, *Emancipation*, 35, 102–3. For the role of New England in the history of the nation, see Douglass's assertion that the Civil War transplanted "the whole south with the higher civilization of the north. The New England schoolhouse is bound to take the place of the Southern whipping-post. Not because we love the Negro, but the nation; not because we prefer to do this, because we must or give up the contest, and give up the country." (Foner, ed., *Douglass*, III: 397.)

55. See Bancroft's November 1861 letter to Lincoln in Howe, *Letters*, II: 143. See also Bancroft's 15 August 1861 letter (133). The extent to which Douglass shared Bancroft's belief in the importance of America's mission in the world is revealed in Douglass's interpretation of the Civil War as the noblest and grandest war that the world had ever witnessed. Americans were fighting, Douglass wrote, "not merely to free a country or continent—but the whole world from Slavery—for when Slavery fails here—it will fall everywhere." (See Foner, *Douglass*, III: 390.) Robert Purvis also believed that the abolition of slavery in the United States was related to the abolition of slavery the world over. See

founding ideal of liberty had been tried by the dogged reality of slavery, and the Civil War validated the ideal of American liberty by proving its irreconcilability with slavery.

Charles B. Ray, pastor of Bethesda Congregational Church and former editor of the *Colored American,* extended this logic one step further. The Fifteenth Amendment fulfilled the revolutionary ideal of equality in the same way that the Civil War completed the revolutionary ideal of freedom. Without the amendment "the nation would not have completed the fabric of government which it commenced to build on the principles enunciated in 1776, as the chief cornerstone of the government, namely: 'All men are created free and equal.' "[56]

While sharing the optimism about the war that characterized his black contemporaries, Frederick Douglass added a note of caution. "You and I know that the mission of this war is National regeneration," he observed in 1864.[57] And he rejoiced at the abundance of signs which promised "the return of our common country again to those peaceful, progressive, and humanizing activities of true national life, from which she had been so wantonly diverted by the insurrection of slaveholders."[58] Nevertheless the war itself was not the final purification of the nation's mission and destiny. The war constituted simply "a great national opportunity, which may be improved to national salvation, or neglected to national ruin." The abolition of slavery was but the beginning of the process

---

his 1864 speech before the annual meeting of the American Anti-Slavery Society, 1864, in Purvis, *Speeches and Letters,* 9. After admitting that "for the first time . . . is it an honor to be a citizen of the United States! Sir, old things are passing away, all things are becoming new" (7), Purvis argues that the Civil War "is a war between freedom and despotism the world over" (9).

56. *Sketch of the Life of Reverend Charles B. Ray* (New York, 1887), 52.

57. Foner, ed., *Douglass,* III: 401.

58. See the address to the "Colored National Convention," October 4–7, 1864, entitled "The Cause of the Negro People," reprinted in Foner, ed., Douglass, III: 409. The address was written largely by Douglass.

of American "regeneration." The annihilation of prejudice, discrimination, and inequality must follow for the nation's mission to be truly complete. The "Abolition war" for Douglass had a mission which transcended the abolition of slavery.

I end where I began—no war but an Abolition war; no peace but an Abolition peace; liberty for all, chains for none; the black man a soldier in war, a laborer in peace; a voter at the South as well as at the North; America his permanent home, and all Americans his fellow-countrymen. Such, fellow-citizens, is my idea of the mission of the war. If accomplished, our glory as a nation will be complete, our peace will flow like a river, and our foundations will be the everlasting rocks.[59]

59. Foner, ed., *Douglass,* III: 386–87; 403.

8
Conclusion

ETCHED ON THE bindings of George Bancroft's volumes on the *History of the United States* stands an eagle on top of the globe surrounded by words, immortalized by Bishop Berkley's famous poem, which summarized Bancroft's image of American mission and destiny: "Westward the Star of Empire takes its way." Frederick Douglass also relied on these words when describing America's destiny in the world, but not without adding greater definition: "Westward, the star of empire takes its way as well for the black man as for the white man." In countering the colonizationist claim that the image America projected to the world should be lily-white, Douglass affirmed that America was as much a "land of progress and enlightenment" for the black American as it was for the white American.[1]

The vision of the ideal America in the nineteenth century as seen through the eyes of George Bancroft and Frederick Douglass was identical. Both black leaders and white historians shared a common belief that history recorded the guiding hand of Providence working for the advancement of mankind and the special role of America in that advancement. Among white historians this doctrine of Providence manifested itself in explanations of why America had been chosen to be the special purveyor to the world of the highest ideals of civilization. Among black leaders the providential

1. *New National Era*, 19 December 1872, reproduced in Foner, ed., *Douglass*, IV: 301.

understanding of history was reflected in their explanations of why it was part of the divine plan that blacks should come to the New World—to participate in these high ideals.

When George Bancroft began writing about American history, he did so in terms of a nation which God had chosen to fulfill his plan for mankind. America was assumed to be a nation uniquely blessed by God, but a nation equally of signal responsibilities. The focus of white historians was upon the future, upon the fulfillment of God's design through the impact of American principles on the world's development.

When black leaders looked at America, they had to begin with the past. They had to begin with their relationship to America, with the most elemental question conceivable: Were they Americans? They did not begin here because it was a question to them. They began here because it was a question to whites. Before blacks could discuss America's relationship to the world, they first had to discuss their relationship to America, which, according to their reasoning, had to be solved before America's mission to the world could be fulfilled. America could not play any meaningful part in world history until she recognized the equal part that blacks had played in American history.

One cannot talk about the black image of America without first talking about black definitions of selfhood, since blacks were told by many white Americans that they were too inferior to be equal partners in the destiny of America. The black image of America entailed the black self-image, because whites excluded blacks from their image of America.

If blacks were to refute this denial of their American nationality, they first had to refute the negative image which whites had of blacks. Put positively, black nationalism was an indispensable ingredient in black assertions of American nationality. Black nationalism can best be understood as pride in color, pride in capabilities, an inverse pride in the common heritage of slavery and oppression (blacks were

proud that they were the enslaved and not the enslavers),
and a pride in the black contribution to world history and to
American history, all of which coalesced in expressions of
racial solidarity. Black nationalism profided the creative thrust
for black demands of American nationality.

In the preface to his 1855 edition of *Leaves of Grass,*
Walt Whitman characterized America as "not merely a nation but a teeming nation of nations," and therefore a nation
of teeming subgroup nationalisms. New England nationalism,
southern nationalism, western nationalism, white nationalism,
black nationalism, and various other ethnic nationalisms all
existed as sub-nationalisms within the overarching American
nationalism of a multinational state. It was within such a context that black spokesmen throughout the nineteenth century
referred to themselves as a "nation,"[2] and that black antagonists such Frederick Douglass and Martin Delany, Booker
T. Washington and W. E. B. Du Bois classified black Americans
as a "nation within a nation."[3]

The alleged nineteenth-century black soul-searching, identity
crisis is more an optical illusion of modern myopia than it is a
true picture of the self-image of blacks, for nineteenth-century
black leaders knew who they were and what they were about.
They were blacks, they were Americans, and they were committed through varying means to the ends of emancipation,
elevation, and equality. The trouble was in trying to convince
whites who they were, what they claimed as their inheritance,
and the seriousness of what they were about.[4]

Nationalistic components such as self-pride, self-conscious-

2. For expressions of this sentiment, see Aptheker, "Consciousness
of Negro Nationality" in *Toward Negro Freedom,* 105–9.
3. Booker T. Washington's speech in 1896, which used this phrase,
referred specifically to black people in the south. See Aptheker, *Toward
Negro Freedom,* 105.
4. John Mercer Langston demanded of the Ohio State legislature in
1857 that "your history and your destiny shall be ours." (Cited by William F. Cheek, "John Mercer Langston: Black Protest Leader and
Abolitionist," in Bracey Jr., Meier, and Rudwick, ed., *Blacks in the Abolitionist Movement,* 35–36.

ness, self-knowledge, and group identity were not the limited preserve of a few black emigrationists or colonizationists who planned to establish a "Negro Nationality"—those whom it has become fashionable to hail as black nationalists.[5] When it came to the means of ending racism in America, Booker T. Washington, for example, could be as compromising and unoffending as it was possible for any black man to be. When it came to the point of personal identity, however, Washington was as unflinchingly nationalistic as any of the other black leaders. "From any point of view," he wrote in his autobiography, "I had rather be what I am, a member of the Negro race, than be able to claim membership with the most favoured of any other race." Beneath Washington's sugar-coated curatives for racism, which he felt whites would swallow most readily, lay a hard inner core of nationalistic pride, which manifested itself in his furtive financial support for T. Thomas Fortune's more aggressive journalistic campaign against discrimination; in his call for the development of "race pride and race consciousness"; and in his gentle rebuke of Harvard University for its complete neglect of courses which directly related to the concerns of black students, especially in the field of black history.[6]

The blanket concept of black nationalism which is used to denote "the belief of a group that it possesses, or ought to possess a country; that it shares, or ought to share, a common heritage of language, culture, and religion; and that its heritage, way of life, and ethnic identity are distinct from other groups"[7] can be applied with accuracy to few blacks

5. See, for example, Howard H. Bell, "Negro Nationalism: A Factor in Emigration Projects, 1858–1861," *Journal of Negro History,* XLVII (January 1962): 42 ff.; and Theodore Draper, *The Rediscovery of Black Nationalism* (New York 1970), 3–47.

6. See Harlan, ed., *Washington Papers* I: 234–35, 405, 406–7.

7. This is the definition of black nationalism used by E. U. Essien-Udom, *Black Nationalism* (Chicago, 1962), 6; also Wilson Record, "The Negro Intellectual and Negro Nationalism," *Social Forces,* XXX (October 1954): 10.

before the West Indian immigrant Marcus Garvey, and then
only with severe restrictions and reservations. Their country
was America, their language was English, their religion was
Protestant; and, as the Constitution of the American Society
of Free Persons of Color contended in 1830, their "habits,
manners, and customs are the same in common with other
Americans."[8]

The dilemma of blacks in the nineteenth century was
how to assert one's position as an American, with equal rights
and privileges in common with other Americans, when the
American nation for the most part did not want blacks included within its nationality. Blacks did not concede America to the whites; neither did they succumb to the white stereotype of themselves as non-American and non-persons. While
aspiring to inclusion in American society, nineteenth-century
free-blacks both affirmed their blackness and denounced the
nation which rejected their blackness for perverting the "principles of civil and religious liberty" upon which that nation
was founded. They did not barter away their birthright for
a mess of popularity and acceptance, all of which would have
been given to them on a silver platter if only they had allowed themselves to be colonized and had renounced their
claim to parity with whites in the American nation and in
the American goal of creating a Christianized society
through religion, morality, and education.

Blacks were nationalistic about their color and about
their capabilities, indispensable ingredients in self-pride and
creativity. Yet their nationalism did not preempt their demands for inclusion as Americans. Blacks realized that they
had a common history of suffering and oppression which dif-
ferentiated them from other groups and that, as a proscribed
minority, they had special interests and special needs which
required them to band together as a unit. In Philadelphia

8. See *Constitution of the American Society of Free Persons of
Color,* 10, cited by Pease and Pease, "Organized Negro Communities,"
32–33.

alone, William Lloyd Garrison, in 1832, counted at least fifty black societies for literary, scientific, benevolent, and moral purposes. And by 1858, Baltimore boasted over forty benevolent and fraternal associations, attesting to their enormous popularity, especially among the upwardly mobile free-blacks.[9] Yet at the same time, blacks recognized that separatist demands seemed to contradict what their ancestors who had fought in the American Revolution had helped to found —the American dream of equality based on the ideal of color-blind institutions. Without autonomous actions for their own emancipation, elevation, equality, and leadership training, however, black identity, respectability, and self-confidence would be seen as the artificial product of white abolitionist tutelage. Hence the importance of black newspapers and especially the black convention movement, the greatest social movement among free blacks in the antebellum period.

Blacks gathered in national conventions annually from 1830 to 1835. After 1840 "colored national conventions" occurred only intermittently until the onset of the Civil War, although there were frequent local and state conventions. These conventions were immensely important in the development of a positive self-image, aggressive confidence, and an historic tradition of heroes and events. It was at these conventions that allegations of inferiority received their first corporate rebuke. It was at these conventions that addresses were given which lauded Afro-American heroes like Nat Turner, Madison Washington, Crispus Attucks, and others whom white Americans were denouncing or ignoring. It was at these conventions that blacks could release their pent-up anger at their own nation, which refused to acknowledge their citizenship and contribution of "blood, sweat, and tears" to American history. It was these conventions which trained

9. Ira Berlin has argued convincingly that by institutionalizing variations in occupation, status, wealth, and interests, benevolent societies often had the adverse affect of exacerbating class divisions within the free black caste. (See his *Slaves Without Masters,* 312–13.)

and demonstrated black leadership, thereby instilling greater self-confidence and self-pride. And it was these conventions which reinforced a powerful sense of community, commonality, common heritage, and group pride. By enabling blacks to establish traditions of value to themselves which would in turn elicit respect from others, these conventions kindled national pride and helped to fashion what Charles H. Wesley referred to as "an heroic tradition for Negro Americans,"[10] a tradition which fostered a deep sense of self-worth and self-esteem.

The demands of blacks for recognition of their full American nationality were not made from a position of weakness. They based their claims for American citizenship on pride in themselves and pride in their history. Nearly every effort of black leaders was directed to prove that blacks were equal partners in American history with whites. When blacks began to write history, the first topics they chose were those which would prove themselves equal to whites in the history of civilization as well as the history of America. The writing of history was thus a strongly pragmatic enterprise for such nineteenth-century blacks as William Cooper Nell, James W. C. Pennington, Robert Benjamin Lewis, William Wells Brown, George Washington Williams, Booker T. Washington, and even W. E. B. Du Bois. Here was recovery of the past not for its own sake, but rather for the sake of discovering models who could be used in the struggle for full participation in American society. What history provided, according to Earl E. Thrope, was "a weapon in the fight for racial equality."[11]

The black nationalism that expressed itself in the nineteenth century can best be interpreted not as a pathological reaction to white racism or to the failure of white nationalism, but as a sentiment that emerged from within the black ex-

10. Charles H. Wesley, "Creating and Maintaining an Historical Tradition," *Journal of Negro History*, XLIX (January 1964): 21.

11. Earl E. Thrope, *Black Historians: A Critique* (New York, 1971), 18.

perience and consciousness which professed pride in color, confidence in one's abilities, pride in one's contribution to American history, and the remedial imperative of racial solidarity in the struggle for acceptance by white Americans. It is hard to find a black leader in the nineteenth century who did not exhibit such nationalistic qualities.

Thus blacks combined two distinct but harmonious themes in the nineteenth century. They asserted both their identity as blacks and their identity as Americans. At the same time that blacks were nationalistic in their pride of color, pride of black capabilities, and pride of a culture which was free of the moral imperfections of the broader American society, they were nationalistic about the superiority of American ideals, their stature as Americans, and their rights as citizens of the American nation. Blacks were bifocal in their identification and affections.

I

The major thrust of black leadership in the nineteenth century was integration. Black Americans, sure of their identity as blacks and as Americans, demanded acceptance as full-fledged, loyal, and competent Americans. Moreover, despite dissenting voices from a few African colonizationists, typified by Bishop Henry McNeal Turner, black leaders at the turn of the century were optimistic about the outcome of the struggle to achieve equal American status. The lead editorial in the first issue of the *Crisis* presented their optimistic millennial vision: "Catholicity and tolerance, reason and forebearance can to-day make the world-old dream of human brotherhood approach realization . . . We strive for this higher and broader vision of Peace and Good Will."[12]

One source of optimism in the early twentieth century was the promise of the bourgeoning Progressive movement. W.

12. *Crisis,* I (November 1910): 10, cited by Francis L. Broderick, *W. E. B. DuBois: Negro Leader in Time of Crisis* (Stanford, California, 1959), 94; see also Lester, ed., *Seventh Son,* I: 64–67.

E. B. Du Bois, editor of the *Crisis,* leaped aboard Theodore Roosevelt's third-party campaign in 1912, bringing with him a proposed plank on race which he had written expressly for the Progressive Convention in Chicago. In short order, however, Du Bois was bumped off the "Bull Moose" crusade by Roosevelt's rejection of him as a "dangerous person" and by Roosevelt's lily-white southern campaign strategy. Du Bois then turned to the Democrats, repeating his performance in the previous presidential election.[13] Through the *Crisis* Du Bois tendered his support to Wilson's Progressive campaign, as did many other black leaders, such as William Monroe Trotter, editor of the Boston *Guardian,* and Bishop Alexander Walters. While blacks like T. Thomas Fortune and Assistant Attorney General William H. Lewis (who had been patronized by the Republican party administration) supported Taft, the election of 1912 witnessed a greater number of blacks turning away from their historic hitch to the Republicans than any previous presidential election.[14]

Wilson's first inaugural address in 1913 struck a classical Progressive note by declaring a return of America to her original "vision."[15] The clashing dictions between aims and attainments, which blacks knew all too well, remained outside the vision of Wilson's "New Freedom," and this Progressive President proceeded to outdo any previous president in anti-black legislation and executive orders. Black supporters of Wilson, like Du Bois, had overrated the power of Wilson's Progressive convictions and underrated the power of his southern upbringing. Once again, blacks had been led to the

13. W. E. B. Du Bois, *The Autobiography of W. E. B. Du Bois* (New York, 1971), 262–64; also Arthur S. Link, "The Negro as a Factor in the Campaign of 1912," *Journal of Negro History,* XXXII (January 1947): 81–99.
14. Thornbrough, *T. Thomas Fortune,* 340–41; Walters, *Life and Work,* 177; Fishel, Jr., and Quarles, ed., *Black American,* 390.
15. Broderick, *Du Bois,* 92. For Wilson's first inaugural address, see Albert Shaw, ed., *President Wilson's State Papers and Addresses* (New York, 1917), 1–5.

trap of an ever-widening cleft between American preachments and American policy.

A curious feature of the Progressive movement and the parallel Social Gospel movement was the blindness exhibited to the race issue. As C. Vann Woodward has noted, the Progressive era was actually retrogressive in matters of race.[16]

Although Du Bois would never again let himself be betrayed by the vapid promises of a Republican, Democratic, or Progressive party, he still retained a sanguine faith in the eventual triumph of the millennium. "Evolution is evolving the millennium," he prophesied in 1914, "but one of the unescapable factors in evolution are the men who hate wickedness and oppression with perfect hatred, who will not equivocate, will not excuse, and will be heard."[17]

Before the dismay over the slovenly treatment afforded blacks by Progressives turned to utter despair, the war intervened to bolster the hopes of black Americans. One of the most pertinacious myths blacks shared in the nineteenth century was the belief that as blacks fought valiantly for their country, white Americans would be forced to face up to the truth about the equality and humanity of black Americans. In supporting the nation in the time of peril, blacks saw an avenue to the attainment of full American status. Du Bois shared this belief, writing at the peak of his optimism, in 1918, a controversial editorial entitled "Close Ranks." Emboldened by his "New Patriotism," Du Bois challenged blacks to "close ranks shoulder to shoulder" with those who were "fighting for democracy," admitting in the process that "we make no ordinary sacrifice, but we make it gladly and willingly with our eyes lifted to the hills." In later years Du Bois would reminisce, in his autobiography, about his motivations for supporting so vigorously this war to end all wars. He had mistakenly hoped, he revealed, that "in a fight with America

16. See Glenn R. Bucher, "Social Gospel Christianity and Racism," *Union Seminary Quarterly Review,* XXVII (Winter 1973): 146–57.

17. *Crisis,* VIII (May 1914): 26, cited by Broderick, *Du Bois,* 94.

against militarism and for democracy we would be fighting for the emancipation of the Negro race. With the Armistice came disillusionment."[18]

In the aftermath of the "Great War," virtually all things became new. Exhaustion replaced exuberance; normalcy replaced novelty; isolationism replaced internationalism; pessimism replaced optimism; and cynicism replaced innocence. Most Americans were left disenchanted, dispirited, and disillusioned. Throughout her history America had woven a silken shroud of millennialist hopes only to be transformed, in the welter of war, not into a radiant millennium, but into a broken-down counterfeit. White and black leaders who had supported enthusiastically the war to end all wars, now turned an about-face, scorning war as a means to end any conflict. Americans had sapped their resources and energies to make the world safe for democracy, only to end up completely dry. In addition blacks had fought to make America safe for democracy, and it too eluded them. Progressive optimism, which had culminated a century of faith in the possibility of progress and the superintendency of divine providence over history, dissipated in disillusionment, and Americans were left spiritually and idealistically jaded.

The ideological disillusionment over the war coincided for many blacks with economic disillusionment over the North as a Promised Land. Southern blacks who had migrated to the North during the war found out that racism and discrimination were national, not sectional. Concentrated into northern ghettos, black masses became more and more sensitive to the intransigence of American racism. Even in the North, American principles could not be budged from their high and lofty pedestals. Suspicions simmered that perhaps there was more rotten with America than just her policies—perhaps her principles were not all that pure. William

18. *Crisis,* XVI (1918): 111, cited by Elliott M. Rudwick, "An Accommodationist in Wartime," in Rayford W. Logan, ed., *W. E. B. Du Bois: A Profile* (New York, 1971), 177; Du Bois, *Autobiography,* 274.

Pickens, in detailing the characteristics of the nascent "New Negro," observed that the black man's idea of the nation had changed gradually. "In 1878 the Negro regarded the oppressor as local—'Uncle Sam' as being some personality separate and apart from the oppressor." Increasingly, however, blacks began to wonder if the nation itself was the oppressor.[19] At this point, the pristine vision of America and the pristine quality of her ideals, which had so infused the writings of white historians and black leaders in the nineteenth century, was lost. Du Bois in the 1920s abandoned his early hopes and aspirations and came to identify racism no longer with ignorance and prejudice, but with capitalism and democracy itself. The nineteenth-century black hope that "if only Americans lived up to their principles" was replaced for Du Bois with the feeling that Americans in fact were living up to their principles, for their principles were racist.[20]

Many blacks were thus led to reject the Anglo-Saxon myth of a homogeneous Christian republic, which for white historians from Bancroft to Wilson involved, at least in principle, less a blend of blood than it did a set of shared beliefs and modes of action. These were the beliefs and actions which were questioned by the emerging ethnic enthusiasts. Black leaders no longer drooled over American ideals; no longer did they dust off the pages of American military history to document their right to an equal partnership in America's mission and destiny; no longer could they decipher meaning in slavery as a school for Christianity and civilization.

Heroes and traditions, long held sacrosanct, were now held up for ridicule. In the white community of the 1920s, the debunking of both the Puritan ethic and the Puritan belief in divine providence became a favorite pastime of the American intelligentsia. The waves of Puritan belief in the mission and destiny of America, which had washed over American society throughout the nineteenth century, were stilled. In-

19. William Pickens, *The New Negro* (New York, 1916), 233–35.
20. See Du Bois's *Autobiography,* 289–90.

deed, "Puritanism" became a pejorative catch-all epithet, especially through the writings of H. L. Mencken and the *American Mercury*.[21] Nothing was sacred, not even patriotism. Americans felt guilty about being hoodwinked so completely by the patriotic belief in America as the last best hope of the world, and they resolved never to be sucked in again by the lure of an idealistic nationalism.

While white Americans were shedding their traditions and heroes, black Americans were discovering and affirming traditions and heroes of their own, especially in Africa. The price nineteenth-century immigrants had to pay to be accepted as Americans was to become Anglo-Saxon in ideology, culture, and religion. Blacks in the 1920s were no longer willing to pay that price. They would be accepted as Americans, but of a different cultural stripe than white Americans. The "New Negro" who emerged in the aftermath of the first world war was bent not on attaining integration into American life so much as attaining an identity independent of white American society. Separatism, which was justified in the nineteenth century for reasons of integration, was justified in the twentieth century for reasons of identity. The goal of the "New Negro" was not integration but identity.

The Garveyite movement of the 1920s rejected the goal of integration and forbade any dual loyalty. Its loyalty was to things African. Before Garvey, the black convention movement of the 1830s through the 1850s came closest to approximating a black mass movement. But here the aim was to seek self-improvement through middle-class, white values leading toward integration into American life. Garvey's Universal Negro Improvement Association rejected both integration and the white values of self-improvement. African identity and separatism were the goals to be courted.[22]

Africa also became a proud source of black culture and

21. Dixon Wecter, *The Hero in America* (New York, 1941), 36 ff., 46–47, 490–91.
22. For an analysis of the differences that marked the thought of Garvey from Du Bois, see Elton C. Fax, *Garvey* (New York, 1972),

identity for the "New Negro" of the Harlem Renaissance, who sought to emphasize the racial-cultural heritage of Afro-Americans.[23] The nineteenth century witnessed a twofold interest in Africa: the first was apologetic, as the ancient glory of Africa served to marshall proof of the equality of blacks with whites; the second was missionary, as black Americans felt the tug of responsibility for sharing the fruits of Christianity and civilization with their African roots. The interest in Africa which blossomed with the Harlem Negro Renaissance of the 1920s and the Garveyite movement was not missionary-oriented, but culturally oriented.

Charles Flint Kellogg, the historian of the National Association for the Advancement of Colored People, has attached added significance to the year 1919 beyond the race riots and other incendiary racial events. It was this year, he observed, which "marked a turning point in the history of the NAACP." The primarily "white-oriented" social reformist and philanthropic founders, who had originally referred to themselves as the "new abolitionists," were being shoved out by a "New Negro" who was less talkative and more militant than the "new abolitionists." The year 1919 witnessed the genesis of the National Association for the Advancement of Colored People–Pan-African Congress in Africa, demonstrating that its concern transcended the upgrading of the black status in America into a concern for race oppression and imperialism in Africa and in the world.[24]

II

Sutton E. Griggs, the black novelist, sensed the direction in which blacks were headed in his 1899 novel entitled *Imperium in Imperio*. The novel presents three major pro-

---

143 ff. For the bitter acrimony between Garvey and Du Bois, see Ben F. Rogers, "William E. B. Du Bois, Marcus Garvey, and Pan-Africa," *Journal of Negro History*, XL (January 1955): 154–65.

23. Thorpe, *Mind of Negro*, 33.

24. Charles Flint Kellogg, *NAACP: A History of the National Association for the Advancement of Colored People*, Vol. I (Baltimore, 1967), 291–93.

tagonists: Belton Piedmont, the antebellum child of slavery (a rough casting of Booker T. Washington), who when forced to choose between his color and his country, refused to his death to admit the necessity of the choice; Bernard Belgrave, the post-Civil War mulatto child of growing awareness and confidence (a rough casting of W. E. B. Du Bois), who when forced to choose between his color and country, chose his color; and Viola Martin, who when forced to choose between her color and her lover, resolved her vacillation in suicide.

The story involved a secret black nation within the American nation, organized "according to the teachings of Thomas Jefferson," its capital "Jefferson College," and its constitution closely "modeled after that of the United States." During the Spanish American War, the Congress of the Imperium met to debate the future relationship between blacks and Anglo-Saxons. Some suggested amalgamation, others proposed African emigration, but eventually everyone settled on a race war. There was, however, one exception—Belton Piedmont.[25]

Piedmont rose to defend his opposition to a race war. Because he felt that he had proven his "patriotism" to the cause of the Imperium, he spoke freely. He was born, raised, and hoped to die in the South. And although blacks were enslaved mercilessly in America, forcibly employed without monetary compensation, yet Piedmont believed that God had not allowed slavery to obstruct his plan for blacks:

He [the black man] received that from the Anglo-Saxons which far outweighs in value all the gold coin on earth. He received instruction in the arts of civilization, a knowledge of the English language, and a conception of the one true God and his Christ. While all of the other races of men were behind the ball of progress rolling it up the steep hill of time, the negro was asleep in the jungles of Africa. . . . So, beloved fellow citizens, when we calmly survey the evil and the good that came to us through American slavery, it is my opinion

25. Sutton E. Griggs, *Imperium in Imperio* (Cincinnati, 1899), 190–98. (For the best interpretation of Griggs's intentions in writing the novel, see Robert E. Fleming, "Sutton E. Griggs: Militant Black Novelist," *Phylon,* XXXIV [March 1973]: 73–77.)

that we find more good for which to thank God than we find evil for which to curse man.[26]

In an attempt to fend off the proposed war between blacks and whites, Piedmont submitted a series of counter resolutions. He suggested that blacks cease to conceal the existence of the Imperium, thereby showing the Anglo-Saxons that what had been seen as weakness and docility in the black character was actually strength. Thus in the open, blacks could try to convince whites that they had to reckon with a "New Negro" who demanded—not requested—his rights. In case this failed, Piedmont proposed that all seven and one half million members of the black nation within a nation migrate to Texas, take control lawfully of the state government through outnumbering whites at the polls, and there "work out our destiny as a separate and distinct race in the United States of America."[27]

Bernard Belgrade, the President of the Imperium and Piedmont's closest friend, immediately submitted the details of his plan to wage war against Anglo-Saxon Americans. When asked his opinion of the plan, Piedmont labeled it "treason," adding that

I am no traitor and never shall be one. Our Imperium was organized to secure our rights within the United States and we will make any sacrifice that can be named to attain that end. Our efforts have been to wash the flag free of all blots, not to rend it; to burnish every star in the cluster, but to pluck none out.

Candidly, Bernard, I love the Union and I love the South. Soaked as Old Glory is with my people's tears and stained as it is with their warm blood, I could die as my forefathers did, fighting for its honor and asking no greater boon than Old Glory for my shroud and native soil for my grave. . . . I shall never give up my fight for freedom, but I shall never prove false to the flag.[28]

For this dual loyalty, the penalty was death.

As he stood before a black firing squad and awaited

26. Griggs, *Imperium,* 228–29. The quote is found on 231–32.
27. *Ibid.,* 245.
28. *Ibid.,* 251–53.

execution, Piedmont was given the customary courtesy of a few last words. "Tell posterity," said Piedmont,

that I loved the race to which I belonged and the flag that floated over me; and, being unable to see these objects of my love engage in mortal combat, I went to my God, and now look down upon both from my home in the skies to bless them with my spirit.[29]

Belton Piedmont stood squarely on his dual identity as a black man and as an American, refusing to be budged from either. His goal was integration into the mainstream of American life, and he refused to abandon hope that his goal was attainable. Bernard Belgrave stood ready to give the execution orders, squarely on the grounds of his proud black identity. "I know the Anglo-Saxon race," he retorted to Piedmont. "He will never admit you to equality with him."[30]

Without any tie of hope to a future in America, the time had arrived for a life and death struggle. With Bernard Belgrave as its apotheosis, the "New Negro" had come alive. The nineteenth-century vision of a colorless, democratic, Christian America, which would stand as a beacon to the world's benighted, was put to rest with the execution of Belton Piedmont by a black firing squad. Americans now had a new type of black man on their hands.

29. *Ibid.,* 259.
30. *Ibid.,* 253.

A Bibliographical Review

Bibliographic Guides

FORTUNATELY, THE STUDENT of Afro-American history is not without bibliographical assistance. Even in 1955 the plethora of bibliographical resources available necessitated a bibliography of the bibliographies, compiled by S. H. Kessler in "American Negro Literature, A Bibliographic Guide," *Bulletin of Bibliography,* 21 (September 1955): 181–85. The most imaginative, exhaustive, and best interpretive bibliographical guide to Afro-American history, arranged chronologically and topically, is James M. McPherson, et al., *Blacks in America: Bibliographical Essays* (Garden City, New York, 1972). Monroe N. Work ploughed untilled soil when he compiled his *Bibliography of the Negro in Africa and America* (New York, 1928; reprinted New York, 1965), which should be consulted in tandem with two other equally indispensable reference books: Erwin K. Welsch, *The Negro in the United States: A Research Guide* (Bloomington, Indiana, 1965), and Dorothy B. Porter, comp., *The Negro in the United States: A Selected Bibliography* (Washington, 1970). The explosion of interest in Afro-American studies is evidenced in Earle H. West's handy compilation of *A Bibliography of Doctoral Research on the Negro, 1933–1966* (Ann Arbor, Michigan, 1969), which should be supplemented by referring to the subject indexes of post-1966 *Dissertation Abstracts.*

Much of the research for this volume was conducted at the renowned Schomburg branch of the New York Public Library. Of immense value is the reproduction of their vast card file, *Dictionary Catalog of the Schomburg Collection of Negro Literature and History,* 9 vols. (Boston, 1962), with a two volume *Supplement* (1967). Related resources of particular value to those teaching Afro-American studies include Elizabeth W. Miller and Mary L. Fisher, comp., *The Negro in America: A Bibliography* (Cambridge, Massachusetts, 1970); Capital University Library's *Black Culture* (Columbus, Ohio, 1969); William L. Katz's annotated *Teacher's Guide to American Negro History* (Chicago, 1968); Dorothy R. Homer and Ann M. Swarthout, comp., *Books about the Negro: An Annotated Bibliography* (New York, 1966); The American Jewish Committee's *Negro History and Literature: A Selected Annotated Bibliography* (New York, 1968); and Peter M. Bergman, *The Chronological History of the Negro in America* (New York, 1969).

Historians involved in Afro-American religious studies are indebted to Ethel L. Williams and Clifton F. Brown for their compilation of *Afro-American Religious Studies: A Comprehensive Bibliography with Locations in American Libraries* (Metuchen, New Jersey, 1972). Far less exhaustive is the pamphlet put out by The Fund for Theological Education, *A Bibliography of African and Afro-American Religions* (Princeton, New Jersey, n.d.).

General Histories

Gunnar Myrdal's skillful survey of race relations in *An American Dilemma: The Negro Problem and Modern Democracy* (New York, 1944), gets better with age. There are any number of adequate textbooks, although John Hope Franklin's *From Slavery to Freedom: A History of Negro Americans,* 4th ed. rev. (New York, 1974) has still not been surpassed. Benjamin Quarles, *The Negro in the Making of America* (New York, 1964) and August Meier and Elliott Rudwick, *From Plantation to Ghetto* 2nd ed. rev. (New York, 1970) have written solid studies.

There have been a number of excellent anthologies of reprinted articles and essays of Afro-American history, notably: Dwight W. Hoover, ed., *Understanding Negro History* (Chicago, 1968); August Meier and Elliott Rudwick, ed., *The Making of Black America,* 2 vols. (New York, 1969); Melvin Drimmer, ed., *Black History: A Reappraisal* (Garden City, New York, 1968); and Eric Foner, ed., *America's Black Past: A Reader in Afro-American History* (New York, 1970). Deserving of special note is an assortment of several of Eugene D. Genovese's noteworthy essays, *In Red and Black: Marxian Exploration in Southern and Afro-American History* (New York, 1971).

Although Robert C. Dick's perceptive analysis of the rhetoric of antebellum black protest literature entitled *Black Protest: Issues and Tactics* (Westport, Connecticut, 1974) purports to be an overview of black intellectual history, the only holistic treatment of the field is Earl E. Thorpe, *The Mind of the Negro: An Intellectual History of Afro-Americans* (Baton Rouge, Louisiana, 1961). Two articles of particular importance to this study are Robert Ernst, "Negro Concepts of Americanism," *Journal of American History*, XXXIX (July 1954): 206–19, and Herbert Aptheker, "Afro-American Superiority: A Neglected Theme in the Literature," *Phylon*, XXXI (Winter 1970): 336–42.

In many ways my book is a counterpart to George M. Frederickson's sinewy investigation of the interrelation between sociopolitical issues and white racial ideology in *The Black Image in the White Mind: The Debate on Afro-American Character and Destiny, 1812–1914* (New York, 1971). The unseemly picture of white church leaders promulgating racist doctrines and the linkage of religious racism to theologico-political issues is presented by H. Shelton Smith, *In His Image, But . . . Racism in Southern Religion, 1780–1910* (Durham, North Carolina, 1972). For a vigorous inspection of white attitudes toward black Americans, see Winthrop D. Jordon, *White Over Black: American Attitudes Towards the Negro, 1550–1812* (Chapel Hill, North Carolina, 1968).

Collection of Primary Sources

The Afro-American historian's task of burrowing in the archives has been made easier by a number of excellent anthologies. These include: Dorothy Porter, ed., *Negro Protest Pamphlets* (New York, 1969) and *Early Negro Writing 1760–1837* (Boston, 1971); Carter G. Woodson, ed., *The Mind of the Negro as Reflected in Letters Written During the Crisis 1800–1862* (Washington, D.C., 1926), and *Negro Orators and Their Orations* (Washington, D.C., 1925; reprinted New York, 1970); Leslie H. Fishel, Jr., and Benjamin Quarles, ed., *The Black American: A Documentary History* (New York, 1970); Joanne Grant, ed., *Black Protest: History, Documents, and Analyses 1619 to the Present* (Greenwich, Connecticut, 1968); Thomas R. Frazier, ed., *Afro-American History: Primary Sources* (New York, 1970); John H. Bracey, August Meier, and Elliott Rudwick, ed., *The Afro-Americans: Selected*

Documents, 2 vols. (Boston, 1970); and Henry Steele Commager, ed., *The Struggle for Racial Equality: A Documentary Record* (New York, 1967). The most ambitious project is Maxwell Whiteman, gen. ed., *Afro-American History Series,* 10 vols. (Wilmington, Delaware, 1971). Howard Brotz has done a superb job of sampling black intellectual history in his editing of *Negro Social and Political Thought, 1850–1920: Representative Texts* (New York, 1966).

The Black Press

Much of the research for this volume came from abolitionist periodicals and newspapers. The first black newspaper, *Freedom's Journal* (1827–29), was founded by John Russwurm and Samuel Cornish. Two months after its demise on March 28, 1829, Cornish briefly revived *Freedom's Journal* under the new title *Rights of All.* David Ruggles edited the *Mirror of Liberty* (1837– ?) in 1837, the same year in which Philip A. Bell founded *The Weekly Advocate.* When Bell relinquished editorial responsibilities to Cornish one month after its founding, the newspaper's name was changed to the *Colored American* (1837–42). Other black newspapers include: the *Mystery* (1843–47); the *North Star* (1847–50), which subsequently changed to *Frederick Douglass' Paper and Douglass' Monthly;* the *Aliened American* (1852–56); and the *Weekly Anglo-African,* which changed its title to the *Anglo-African* (1859–62). For the history of the black press and a good collection of articles selected from it, see Martin L. Dann, ed., *The Black Press, 1827–1890: The Quest for National Identity* (New York, 1971).

Minutes and Proceedings of Black Conventions

Local, state, and national black conventions, which began systematically in 1830 and lasted throughout the nineteenth century, reveal a leadership consensus on a wide range of topics affecting the black community. Howard H. Bell has performed a beneficial service in editing the *Minutes of the Proceedings of the National Negro Conventions, 1830–1864* (New York, 1969). What Bell has done on a national level (national black conventions met regularly between 1830 and 1835 and irregularly thereafter) needs to be done on a state and local level as well. See also Bell's *Survey of the Negro Convention Movement, 1830–1861* (New York, 1969): and William H. Pease and Jane H. Pease, "The Negro Convention Movement" in Nathan I. Higgins, Martin Kilson, and David M. Fox, ed., *Key Issues in the Afro-American Experience,* 2 vols. Vol. I, 191–205 (New York, 1971).

Slave Narratives and Autobiographies

According to Theodore Parker, the only "wholly indigenous and original" form of American literature is the fugitive slave narrative (Robert E. Collins, ed., *Theodore Parker: American Transcendentalist* [Metuchen, New Jersey, 1973], 128). Although slave narratives were of only limited usefulness to this study, a number of them deserve special note. Second only to dime novels in mass circulation in the nineteenth century, the genre of fugitive slave narratives found classic illustration in Frederick Douglass's *Narrative of the Life of Frederick Douglass* (Boston, 1845; reprinted Cambridge, Massachusetts, 1960). Two handy anthologies of slave narratives are Benjamin Drew, ed., *A North Side View of Slavery. The Refugee: or the Narratives of Fugitive Slaves in Canada. Related by Themselves, with an account of the history and condition of the colored population of upper Canada* (Boston, 1856); and Gilbert Osofsky, ed., *Puttin' On Ole Massa: The Slave Narratives of Henry Bibb, William Wells Brown, and Solomon Northup* (New York, 1969). A review article on "History from Slave Sources" by C. Vann Woodward is in the *American Historical Review,* 79 (April 1974): 470–81. An example of the fruitful rewards of reading and using slave narratives with caution and discernment is John W. Blassingame's extraordinarily perceptive *The Slave Community: Plantation Life in the Antebellum South* (New York, 1972).

With painstaking precision and exhaustiveness, Russell C. Brignano has provided historians with an extremely valuable tool entitled *Black Americans in Autobiography: An Annotated Bibliography of Autobiographies and Autobiographical Books Written Since the Civil War* (Durham, North Carolina, 1974). A partial listing of autobiographies and autobiographical writings used in the preparation of this essay include: Richard Allen's memoirs, discovered by Daniel A. Payne, *The Life, Experience, and Gospel Labors of the Rt. Rev. Richard Allen* 2nd ed. (New York, 1960); Jeremiah Asher, *An Autobiography, With Details of a Visit to England, And Some Account of the History of the Meeting Street Baptist Church, Providence, Rhode Island, and of the Shiloh Baptist Church, Philadelphia,*

Pennsylvania (Philadelphia, 1862); Frederick Douglass, *My Bondage and My Freedom* (New York and Auburn, 1855; reprinted New York, 1968); *Five Black Lives: The Autobiographies of Venture Smith, James Mars, William Grimes, the Rev. G. W. Offley, James L. Smith* (Middletown, Connecticut, 1971); L. H. Holsey, *Autobiography, Sermons, Addresses, and Essays* (Atlanta, Georgia, 1898); Daniel Alexander Payne, *Recollections of Seventy Years* (Nashville, 1888; reprinted New York, 1968); James W. C. Pennington, *The Fugitive Blacksmith; or, Events in the History of James W. C. Pennington, Pastor of a Presbyterian Church, New York, Formerly a Slave in the State of Maryland, United States* 2nd ed. (London, 1849); Austin Steward, *Twenty-Two Years a Slave, and Forty Years a Freeman; Embracing a Correspondence of Several Years, While President of Wilberforce Colony, London, Canada West* 4th ed. (Canandaigua, New York, 1867); Bishop Alexander Walters, *My Life and Work* (New York, 1917); and Samuel Ringgold Ward, *Autobiography of a Fugitive Negro: His Anti-Slavery Labours in the United States, Canada, and England* (London, 1855; reprinted New York, 1968).

George Bancroft and Black Historians

Students who wish to share in the modest Bancroft revival (which is described by Robert M. Patterson "American Historian: George Bancroft," *American Chronicle,* I [January 1972]: 18–19) are not at a loss for widely accessible sources, including Bancroft's *History of the United States,* 10 vols. (Boston, 1834–74); *History of the Formation of the Constitution of the United States of America,* 2 vols. (New York, 1882); *Literary and Historical Miscellanies* (New York, 1855); and M. A. DeWolfe Howe, ed., *The Life and Letters of George Bancroft,* 2 vols. (New York, 1908). Distinguished interpretations of Bancroft include David W. Noble, *Historians Against History: The Frontier Thesis and the National Covenant in American Historical Writing Since 1838* (Minneapolis, 1965); David Levin, *History as Romantic Art* (Stanford, California, 1959); and Russell B. Nye, *George Bancroft: Brahmin Rebel* (New York, 1966). George Livermore acknowledged Bancroft's recording of black participation in the Revolutionary War in Livermore's *Historical Research Respecting the Opinions of the Founders of the Republic on Negroes as Slaves, as Citizens, and as Soldiers. Read*

Before the Massachusetts Historical Society, August 14, 1862 (Boston, 1862; reprinted New York, 1969). Bancroft's mere chronicling of black involvement was not enough for Theodore Parker, who felt it necessary to call to Bancroft's attention (John Weiss, ed., *Life and Correspondence of Theodore Parker*, Vol. II [New York, 1864], 234–35) the pioneer source books on Afro-American history by the black historian William Cooper Nell—*Colored Patriots of the American Revolution* (Boston, 1855) (an expanded version of Nell's earlier work, *Services of Colored Americans in the Wars of 1776 and 1812* 2nd ed. [Boston, 1852]). Biographical information on Nell can be found in Robert P. Smith, "William Cooper Nell: Crusading Black Abolitionist," *Journal of Negro History*, LV (July 1970): 182–99. Benjamin Quarles's *The Negro in the American Revolution* (Chapel Hill, North Carolina, 1961) is the standard authority on blacks in the Revolutionary period.

The only extended study of black historians and their contributions to American historiography is Earl E. Thorpe's *Black Historians: A Critique* (New York, 1971, rev. ed. of *Negro Historians in the United States* [Baton Rouge, Louisiana, 1958]). Charles H. Wesley has traced the efforts to preserve black history in "Racial Historical Societies and the American Heritage," *Journal of Negro History*, XXXVII (January 1952): 11–35. The black historical interest in revolutions is exemplified by James McCune Smith, *A Lecture on the Haitian Revolution; with a Sketch of the Character of Toussaint L'Ouverture. Delivered at the Stuyvesant Institute, for the Benefit of the Colored Orphan Asylum, February 26, 1841* (New York, 1841); William Wells Brown, *St. Domingo: Its Revolutions and its Patriots. A Lecture Delivered Before the Metropolitan Athenaeum, London, May 16, at St. Thomas' Church, Philadelphia, December 20, 1854* (Boston, 1855); and James Theodore Holly, *A Vindication of the Capacity of the Negro Race as Demonstrated by Historical Events of the Haitian Revolution* (New Haven, Connecticut, 1857), reprinted in Howard Brotz, ed., *Negro Social and Political Thought 1850–1920: Representative Texts* (New York, 1966), 141–70. Historical accounts of the black man in the Civil War were made by William Wells Brown, *The Negro in the American Rebellion: His Heroism and His Fidelity* (Boston, 1867); George Washington Williams, *A History of the Negro Troops in the War of the Rebellion 1861–1865. Preceded By a Review of the*

Military Services of Negroes in Ancient and Modern Times (New York, 1888); and Joseph T. Wilson, *The Black Phalanx* (Hartford, Connecticut, 1887). See also Wilson's *Emancipation: Its Course and Progress, From 1481 B.C. to A.D. 1875, With a Review of President Lincoln's Proclamations, The XIII Amendment, and the Progress of the Freed People Since Emancipation; With a History of the Emancipation Monument* (Hampton, Virginia, 1882). The first attempt by a black author at popularizing Afro-American history was James W. C. Pennington's *Text Book of the Origin and History of the Colored People* (Hartford, Connecticut, 1841: reprinted Detroit, Michigan, n.d.). Subsequent black overviews of Afro-American history include William Wells Brown, *The Rising Son; or the Antecedents and Advancement of the Colored Race* (Boston, 1874); George Washington Williams, *A History of the Negro Race in America from 1619–1880,* 2 vols. (New York, 1883; reprinted New York, 1968); and John W. Cromwell, *The Negro in American History; Men and Women Eminent in the Evolution of the American of African Descent* (Washington, D.C., 1914: reprinted New York, 1969).

Colonization and Emigration

Any examination of black images of America must begin with the second political and social question to confront the black community. Second only to the problem of slavery, the issues of emigration and colonization gripped the emotions and minds of black leaders during the first two-thirds of the nineteenth century. Virtually every black publication from the formation of the American Colonization Society in 1817 to the onset of the Civil War grappled in some way with the question of emigrationism or colonizationism. Besides the obvious usage of black convention minutes and the black press, two other black publications that deal exclusively with the colonizationist controversy should be singled out: Samuel E. Cornish and Theodore S. Wright, *The Colonization Scheme Considered, in its Rejection by the Colored People—in its Tendency to Uphold Caste—in its Unfitness for Christianizing and Civilizing the Aborigines of Africa, and for Putting a stop to the African Slave Trade: In a Letter to the Honorable Benjamin F. Batter and the Honorable Theodore Frelinghuysen* (Newark, 1840); and David Ruggles, *The "Extinguisher" Extinguished! or David M.*

Reese, M.D. "Used Up." Together with Some Remarks Upon a Late Production, entitled 'An Address on Slavery and Against Immediate Emancipation with a Plan of their Being Gradually Emancipated and Colonized in Thirty-Two Years. By Herman Howlett' (New York, 1834). For a scissors-and-paste sampling of black anti-colonizationist writings, most likely compiled by James E. Forten, see William Lloyd Garrison, *Thoughts on African Colonization: or an Impartial Exhibition of the Doctrines, Principles and Purposes of the American Colonization Society. Together With the Resolutions, Addresses and Remonstrances of the Free People of Color* (Boston, 1832; reprinted New York, 1968).

As Howard Bell's numerous studies have shown, a faint undercurrent of black support for colonization splashed alongside the swell of black leadership opposition to the American Colonization Society. But for the most part, in the interest of anchoring black nationalist ideology as firmly in the past as possible, historians have failed to look beyond the act of colonization to examine the attitudes and avowed motives which prompted black transplantation to Africa. Were blacks impelled to Africa by a quest for racial or national identity? Or did blacks envision colonization as an escape from oppression, propelled to Africa by a despair of ever obtaining equality in America? Was there a development from the latter to the former? To what extent did missionary motives lubricate the slide toward African colonization? Once in Africa or in the Caribbean, did black colonizers reject white standards of success and renounce white values, affirming a distinctly African identity? Or did they conceive of themselves as Americans in exile?

It is clear that for most black leaders, the Christianization and civilization of Africa was a dream that glowed like the Grail, although few were as dedicated as Paul Cuffe to the redemption of Africa—albeit a redemption along the lines of a distinctly American culture. In an important study, Sheldon H. Harris's *Paul Cuffe: Black America and the African Return* (New York, 1972) (which utilizes the Cuffe Manuscripts as well as the more available *Memoir of Captain Paul Cuffee, A Man of Colour: To Which is Subjoined the Epistle of the Society of Sierra Leone, in Africa* [London, 1811] and *Narrative of the Life and Adventures of Paul Cuffe, a Pequot Indian: During Thirty Years Spent at Sea, and in Traveling in Foreign Lands* [Vernon, 1839]) convincingly criticizes P. J. Staudenraus for exaggerating Cuffe's economic motivation behind his interest in Africa and for belittling the missionary impulse. Nevertheless, Harris purports to see a transition in Cuffe's thought from an African regenerationist to a "black nationalist." Yet Harris' own account reveals that Cuffe's concern for the plight of Africans preempted his concern for the enslavement of American blacks, who in Cuffe's mind were at least blessed with Christianity and civilization. Drawn into colonization by his interest in African mission, Cuffe envisioned black Americans as destined to perform a messianic role in the redemption of Africa. Cuffe can perhaps best be classified as a missionary emigrationist.

The black Baptist lay preacher from Virginia, Lott Cary, also was led to the American Colonization Society because of his interest in African missions. Lott Cary's life is recounted in Miles Fisher's "Lott Cary, the Colonizing Missionary," *Journal of Negro History,* VII (October 1922): 380–418. Having embarked in 1821 with Collin Teague as missionaries to Liberia, Cary began complaining soon after his arrival that the demands of colonizationist activities eclipsed his missionary labors, a remonstrance that Wlbur Christian Harr reveals was echoed by another early black missionary, James M. Priest ("The Negro as an American Protestant Missionary in Africa" [Ph.D. dissertation, University of Chicago Divinity School, 1945]). Parenthetically, the whole dispute over the indigenousness of missionaries to Africa has not been broached by historians; typically, Delany advocated black missionaries for black peoples, whereas Cornish and Wright believed that color was of no moment in African missionary endeavors.

Daniel Coker's *Journal of Daniel Coker, A Descendant of Africa* (Baltimore, 1820) reveals further this image of a black messianic vocation in Africa. The affiliation of both Coker and J. B. Russwurm with the Maryland State Colonization Society (which subsidized Coker and sponsored the Cape Palmas Colony, of which Russwurm was governor) is traced by Penelope Campbell, *Maryland in Africa: The Maryland State Coloniation Society, 1831–1857* (Urbana, 1971). She presents an unflattering portrait of black colonists who often mirrored in Africa the same sentiments they fled from in America, a view which is corroborated by the nineteenth-century black mathematics professor and general agent for industrial education in Liberia, T. McCants Stewart, *Liberia: The Americo-*

African Republic. Being Some Impressions of the Climate, Resources, and People, Resulting from Personal Observations and Experiences on West Africa (New York, 1886). While antebellum black leaders believed that neither emigration nor colonization offered a solution to the race problem in America, they did distinguish clearly between the two. In sum, nearly all black opponents of African colonization endorsed two forms of emigration from America: missionary emigrationism, with its motive of salvation, and existential emigrationism, with its motive of survival.

A complex of views surrounded the acceptance of colonization or emigration by antebellum blacks. A few blacks justified their departure by citing the race view of history promulgated by the American Colonization Society, which has been studied meticulously by Early Lee Fox, *The American Coloniation Society, 1817–1840* (Baltimore, 1919); P. J. Staudenraus, *The African Colonization Movement 1816–1865* (New York, 1961); and Frederic Bancroft, in Jacob E. Cooke's *Frederic Bancroft, Historian* (Norman, Oklahoma, 1957). Apologetic analyses of the colonization movement can be found in *Claims of the Africans: or the History of the American Colonization Society* (Boston, 1832), and in Archibald Alexander's *History of Colonization on the Western Coast of Africa* (Philadelphia, 1846). According to colonizationist reasoning, which was propounded by the official publication of the A.C.S. (*The African Repository and Colonial Journal* [*1826–60*]), Providence had ordained that the races be separate. John H. B. Latrobe gave this view resounding expression in his *African Colonization. An Address Delivered by Honorable John H. B. Latrobe, President of the American Colonization Society, at the Anniversary Meeting of the American Colonization Society, Held in the Hall of the House of Representatives, Washington City, January 21, 1862* (Washington, D.C., 1862). This theme of the natural aversion of the races developed early in white circles. It is apparent in the reasons given by Thomas Branagan for his proposal that a self-governing black state be sculpted out of territory purchased from France (*Serious Remonstrances, Addressed to the Citizens of the Northern States, and their Representatives, Being an Appeal to their Natural Feelings and Common Sense; Consisting of Speculations and Animadversions, on the recent revival of the Slave Trade, in the American Republic* [Philadelphia, 1805]); in the colonizationist proposals of John Parrish (*Remarks on the Slavery of the Black People Addressed to the Citizens of the United States, Particularly to Those Who are in Legislative or Executive Stations in the General or State Governments; and Also to Such Individuals as Hold Them in Bondage* [Philadelphia, 1806]); and in the influential book by Jacob Dewees (*The Great Future of America and Africa; An Essay Showing Our White Duty to the Black Man, Consistent with Our Own Safety and Glory* [Philadelphia, 1854; reprinted Freeport, New York, 1971]). John Mercer Langston, who, with his brother Charles, spurred emigrationist sentiment in the 1850s, also theorized concerning the mutual repellency of the races, though much of this speculation is missing in his mellow *From the Virginia Plantation to the National Capitol* (Hartford, Connecticut, 1894; reprinted New York, 1968). The black barber and poet from Buffalo James M. Whitfield, whose collection of poems, *America and Other Poems* (Buffalo, 1853), has received undeserved neglect, shared a similar view in the 1850s and underwent a similar mellowing as did Langston. (See Joan R. Sherman, "James Monroe Whitfield, Poet and Emigrationist: A Voice of Protest and Despair," *Journal of Negro History,* XVII [April 1972]: 165–76.) The tenacity of this interpretation of the natural repellency of the races is revealed in the rationale for the early twentieth-century proposal for the creation of separate black states within the United States by the Georgia Bishop of the Colored Methodist Episcopal Church, Lucius H. Holsey, in "Race Segregation" in Willis B. Parks, ed., *The Possibilities of the Negro in Symposium* (New York, 1904), 102 ff.

Howard H. Bell has analyzed the emergence in the 1850s of a less academic and missionary-oriented, more positive and nationalist interest in emigration for the purpose of forming a "Negro nationality" in his "Negro Nationalism: A Factor in Emigration Projects, 1858–1861," *Journal of Negro History,* XLVII (January 1962): 42–53. A handy pro-and-con debate on this subject between William Nesbit (*Four Months in Liberia: or African Colonization Exposed* [Pittsburgh, 1855]) and Samuel Williams (*Four Years in Liberia: A Sketch of the Life of the Reverend Samuel Williams, With Remarks on the Missions, Manners and Customs of the Natives of Western Africa. Together with an Answer to Nesbit's Book* [Philadelphia, 1857]) has been published under one cover as *Two Black Views of Liberia* (New York, 1969). Howard Bell has also edited the pamphlets of two publicists for interpropical emigration, J. Dennis Harris and James Theodore Holly (both of whom explain their reasons for rejecting Africa in favor of building what Harris termed an "Anglo-African" empire which would parallel the "Anglo-American" empire), in *Black Separatism and the Caribbean, 1860* (Ann Arbor, Michigan, 1970). This should be read in conjunction with Bell's *Search for a Place: Black Separatism and Africa, 1860* (Ann Arbor, Michigan, 1969). Holly's reading of the black community's differentiation between colonization to Africa and emigration within the New World underlines a crucial distinction that is necessary for a clear understanding of black emigrationism in antebellum America. At the same time blacks voiced their vociferous opposition to African colonization through resolutions, speeches, and letters, the related question of settlements in North America, especially in Canada or in the frontier regions of America, generated great excitement in similar forums. This exception of Canada and the New World from the near blanket hostility to colonization needs further study. Suggestive are the works by the Peases and Robin Winks on blacks in Canada. Winks's majesterial study on *The Blacks in Canada* (New Haven, Connecticut, 1971) analyzes the "exile mentality" of black American refugees. Jane H. Pease's and William H. Pease's "Organized Negro Communities: A North American Experiment," *Journal of Negro History,* XLVII (January 1962) (later expanded into *Black Utopia: Negro Communal Experiments in America* [Madison, Wisconsin, 1963]), traces the maze of motivations—prominent among which were the apologetic goals of creating a society which would serve as visual proof that blacks were equal to compete with whites in American life—which led blacks to settle in a Canadian Canaan.

Black Images of Africa

Until recently, historians have not appreciated the early black interest in Africa which withstood the identification of Africa with colonization. The position of such black leaders as W. E. B. Du Bois, J. C. Smith, and Edward Wilmot Blyden has been that because most nineteenth-century black Americans rejected Africa as a homeland, they did not take pride in their African ancestry. W. E. B. Du Bois's remarkably gratuitous assertion that "interest in Africa did not begin with anyone until after 1880 or so," an assessment grounded in

Du Bois's belief that since nineteenth-century blacks boasted an American self-identity, they resented reminders of their African ancestry, is discussed in Harold R. Isaacs's "Pan-Africanism as 'Romantic Racism,' " in Rayford W. Logan, ed., *W. E. B. Du Bois: A Profile* (New York, 1971). Edward Wilmot Blyden, who has fared well by his two biographers, Edith Holden (*Blyden of Liberia* [New York, 1966]) and Hollis R. Lynch (*Edward Wilmot Blyden: Pan-Negro Patriot 1832–1912* [London, 1967]), lamented the same African amnesia among Afro-Americans in his *Liberia's Offering* (New York, 1862), especially the chapter entitled "The Call of Providence to the Descendants of Africa in America" (which has been reprinted by Howard Brotz, *Negro Social and Political Thought 1850–1920: Representative Texts* [New York, 1966], 112–26). The widely overlooked conference on Africa held at Gammon Theological Seminary in 1895 echoed this same refrain, particularly in the speech by the Richmond, Virginia editor and former minister to Liberia, J. C. Smyth. (See John W. E. Bowen, ed., *Africa and the American Negro: Addresses and Proceedings of the Congress on Africa Held under the Auspices of the Stewart Missionary Foundation for Africa of Gammon Theological Seminary in Connection with the Cotton States and International Exposition December 13–15, 1895* [Atlanta, Georgia, 1896; reprinted Miami, Florida, 1969].)

Fortunately, historians such as Howard H. Bell, Earl Ofari, Sheldon H. Harris, and Robert G. Weisbord have begun to puncture the myth that Africa did not occupy a compelling place in the minds of black Americans until late in the nineteenth century. Renewed attention to the role of the black press in disseminating information on Africa and the ironic contribution of colonizationist publications toward illuminating the history and cultural heritage of Africa have sparked a growing interest in the attitude of black Americans toward Africa. The trend has culminated in two books, Adelaide Cromwell Hill's and Martin Kilson's collection of documents entitled *Apropos of Africa: Afro-American Leaders and the Romance of Africa* (Garden City, New York, 1971), and Robert G. Weisbord's *Ebony Kinship: Africa, Africans, and the Afro-American* (Westport, Connecticut, 1973), in which he traces the complex and "multifaceted" connection between black Americans and Africans. Although the bulk of Weisbord's study deals with the twentieth century, his first chapter, surveying "Back-to-Africanism before Garvey," argues for the facile equation of repatriation programs with black nationalist ideology.

An interesting feature of nineteenth-century black attitudes toward Africa is the absence of any correlation between one's stance on emigration and one's pride and estimation of Africa. As variegated in perspectives as James W. C. Pennington, R. B. Lewis, and Alexander Crummell, they waxed romantic in a nostalgic vision of primitive Africa in their respective volumes entitled *A Text Book of the Origin and History of the Colored People* (Hartford, 1841; reprinted Detroit, Michigan, n.d.), *Light and Truth, Collected from the Bible and the Ancient and Modern History, Containing the Universal History of the Colored and Indian Races* 2nd ed. (Portland, Maine, 1844), and *The Future of Africa. Being Addresses, Sermons, etc., etc., Delivered in the Republic of Liberia* (New York, 1962; reprinted New York, 1969). The widespread conviction that European greed had exploited and crushed the grand nobility and innocent tranquility of African life is revealed in the formal lectures on the history of Africa by Amos Beman and Jeremiah Sanderson, as well as the scattered speeches of black leaders such as David Nickens, William G. Allen, and Frederick Douglass. For a conflicting viewpoint based on much later data, see James W. Ivy's article "Traditional NAACP Interest in Africa as Reflected in the Pages of 'The Crisis,' " in John A. Davis, ed., *Africa From the Point of View of American Negro Scholars* (n.p., n.d.), 230 ff., in which he asserts that the black intellectual's repudiation of "back to Africa" spelled the repudiation of Africa. Walter L. Williams implies this same thesis in his informative article on "Black Journalism's Opinions About Africa During the Late Nineteenth Century," *Phylon,* XXXIV (December 1973): 224–35.

Black orations celebrating the abolition of the slave trade also provided a favorite forum for expounding the primitive bliss and cultural genius of Africans before the onslaught of the slave traders. Some of these anniversary accolades to Africa are reprinted in Dorothy Porter, *Early Negro Writing 1760–1837* (Boston, 1971). For two white arguments marshalling evidence of the departed glory of Africa as proof of black intellectual parity with whites, see Harvey Newcomb, *The 'Negro Pew': Being an Inquiry Concerning the Propriety of Distinctions in the House of God, on account of Color* (Boston, 1837; reprinted Freeport, New York, 1971), and Theodore

Dwight, "Condition and Character of Negroes in Africa," *Mercersburg Review,* VI (January 1864): 77ff.

Antebellum Black Nationalism

The title of Sterling Stuckey's essay and anthology tracing *The Ideological Origins of Black Nationalism* (Boston, 1972) aptly summarizes the prevailing preoccupation of historians involved in Afro-American intellectual history during the past decade. Unfortunately, all too often the rigor of historical analysis has become a casualty of the pell-mell rush to dig up the roots of black nationalism in the soil of antebellum black thought. This search for historical antecedents, methods, and tactics to satisfy present political and social objectives has led to a sad isolation of black protest literature from the mainstream of black intellectual history—a trend which has been halted somewhat by Frederick Cooper's important article on "Elevating the Race: The Social Thought of Black Leaders, 1827–1850," *American Quarterly,* XXIV (December 1972): 604–25. The indiscriminate pairing of black protest with black nationalism has created a forced inflation in the conceptual currency of black nationalism. The shallow search for the true claimant to the title "the father of black nationalism," for example, has produced a bumper crop of candidates as diverse as Paul Cuffee (Sheldon H. Harris and Sally Loomis), Lewis Woodson (Floyd Miller), Martin R. Delany (Theodore R. Draper), Alexander Crummell (Rodney Carlisle), and Henry McNeal Turner (Robert G. Weisbord). Two exceptions to this lack of definitional precision and contextual integrity in discussions of black nationalism are E. U. Essien-Udom's *Black Nationalism: A Search for an Identity in America* (Chicago, 1962) and John H. Bracey, Jr., August Meier, and Elliott Rudwick's attempt to construct typologies within the framework of black nationalism in their editing of black nationalist documents entitled *Black Nationalism in America* (Indianapolis and New York, 1970).

The literature on black nationalism is immense. It would behoove the interested student to begin with the bibliography on "Black Nationalism and Black Power" in Elizabeth W. Miller and Mary L. Fisher, comp., *The Negro in America: A Bibliography* (Cambridge, Massachusetts, 1970), 283–89. Other germane studies include Howard H. Bell, "The Negro Emigration Movement, 1849–1854: A Phase of Negro Nationalism," *Phylon,* IX (Summer 1959):

132–43, and "Negro Nationalism: A Factor in Emigration Projects, 1858–1861," *Journal of Negro History*, 47 (January 1962): 43–53; Eugene D. Genovese, "The Legacy of Slavery and the Roots of Black Nationalism," *Studies on the Left*, 6 (November–December 1966): 3–26; J. Herman Blake, "Black Nationalism," *Annals of the American Academy of Political and Social Sciences*, 382 (March 1969), 15–25; James A. Gregor, "Black Nationalism," *Science and Society*, XXVII (Fall 1963): 415–32; August Meier, "Emergence of Negro Nationalism; A Study in Ideologies," *Midwest Journal*, IV (Winter 1951–52): 96–104; IV (Summer 1952): 95–111; Murapa J. Rukudzo, "Negro Nationalism in the 1850's," *Journal of Negro Education*, 35 (Winter 1966): 100–104.

Antebellum Free Blacks and Black Abolitionism

Leon F. Litwack's erudite yet sparkling study of blacks in the antebellum North, *North of Slavery: The Negro in the Free States, 1790–1860* (Chicago, 1961), has finally found a worthy counterpart in Ira Berlin's fine study of Southern freemen, *Slaves Without Masters: The Free Negro in the Antebellum South* (New York, 1975) (although for many years numerous monographs and articles have appeared recounting the history of free blacks in various states and regions).

Good starting points for understanding recent historiographical trends in abolitionist studies are Morton L. Dillon, "The Abolitionists: A Decade of Historiography, 1959–1969," *Journal of Southern History*, XXXV (November 1969): 500–522; Hugh Hawkins, ed., *The Abolitionists: Immediatism and the Question of Means* (Boston, 1964); Martin Duberman, ed., *The Antislavery Vanguard: New Essays on the Abolitionists* (Princeton, 1965); and William H. Pease and Jane H. Pease, "Antislavery Ambivalence: Immediatism, Expediency, Race," *American Quarterly*, XVII (Winter 1965): 682–95. The best recent studies are Aileen Kraditor's *Means and Ends in American Abolitionism: Garrison and His Critics on Strategy and Tactics, 1834–1850* (New York, 1969), and Lewis Perry's endorsement and expansion of Kraditor's analysis to underline the Puritan roots and millennial outcropping of abolitionist ideology, *Radical Abolitionism: Anarchy and the Government of God in Antislavery Thought* (Ithaca, New York, 1973).

There are numerous biographies of abolitionists. Three of the best are John L. Thomas, *The Liberator: William Lloyd Garrison* (Boston, 1963); Bertram Wyatt-Brown, *Lewis Tappan and the Evangelical War Against Slavery* (Cleveland, 1969); and Stephen B. Oates, *To Purge this Land with Blood: A Biography of John Brown* (New York, 1970). Benjamin Quarles has compiled a book of readings, *Blacks on John Brown* (Urbana, Illinois, 1972), and has written a monograph, *Allies for Freedom: Blacks and John Brown* (New York, 1974), with the mastery and care which historians have come to expect from him. Quarles's provocative study of *Black Abolitionists* (New York, 1969) has been supplemented, but not supplanted, by Jane H. Pease and William H. Pease, *They Who Would Be Free: Blacks' Search for Freedom, 1830–1861* (New York, 1974). For other important studies of black abolitionists, see Herbert Aptheker's brief *Negro in the Abolitionist Movement* (New York, 1974), and James M. McPherson's *Struggle for Equality: Abolitionists and the Negro in the Civil War and Reconstruction* (Princeton, 1964).

Biographies

There exists a pressing need for biographies of many nineteenth-century black leaders, fifty-seven of whom were given short biographical treatment by William Wells Brown in his *Black Man, His Antecedents, His Genius, and His Achievements* 2nd ed. (New York, 1863; reprinted New York, 1968). Benjamin Quarles's exceptional study of Frederick Douglass, published over a quarter of a century ago as *Frederick Douglass* (Washington, D.C., 1948) is still unsurpassed, even by the more recent, pedestrian, and disappointing attempt by Arna Bontemps, *Free at Last: The Life of Frederick Douglass* (New York, 1971). Indispensable to understanding Douglass is Philip S. Foner's collected edition of Douglass's speeches, letters, editorials, and writings (*The Life and Writings of Frederick Douglass,* 4 vols. [New York, 1950]).

One of the best biographies of an antebellum black leader is William E. Farrison's *William Wells Brown: Author and Reformer* (Chicago, 1969)—although Farrison does not always convey to the reader the spirit of restiveness and bitterness that percolated some of Brown's letters and writings. Because of his novel *Clotel, or, the President's Daughter* (London, 1853; reprinted New York, 1969), the first piece of black American fiction, the talented and prolific

Brown occupies an important place in the black belletristic tradition in America. Brown's novel underwent a total of four revisions and renamings and was serialized during the winter of 1860–61 in the *Weekly Anglo-African*. Martin R. Delany's novel *Blake, or The Huts of America* (reprinted Boston, 1970, ed. Floyd J. Miller) was also serialized in the *Anglo-African Magazine,* 1859 and 1861–62. I have given special attention to another novel, *Imperium in Imperio,* by the Baptist minister Sutton E. Griggs (Cincinnati, 1899; reprinted New York, 1969). Although Griggs displayed less artistic ability than his black literary contemporaries Charles W. Chesnutt and Paul Laurence Dunbar, Griggs's promotional skills led to the wide dissemination of his robust novels among the black masses. Those who would pursue further the writing of black fiction should consult Robert Bone, *The Negro Novel in America* rev. ed. (New Haven, Connecticut, 1965); Benjamin Brawley, ed., *Early American Negro Writers* (Chapel Hill, North Carolina, 1935); Vernon Loggins, *The Negro Author: His Development in America to 1900* (New York, 1931; reprinted Port Washington, New York, 1964), and Kenny J. Williams, *They Also Spoke: An Essay on Negro Literature in America, 1787–1930* (Nashville, 1970).

One of the most controversial, complex, and original black figures in the nineteenth century was Martin R. Delany, whose wide-ranging book *The Condition, Elevation, Emigration and Destiny of the Colored People of the United States* (New York, 1852; reprinted New York, 1968) is a landmark in black intellectual history. Unfortunately, Victor Ullman's tendentious, didactic biography of Delany (*Martin R. Delany: The Beginnings of Black Nationalism* [Boston, 1971]) is not worthy of its brilliant subject. A perplexing conjunction of extensive scholarly research without the requisite scholarly apparatus, Ullman's biography belongs to the literature of hagiography more than history. Equally unsatisfying is Theodore Draper's interpretation of Delany and other "black nationalists" in *The Rediscovery of Black Nationalism* (New York, 1970), chaps. 1–2. Those unwilling to labor at separating the wheat from the chaff in Ullman and Draper can find background information on Delany in Howard H. Bell's introductory essay to a new edition of Delany, and Robert Campbell's *Search for a Place: Black Separatism and Africa, 1860* (Ann Arbor, Michigan, 1969). A new study emphasizing Delany's African interests has just appeared: Cyril E.

Griffith, *The African Dream: Martin R. Delany and the Emergence of Pan-African Thought* (University Park, Pennsylvania, 1975).

Earl Ofari has transcended the limitations of his propaedeutic outlook on black history to present a competent biographical account of Henry Highland Garnet in *"Let Your Motto Be Resistance": The Life and Thought of Henry Highland Garnet* (Boston, 1972). Of particular value is the appendix, which includes ten of Garnet's speeches and writings. For a somewhat tamer view of Garnet than that of Ofari's "Prophet of Revolutionary Black Nationalism," see Jane H. Pease and William H. Pease, *Bound With Them in Chains: A Biographical History of the Antislavery Movement* (Westport, Connecticut, 1972), a collection of biographical essays including a frowning assessment of Samuel E. Cornish.

Information on other antebellum black abilitionists can be found in John H. Bracey, August Meier, and Ellottt Rudwick, ed., *Blacks in the Abolitionist Movement* (Belmont, California, 1971); Ray Allen Billington, "James Forten: Forgotten Abolitionist," *Negro History Bulletin,* XIII (November 1949): 31–36, 45; William Brewer, "John B. Russwurm," *Journal of Negro History,* XIII (October 1928): 413–22; Dorothy Porter, "David M. Ruggles, an Apostle of Human Rights," *Journal of Negro History,* XXVIII (January 1943): 23–50; William F. Cheek, "John Mercer Langston: Black Protest Leader and Abolitionist," *Civil War History,* XVI (June 1970): 101–20; Monroe N. Work, "The Life of Charles B. Ray," *Journal of Negro History,* IV (October 1919): 361–71; *Sketch of the Life of Reverend Charles B. Ray* (New York, 1887); and Herbert Aptheker, ed., *One Continued Cry: David Walker's Appeal to the Colored Citizens of the World, 1829–1830* (New York, 1965).

Although not a primary focus of this essay, sufficient attention has been given to black thought between the years 1870–1920 to warrant brief mention of a few seminal studies. August Meier reviews this period in *Negro Thought in America, 1880–1915: Racial Ideologies in the Age of Booker T. Washington* (Ann Arbor, Michigan, 1963). Booker T. Washington's accommodationism, according to revisionist historians August Meier, Louis R. Harlan, Emma Lou Thornbrough, and J. Donald Calista, was motivated less by ideology than by pragmatic realism. Although the revisionists are currently under revision, their assessment of Washington, epitomized by Louis

R. Harlan's astute *Booker T. Washington: The Making of a Black Leader* (New York, 1972), is the most cogent and compelling. The first three volumes of a projected fifteen-volume collection of Washington's writings and correspondence has already been published by Louis R. Harlan, ed., *The Booker T. Washington Papers,* vols. 1–3 (Urbana, Ill., 1971–74). Accorded high praise as a hallmark of historical editing, Washington's career is now covered until 1895. The curious friendship between Washington and the black activist journalist T. Thomas Fortune is analyzed with perspicacity in Emma Lou Thornbrough's capable biography of *T. Thomas Fortune: Militant Journalist* (Chicago, 1972).

Two of the most prominent critics of Washington's accommodationism were William Monroe Trotter and W. E. B. Du Bois. Trotter has been scrutinized by Stephen R. Fox, *The Guardian of Boston: William Monroe Trotter* (New York, 1970). Although there are penetrating biographies and appraisals of Du Bois in Francis L. Broderick's *W. E. B. Du Bois: Negro Leader in a Time of Crisis* (Stanford, California, 1959), Elliott M. Rudwick's *W. E. B. Du Bois: A Study in Minority Group Leadership* (Philadelphia, 1960), and Ratford W. Logan, ed., *W. E. B. Du Bois: A Profile* (New York, 1971), Du Bois is best left to speak for himself in *The Souls of Black Folk* (Chicago, 1903; reprinted Greenwich, Connecticut, 1961); *The Gift of Black Folk: The Negroes in the Making of America* (Boston, 1924); and in the two autobiographies, which reveal his intellectual pilgrimage—*Dusk of Dawn: An Essay Toward an Autobiography of a Race Concept* (New York, 1940), and *The Autobiography of W. E. B. Du Bois: A Soliloquy on Viewing My Life from the Last Decade of Its First Century* (New York, 1968). Selections from Du Bois's writings are widely available: Meyer Weinberg, ed., *W. E. B. Du Bois: A Reader* (New York, 1970); Philip S. Foner, ed., *W. E. B. Du Bois Speaks,* 2 vols. (New York, 1970); and Julius Lester, ed., *The Seventh Son: The Thought and Writings of W. E. B. Du Bois,* 2 vols. (New York, 1971). On the NAACP from 1909–1920, see Charles Flint Kellogg, *NAACP: A History of the National Association for the Advancement of Colored People,* Vol. 1 (Baltimore, 1967).

Two other post-Civil War black spokesmen not already mentioned who are given special consideration in the narrative are Alexander Crummell and Henry McNeal Turner. Most of Crummell's writings can be found in his *Future of Africa: Being Addresses, Sermons, etc., etc., Delivered in the Republic of Liberia* (New York, 1862; reprinted New York, 1969) and his *Africa and America* (Springfield, Massachusetts, 1891; reprinted Miami, Florida, 1969). An exceptionally fine essay on Crummell has been written by Wilson T. Moses, "Civilizing Missionary: A Study of Alexander Crummell," *Journal of Negro History*, LX (April 1975): 229–51. Much of what we know of Henry McNeal Turner comes from the pen of Edwin S. Redkey. See his article "Bishop Turner's African Dream" *Journal of American History*, LIV (September 1967): 271–90; his editing of *Respect Black, The Writings and Speeches of Henry McNeal Turner* (New York, 1971); and his book *Black Exodus: Black Nationalist and Back-to-Africa Movements, 1890–1910* (New Haven, Connecticut, 1969).

Index

Abdy, Edward Strutt, 41, 62n
"Abolition war" (Douglass), 64, 167
Abolitionist movement, 40–41, 106–8, 140, 156, 159, 162, 164; completes "American Revolution," 164–67; politicization of, 130; and purification of American mission, 155–56, 158–59; and tension between white and black segments, 140–41
Adams, Herbert Baxter, 7, 8, 22
Adams, James Truslow, 12
Africa, 38–39, 44–45, 58, 61, 66–68, 74–77; black Christian empire in, 36–67; black messianism and, 121–24; Christianization and civilization of, 25–26, 193–94; colonization of, 28–31; conference on, 81, 82; cultural achievements of, 115; identification with, 36–37, 53; "New Negro" interest in, 180–81; nineteenth-century interest in, 181, 197–200
Afric-American Female Intelligence Society of Boston, 87n
African Baptist Chuch (Albany), 155
African Civilization Society, 61n, 102n, 146
African colonization, 28, 30, 192, 198, 199; and American nationality, 29; black views of, 54n, 79–84, 197; Hopkins's promotion of, 28; Newport black community's support of, 30; Paul Cuffe and, 79–80, 193–94
African Methodist Episcopal Church, 75n, 96n, 126
African Methodist Episcopal Church (Pittsburgh), 66
"African Mission," 22–32
"African" title, 50–53
African Union Society (Newport), 32, 33
"Africo-Americans" (Delany), 89
Afro-American, 52n
Afro-American League, 100n
Agrarianism, 108, 135–38
Albany National Convention (1840), 142
Alcott, Louisa May, 100n
Alexander, Archibald, 36n, 40, 79n
Aliened American, 50, 67n, 76n, 93n, 157n
Allen, Richard, 85, 104, 112, 147; and American nation, 57; elected bishop, 96n; founder, AME Church, 126; influential black leader, 53; providential philosophy of, 85; views on colonization, 64
Allen, William G., 114, 199
Amalgamation, 97–100, 102, 139
American, The, 50n

American and Foreign Anti-Slavery Society, 155n
American Anti-Slavery Society, 65n, 139, 162, 166
American Bible Society, 60
American Colonization Society, 29–30, 31, 34, 36, 44, 56, 60–61, 83, 145; black hostility to, 42, 43, 142; founder, Robert Finley, 36; indoctrinated children, 38; methods of, 34, 37–38; and national policy, 37; organized 1816, 36, 39; on redemption of Africa, 37; resolutions against, 56; spurred black solidarity, 40–41
American Historical Association, 7
American history, 1–22, 44–57; black contributions to, 44–45, 158–63, 173; and black interpretation of founding of America, 138; Frederick Douglass on, 55–56; providential philosophy of, 2–3, 8, 71, 168–69; William Wells Brown on, 57
American independence, 19
American Indian, 25n, 85, 86–89, 102
American Mercury, 180
American Missionary Association, 140
American Moral Reform Society, 52, 64, 73, 112, 128
American nationalism, 29
American Negro Academy, 50n, 110
American Quarterly, 108n
American Revolution, 5, 15, 26–27, 29, 34, 49, 56, 126, 149n, 152–53, 154, 156, 164, 165, 166, 173
American Society for the Promotion of Education in Africa, 68n
American Society of Free Persons of Color, 172
Americo-African empire, 62
Amistad, 139–40
Anglo-African, 93n, 100n, 159, 165n
Anglo-Saxon myth, 15, 117, 179
Anti-party, 130n–31n
Aptheker, Herbert, 41n, 55n, 60n, 93n, 105n, 106n, 112n, 131n, 151n, 153n, 160n, 170n
Asher, Jeremiah, 45, 126n
Asylum image, 157, 162
Atlantic Monthly, 12n
Attucks, Crispus, 45, 109, 149, 153, 173
"Augustine," *see* Woodson, Lewis
Autonomy, *see* Racial autonomy

Baker, Ray Stannard, 16n, 20n
Baltimore, 36n, 46, 67, 138, 173
Baltimore Douglass Institute, 143
Bancroft, Frederick, 7n
Bancroft, George, 2, 7, 10–22, 117, 160,
    161, 162, 165, 168, 179; on cause of
    civil war, 165; covenantalistic view of,
    10, 13; doctrine of progress of, 11–13;
    ignores black contributions to American
    history, 149; and millennium, 12–14;
    philosophy of history, 101; providential
    philosophy of, 10–12; views on slavery,
    65, 164
Banneker, Benjamin, 94
Barbadoes, James, 139
Bassett, John Spencer, 10n
"Begging" controversy, 146, 147
Beecher, Henry Ward, 35
Belgrave, Bernard, 182, 184
Bell, Howard H., 2n–3n, 81n, 116n, 131n,
    134n, 154n, 171n
Bell, Philip A., 52, 57n, 133
Beman, Amos, 199
Benevolent societies, 40, 156, 173
Berkeley, George, 168
Berlin, Ira, 66n, 98n, 173n
Bibb, Henry, 98
Bible, 24, 155n, 160
Billington, Ray Allen, 41n
Birney, James G., 131n
Black, Harold Garnet, 11n
Black abolitionists, 138, 140, 155, 164
Black communities, 39, 135–37
Black convention movement, 39, 128, 129,
    143, 145, 160, 173–74, 180, 188–89;
    Albany (1842), 142; Albany (1851),
    153–54; Buffalo (1843), 3, 92, 107,
    130–31n, 144; Cazenovia, N.Y. (1850),
    153; Cincinnati (1858), 154; Columbus
    (1849), 108n–9n; Columbus (1856),
    160n; Louisville, Ky. (1883), 143n;
    Maryland (1859), 47; Massachusetts
    (1858), 55n; New York City (1833),
    58n; New York City (1834), 60n, 142;
    Ohio (1853), 67; Philadelphia (1835),
    51, 52n; Rochester, N.Y. (1831), 51n;
    Rochester, N.Y. (1848), 126–27;
    Rochester, N.Y. (1893), 35, 146,
    150–51; Sandwich, Ont. (1850), 137;
    Schenectady, N.Y. (1844), 137;
    Troy, N.Y. (1847), 108
Black equality, 134, 135, 143, 162–63,
    164, 170, 174
Black historiography, 149–50, 171
Black identity, 1, 6, 44, 48–50, 62, 175,
    180, 184
Black intellectual history, 187
Black nationalism, 4–5, 116–17, 135, 147,
    169, 170, 171, 172, 174–75, 200–1;
    equated with separatism, 132; and
    Marcus Garvey, 171–72
Black press, 48–50, 128, 129, 132, 173, 188
Black separatism. *see* Separatism
Blyden, Edward Wilmont, 82, 99, 117,
    120; and black messianism, 83, 122–24;
    philosophy of history, 84; romantic
    racism of, 120
Bodo, John R., 38
Boston, 140n, 147, 150, 164
Bowen, John W. E., 50n, 78, 81n
Bracey, John, Jr., 41n, 76n, 127n, 129n
Bradford, William, 21

Branagan, Thomas, 195
Broderick, Francis L., 175n, 176n, 177n
Brooklyn, N.Y., 154
Brotz, Howard, 40n, 87n, 123n, 129n,
    140n
Brown, B. Katherine, 9
Brown, John, 152–53, 154, 155n
Brown, Robert E., 9
Brown, William Wells, 4, 57, 58, 101, 102,
    113n, 130n, 131n, 134, 135n, 136, 146,
    148, 149n, 150n, 151, 152n, 154n, 165n,
    174; agrarian ideal of, 136; on American
    hypocrisy, 157, 159, 160; on autonomous
    action, 134–35; on black role in
    American history, 148–49, 161, 163n;
    on colonization, 57, 63–64; and dispute
    over "begging," 147; on lofty role of
    abolitionist movement, 156–57; pro-
    integration, 100; on racial pride, 96n;
    on slave revolts, 151–52; on slavery, 102
Buchanan, James, 20
Bucher, Glenn R., 177n

Campbell, Penelope, 36n, 39n, 47n
Cape Palmas Colony, 194
Capitalism, 179
Carey, Matthew, 37
Carlyle, Thomas, 9n
Carthagena settlement (Ohio), 136
Cary, Lott, 194
Central College (McGrawville, N.Y.), 114
Channing, Edward, 8
Channing, William Ellery, 41n, 114n,
    118–19
Chapman, Maria Weston, 138
Charleston, S.C., 39
Charlestown, Va., 154
Chauncy, Charles, 24
Cheek, William F., 170n
Chevalier, Michael 14
Chickasaw rescue, 138n
Child, Lydia Maria, 40n, 100n
Christian Recorder, 131n
Church (American Protestant), 126,
    144–45, 156
Church History, 8n, 114n
Cincinnati, 39, 136, 152, 154
Citizenship, 45, 154, 174
Civil War, 5, 17–18, 74n, 93, 132, 135,
    146–47, 149, 150, 164–67, 173
Civilization, 71, 75; advantages of, 80;
    of Africa, 73; confusing conceptions of,
    75n
Clay, Henry, 9n, 37, 59
Coffin, Levi, 61
Coker, Daniel, 98, 126; denounced
    miscegenation, 98; founder, AME
    Church, 126; resignation as bishop, 96n
College of Liberia, 103
Colonization, 192, 195; black opposition
    to, 3, 36n, 172, 192; black support for,
    175–92; distinction from emigration,
    195; motivations in, 34; as panacea,
    29–30; white opposition to, 192; white
    support for, 192
Colored American, 4n, 46, 48, 50, 52, 53n,
    58, 59n, 62, 63n, 67, 95, 101, 107, 112,
    113n, 114n, 125, 128, 131n, 133n, 134,
    135n, 139n, 141, 142, 145n, 147, 157n,
    159
"Colored Baltimorean," 60
Colored Citizen, 50
Colored Methodist Episcopal Church, 77

"Colored Philadelphian," 61, 64n
Compensated emancipation, 17
Constitution, 16n, 19, 154, 162
Continental Congress (1776), 26, 73n
Continentalism, 20
Converse, Philip E., 2n
Cooke, Jacob E., 7n
Cooper, E. E., 4
Cooper, Frederick, 108, 127n, 129n–30n
Cooper's Institute (New York City, 102n
Copeland, John A., 153n
Cornish, Samuel E., 42, 52, 60–61, 63;
  agrarian ideal of, 135; denunciation of
  colonization, 42; as editor, 52; supports
  phrase "Colored American," 53
Covenanted nation, 9n, 13–14, 21, 27, 169
Cox, Samuel, 99n
Cresson, Elliott, 38
Crisis, 175, 176, 177n, 178n
Cromwell, John W., 4n, 52n, 109, 110n
Crummell, Alexander, 74–78, 80, 98n–99n,
  110, 117, 118, 119, 122, 142, 162;
  on Anglo-Saxons, 75–76; attacks Josiah
  Strong, 98n–99n; on black moral
  character, 119; on blacks as testers of
  American democracy, 162; on divine
  providence, 78; philosophy of history,
  74–75; and romantic racism, 118–19;
  on schooling of slavery, 80; on spiritual
  destiny of blacks, 88, 110–11; supports
  designation "Negro," 50n
Cuffe, Paul, 79–80, 193–94
Curtis, George William, 17n

Dana, Charles, 17
Dann, Martin E., 50n, 63n, 140n, 161n
Darwin, Charles, 88
Declaration of Independence, 60, 62, 153,
  154, 160, 162, 164
Delany, Martin R., 4, 40, 71n–72n, 96n, 101,
  102, 113n, 114n, 117, 129n, 140, 146n;
  on abolitionist movement, 40, 140; on
  black autonomy, 145–46; on black
  destiny, 89–91; on black religious nature,
  114; on black as superior race, 113;
  on common cause of blacks and Indians,
  87n; on "nation within a nation," 170;
  quoted, 40, 153; racial pride of, 94, 102;
  supports emigration, 90–91, 93;
  supports quota system, 94
Democratic party, 143n–44n, 176, 177
Democracy, 8–9, 12, 14, 18–19, 20–21,
  162–63, 165, 179
Depew, Chauncey M., 30n
Dewees, Jacob, 30n, 79n, 85
Dexter, Franklin Bowditch, 24n, 25n, 26n
Dickinson, Anna, 100n
Disfranchised American, 50
Dix, John Adams, 30n
Douglass, Frederick, 3, 4, 34, 43, 55–56,
  63n, 64n, 70, 76, 86n, 101, 105, 106–7n
  114, 127, 130n, 143, 199; on "Abolition
  War," 164, 167; on abolitionism and
  American mission, 156, 159; on
  American hypocrisy, 157–58, 163–64;
  applauds John Brown, 154n–55n;
  approves colonization, 36–37; attacked
  for inconsistencies, 145; attacked for
  marrying white, 99; on black destiny,
  84–85, 155, 159, 161; on blacks and
  American destiny, 43, 168–69; on Civil
  War and national regeneration, 166–67;

dispute with Delany, 194; on "nation
  within a nation," 170; philosophy of
  reform, 134; on prejudice and slavery,
  103; pro-integration, 100; racial pride of,
  94; on racial unity, 127; on slave
  equality, 106; supports independent
  institutions, 143, 146
Douglass, Henry Ford, 67, 96n
Douglass, William, 31n, 79n
Douglass' Monthly, 43n, 47n, 94n, 101n,
  113n, 140n, 155n, 161n
Drake, St. Clair, 83n, 84n
Draper, Theodore, 171n
Dred Scott decision, 65n, 145, 154, 161
DuBois, W. E. B., 85, 92n, 98n, 104, 107,
  111, 120, 121, 124n, 147, 162, 174, 176n,
  177, 178n, 182, 197; advances designation
  "Negro," 50n; on black American
  contributions to world, 124; capitalism
  intrinsically racist, 179; denounces interracial marriage, 98n; "dichotomous"
  identity of, 92; and election of 1912,
  176; on "gift of the spirit," 121; on
  messianic ideology of, 122, 124; on
  "nation within a nation," 170; optimism
  of, 177; on self-improvement, 129;
  spiritual role of, 111, 120, 121; supports
  World War I, 177–78; on unique black
  destiny, 85–86, 88, 163
Dunbar, Paul Laurence, 130n, 138

Easton, Hosea, 57n, 101, 102, 105, 110,
  115, 116
Education, 142
Edwards, Jonathan, 12, 13, 21, 23
Ekirch, Arthur A., 15n
Elson, Ruth Miller, 3n
Emigration, 136, 192, 196; and
  agrarianism, 136; and escapism, 62
England, 13, 15
Ennals, Samuel, 57n
Environmentalism, 8, 104
Ernst, James, 8
Essien-Udom, E. U., 171n
"Euthymas," 105n
Everett, Edward, 37
Existential emigrationism, 192–95

Faneuil Hall (Boston), 44n, 47
Farrison, William E., 4n, 96n, 102n, 146n,
  147n, 149n, 152n, 159n, 165n
Fax, Elton C., 180n
Female Anti-Slavery Society (Boston),
  138
Female Anti-Slavery Society (Salem), 156
Fifteenth Amendment, 166
Fillmore, Millard, 131n, 153
Finley, Robert, 36, 51, 63
Fishel, Leslie H., Jr., 176n
Fiske, John, 8
Fleming, Robert E., 182n
Foner, Jack D., 149n
Foner, Philip S., 36n, 43n, 62n, 63n, 93n,
  94n, 103n, 106n, 134n, 143n, 146n, 154n,
  155n, 156n, 159n, 160n, 161n, 164n,
  165n, 166n, 167n
Fort Sumter, 146
Forten, James, 53, 54, 128, 140; influence
  of, 38; views on colonization, 54
Fortune, Timothy Thomas, 13n, 82, 123n,
  142n, 176; discrimination a national
  problem, 161n; on future of African

Fortune, Timothy Thomas (*continued*)
    civilization, 123n, 130n; rejects
    providential-design theory, 82;
    relationship to B. T. Washington, 171;
    supports designation "Afro-American,"
    50n, 100n; supports Taft, 176; views on
    racial amalgamation of, 100
Foster, Charles I., 36n
Fourth of July, 34, 55, 100n, 152
Foxe, John, 11
Frazier, E. Franklin, 118–19
Frederick Douglass' Paper, 45, 134n,
    146n, 156n
Frederickson, George M., 104n, 118
Free African Society (Philadelphia), 30,
    31, 33
Free Soil party, 131n
Freedom, 149, 150–52, 165
Freedom's Journal, 40, 52, 57n, 95, 107,
    127, 131n
Freeman, F., 30n, 37, 79n, 156n
Frontier, 8, 16–18, 38, 161
Fugitive Slave Act (1850), 90, 131n, 145,
    150, 151, 153, 154, 157
Fuller, Richard, 35n, 79n

Gaines, John I., 96n
Gammon Theological Seminary (Atlanta),
    78, 81, 82
Gardner, Caleb, 31, 32, 33
Garnet, Henry Highland, 4, 51n, 58, 86,
    88, 101, 105, 107, 130n, 136, 142; on
    Anglo-Saxon avarice, 110; on black
    equality, 105; compares blacks and
    Indians, 88; on democratic ideals, 158;
    denial of multiple races, 93n; dispute
    over titles, 50n; dispute with W. W.
    Brown, 146–47; on prejudice, 101; on
    racial amalgamation, 98; on racial pride,
    97; on separatism versus integration,
    143n; and white abolitionists, 107, 140n
Garrison, Wendell P., 60n
Garrison, William Lloyd, 36n, 37n, 40, 41,
    51n, 55n, 56n, 59–60, 64, 67n, 91, 127,
    134, 144, 154, 173; advocates black
    equality, 40; attacks Delany, 91;
    publishes *Liberator,* 40, 127
Garvey, Marcus 99, 172, 180
Gatewood, Willard B., 4n
Germ theory, 8, 162
Gibson, A. B., 131n
Gilmore, Al-Tony, 99n
Gloucester, J. N., 130n
Gooch, G. P., 10n
Gorden, C. B. W., 151n
Gossett, Thomas F., 117n
Grant, Joanne, 132n
"Great War," *see* World War I
Griffiths, Julia, 148n
Griggs, Sutton E., 181–84
Grimke, Sarah, 114n
Grund, Francis, 17n
Guardian, 176
Guinea, 23

Hague, Asa, 102–3n
Haiti, 116, 136
Hall, James, 85
Hallam, Henry, 9n
Haller, William, 11n
Hamilton, Thomas, 127n
Hamilton, William, 105, 106, 142

Hamitic theory, 115
Hammon, Jupiter, 65, 69–70
Hampton Institute, 103
Hansen, Marcus L., 117n
Harding, Vincent, 124n
Harlan, Lewis, 103n, 171n
Harlem Renaissance, 181
Harper, George McLean, 13n
Harper, Robert Goodloe, 103
Harper's Ferry, 152–53
Harris, J. Dennis, 81
Hartz, Louis, 16n
Harvard University, 171
Haven, Gilbert J., 110n, 118
Heroic tradition, 173–74, 179
Higginson, Thomas Wentworth, 41n
Hildreth, Richard, 72, 138–39
Hill, Adelaide Cromwell, 93n, 123n
Hill, Leslie Pinckney, 117, 122
History, and historical writing, 174;
    pragmatic use of, 149–50
Hofstadter, Richard, 9n, 21–22
Holden, Edith, 120n
Holly, James Theodore, 4, 81, 116;
    building Negro nationality, 81; and
    solar symbolism, 81
Holsey, L. H., 74n, 75n, 77, 80
Hope, Thomas, 114n
Hopkins, Samuel, 2, 22, 23, 36; and
    "African Mission" project, 22–32;
    father of African colonization, 23;
    interpretation of Revolutionary War,
    28–30; rationale for colonization, 34;
    views on slavery, 27, 73n, 164
Howe, M. A. DeWolfe, 9n, 11n, 20n, 165n
Hudson, Winthrop S., 9n
Hutchinson, William T., 8n
Hypocrisy, 157–60

Identity, *see* Black identity
Immigrants, 53–54, 158, 180
Impartial Citizen, 50
Indians, *see* American Indian
Insanity, 47
Insurrections, 76–77; *see also* Slavery
Integration, 131, 132, 142, 144–45, 146–47,
    175, 180

Jackson, Andrew, 17, 37
Jackson, Bruce, 95n
Jacksonian democracy, 9, 10, 18
Jameson, John Franklin, 9
Jay, William, 105n
Jefferson, Thomas, 94–95, 105, 133, 135
Jim Crow system, 43, 142n
Jocelyn, Simeon S., 139
Johns Hopkins University, 16n
Johnson, Jack, 99
Johnson, O. C., 9n
Jones, Absalom, 65, 76n, 79, 104, 112, 121,
    122n
Jordan, Winthrop D., 104n
Journal of Negro History, 3n, 17n, 26n, 36n,
    55n, 99n, 119n, 131n, 134n, 136n, 154n,
    171n, 174n, 176n, 181n
Journal of Presbyterian History, 26n
Journal of Southern History, The, 5n
Judeo-Christian morality, 114
Judgment, 28, 164

Kammon, Michael G., 9n
Katz, William Loren, 152n

Kellogg, Charles Flint, 181
Key, Francis Scott, 37, 60
Kilson, Martin, 93n, 123n
Kristol, Irving, 16n
Kraus, M. G., 8n

Ladies' Anti-Slavery Society, 160n
Lane, Ann J., 111n
Lane Seminary, 136
Langston, John Mercer, 4, 65, 162; on
    America as asylum, 162; mellowing of,
    130n, 196
Latrobe, John H. B., 38
Lawrence, George, 65, 105–6
League of Nations, 13n
Lester, Julius, 86n, 111n, 121n, 129n, 163n,
    175n
Levin, David, 8n, 9n, 12n
Lewis, Robert Benjamin, 174
Lewis, William H., 176
Liberator, 40, 44n, 46n, 47n, 55n, 58, 60,
    61, 64n, 91, 92n, 96n, 97n, 105n, 107n,
    109n, 113n, 127, 129n, 131n, 150n, 153n,
    156n, 164n, 165n, 167
Liberia, 32, 38, 39, 43, 46, 62, 66, 76
Liberty Bell, The, 131n, 139n
Liberty party, 2n, 130n, 159
Lincoln, Abraham, 17, 74n, 146, 165
Lincoln Monument (Washington, D.C.),
    72n
Link, Arthur S., 11n, 13n, 176n
Litwack, Leon F., 41n, 107n
Livermore, George, 65n
Locke, Alain, 121n
Logan, Rayford W., 124n, 178n
L'Ouverture, Toussaint, 149
Lovejoy, David S., 28n
Lundy, Benjamin, 95
Lutz, Alma, 41n, 138n
Lynch, Hollis R., 83n, 100n, 120n, 123n,
    124n

McCrummill, James, 45, 139
McMaster, John Bach, 8n
McPherson, James M., 159n
Madison, James, 37
Magaw, Samuel, 79n
Mann, Horace, 114
Marshall, John, 37
Martin, Viola, 182
Maryland Colonization Society, 36n, 39,
    46, 194
Massachusetts General Colored Associa-
    tion, 144
Massachusetts Sabbath School Union, 39
Materialism, 109–11, 121
Mather, Cotton, 21
Mays, Benjamin E., 72n
Meier, August, 41n, 76n, 127n, 129n
Mencken, H. L., 180
Messianism, 121–24
Methodist Episcopal Church, 118
Millennialism, 6, 10, 12–14, 18–20, 28, 30,
    122–24, 168–69, 176, 177, 178; and
    colonization, 36–37; and messianism,
    122
Miller, Kelly, 2, 120, 121
Mirror of Liberty, 43
Miscegenation, *see* Amalgamation
Mission and destiny (American), 14–16,
    155–57, 165, 166–67, 169, 179–80

Missionary emigrationism, 29, 32, 130, 194
Moore, LeRoy, Jr., 8n
Moral superiority of blacks, 111–13
Morel, Junius C., 50n
Morton, Robert Russa, 72n
Moses, Wilson T., 118n, 206
"Mother Bethel" Church (Philadelphia),
    56
Motley, John Lothrop, 17, 117
Munro, William C., 130n
Mutual-aid societies, 126
Myer, Stephen, 50
Mystery, 89

National Anti-Slavery Standard, 54n, 107,
    134n, 139n, 141n, 145n
National Association for the Advancement
    of Colored People, 181
National Emigration Convention (1854),
    94
National Federation of Afro-American
    Women, 50n
Nationalism, 170, 180; *see also* Black
    nationalism
"Negro Nationality," 81, 171
Nell, William C., 4, 44, 60, 61n, 107, 130n,
    144, 149, 174; against separationist
    tendencies, 144; opposes colonization,
    44; opposes Douglass, 146; political
    activities of, 131n
"New abolitionists," 181
New Bedford, Mass., 114
New England, 11, 13, 23, 165
New England Anti-Slavery Convention
    (1859), 152
New England Quarterly, 28n
New Era, 49
"New Freedom," 176
New National Era, 168n
"New Negro," 6. 179, 181, 183, 184
New York African Institution, 79
New York Age, 100n
New York City, 39, 57n, 60, 133
New York Globe, 161n
New York Review of Books, 18n
New York State Anti-Slavery Society, 63
New York Tribune, 47, 51n
Newcomb, Harvey, 102, 107n
Newport, R.I., 23, 24, 30, 31, 33
Newton Theological Seminary, 80n
Niagara movement, 1
Nickens, David, 64n, 129, 199
Noble, David W., 9n, 16n, 19
North American Review, 10n
North Star, 44n, 64n, 92, 106n, 127, 144n,
    145, 153n
Northern migration, 178
Northern Star and Freeman's Advocate,
    50
Nubia, Salmar, 30, 32, 33
Nye, Russell B., 9n

Oberlin College, 65n
Ofari, Earl, 85n, 93n
Offley, G. W., 112
Ohio State Anti-Slavery Society, 67n
Oneida Institute, 136
Orion (ship), 46
Owen, Robert, 9n

Paine, Tom, 9n
Pan-African Congress, 181

Park, Edwards A., 24n
Parker, Theodore, 100n, 113, 189
Parkman, Francis, 117
Parrington, Vernon Louis, 8
Parrish, John, 66n
Patriotism, 154, 160, 180
Paul, Nathaniel, 74, 155
Payne, Daniel A., 93n, 96n; on religious
    separatism, 134; speech by, 93n
Peace and Benevolent Society of Afric-
    Americans (New Haven), 68n
Pease, Jane H. and William H., 3n, 97n,
    111n, 135, 136n, 140n, 172n
Pennington, James W. C., 77, 110, 139,
    144n, 174; attacks black religious
    separatism, 144; musings on slavery, 71;
    views on public opinion, 39
Peterson, Daniel A., 71
Philadelphia, 30, 31, 33, 39, 45, 54, 66,
    172–73
Philbrick, Edward, 136n
Phillips, Wendell, 41n, 100n
Phylon, 140n, 182n
Pickens, William, 178–79
Piedmont, Belton, 182, 183
Pine and Palm, 63, 64n
Pittsburgh African Education Society, 105
Pomeroy, S. C., 87n
Porter, Dorothy, 44n, 45n, 46n, 54n, 79n,
    95n, 113n, 122n, 130n, 133n
Prejudice, 100–3, 108, 141
Prescott, William H., 117
Price, Enoch, 160
Priest, James M., 194
Princeton College, 25
Princeton Seminary, 40
Progress, 11–12, 158, 161, 163, 178
Progressive party, 175, 176, 177
Prosser, Gabriel, 152
Providence, R.I., 56
Providential design, theory of, 82, 84
Puritanism, 9n, 20, 179, 180
Purvis, Robert, 4, 55n, 98, 107n, 112, 138,
    139n, 145n, 146; on common cause of
    blacks and native Americans, 87n; and
    Dred Scott decision, 154; as moral
    suasionist, 144; on Civil War, 165–66n

Quamine, John, 23, 24, 25, 26, 32, 33
Quarles, Benjamin, 26n, 152n, 154n, 159,
    176n

Racial autonomy, 133–35, 140, 141, 143,
    173
Racial gifts, 115
Racial solidarity, 40, 66, 128, 129, 131,
    132, 170, 172–73
Racism, 29, 117, 178, 179
Randolph, John, 37
Ranke, Leopold von, 7n, 9n
Ransom, Reverdy C., 1, 151n
Ray, Charles B., 72, 130n, 142, 166;
    career in agriculture, 137; on Fifteen‘h
    Amendment,166
Reason, Charles L., 106
Record, Wilson, 171n
Redkey, Edwin S., 84n, 99n
Redpath, James, 63, 154n
Religion, 70
Remond, Charles Lenox, 3n, 4, 44, 55n,
    107, 130–31n, 146, 161
Repellency of races, 195–96

Republican party, 140, 144n, 176–77
Richmond, Va., 39
Rights of All, 61n, 63, 135n
Rock, John Swett, 95–96, 109, 117, 164,
    165n; on black superiority, 113;
    judgment, 164; on racial pride, 96–97
Rogers, Ben F., 181n
"Romantic racism," 118–21
Roosevelt, Theodore, 176
Rothman, David J., 47n
Rudwick, Elliott, 41n, 76n, 127n, 129n
Ruggles, David, 4, 42, 44, 46, 67n, 95, 112,
    144, 145n; asks people to stop discussing
    colonization, 43; on amalgamation,
    97–98; and *Dred Scott* decision, 154;
    on effects of colonization on blacks,
    42–43; on effects of colonization on
    native populations, 87n; on racial pride,
    95; on women and abolitionism, 130n
Rush, Richard, 37
Russwurm, John B., 67

Sabbatarianism, 108
St. Paul's Episcopal Church
    (Philadelphia), 79n
St. Philip's Episcopal Church
    (New York City), 55
St. Thomas's African Episcopal Church
    (Philadelphia), 79
Sanders, Jennings B., 7n–8n
Sanderson, Jeremiah, 199
Sandwich Islanders, 86
Santo Domingo Revolution, 151
Saratoga Springs (New York), 7
Saveth, Edward N., 117n
Scarborough, W. S., 50n
Schaff, Philip, 15
Schurz, Carl, 14n–15n, 17
Scott, Austin, 21
Scott, Winfield, 37
Self-improvement, 104, 108, 109, 128–32
Separatism, 125–47, 173, 180
Seward, William Henry, 37
Shadd, Abraham, 51n, 58
Sharp, Granville, 28
Shaw, Albert, 176n
Shepard, Eli, 95n
"Sidney," 95; on racial pride, 95, 101;
    on separatist tradition, 125–26, 132–33,
    138, 141
Sidney, Joseph, 121, 122n
Slave narratives ,189
Slave trade, 24, 26–27, 163
Slavery, 17, 102, 110, 115, 117, 118, 157,
    158, 164, 166; black understanding of,
    18, 69–88, 138–39; as blemish on
    America's image, 30, 158–59; as cause
    of Civil War, 164–67; causes of, 109–10;
    divine permission and, 77; Hopkins on,
    26–27; mystery and meaning of, 78–79;
    prejudice involved in, 103; punishment
    of Africa, 71; redemptive purpose of,
    73; as school for Christianity and
    civilization, 80, 179; suffering and, 74;
    violent overthrow of, 154–55
Slaves, 34, 63–68; opposition to
    colonization of, 39; revolts by, 151–53
Smith, David, 96n
Smith, Gerrit, 41, 72, 137
Smith, James L., 64, 74, 146n, 149
Smith, James McCune, 47, 72, 131n, 149n;
    on effects of ACS, 51n; on farming,

137–38; opposes separatism, 128, 144, 145n; response to Sixth Census (1841), 47
Smith, Robert P., 131n, 144n
Smith, Timothy L., 77n, 114n
Social Forces, 171n
Social-gospel movement, 177
Solar symbolism, 81
Song of Solomon, 97
Sorin, Gerald, 129n, 141
Spanish-American War, 3–4
Spirituals, 74
Strange, Douglas C., 93n
Staudenraus, P. J., 28n, 38n, 39n, 51n, 59, 156n
Steward, Austin, 73, 87–88, 98, 128n, 152n, 159n; on agrarian life-style, 136–37; on America as asylum, 158–59; on destiny of blacks, 87–88; on racial pride, 98
Stewart, Maria W., 45, 46n, 56n, 71, 105, 130n, 150; on black autonomy, 133; on black equality, 150; compares blacks and American Indians, 86n; opposes colonization, 45
Stewart, Thomas McCants, 194; on separatism versus integrationism, 143–44n; on slavery and prejudice, 103
Stiles, Ezra, 23–25
Stowe, Harriet Beecher, 59–60, 118
Strong, Josiah, 98n
Stuart, Charles, 57n
Stuckey, Sterling, 111n, 122n, 132n, 140n, 143n
Sumner, Charles, 41n
Superiority, black, 111–24
Sutherland, LaRoy, 139
Swedenborg, Emanuel, 123, 124n
Swift, David A., 26n

Taft, William Howard, 176
Tanner, Benjamin T., 93n
Tanner, Obour, 70n
Tappan, Arthur, 41, 52
Tappan, Lewis, 41, 100n, 139
Teague, Collin, 194
Temperance, 108
Testers of American ideals, 3, 160–63
Thompson, John P., 50n
Thornbrough, Emma Lou, 3n, 176n
Thornton, William, 28
Thorpe, Earl E., 99n, 153n, 174, 181n
Tocqueville, Alexis de, 89
Torrey, Jesse, 58n
Trotter, William Monroe, 176
True American, 50
Truth, Sojourner, 58
Tubman, Harriet, 74n
Turner, Frederick Jackson, 8, 16, 18
Turner, Henry McNeal, 4, 83n, 99; African colonizationist, 175; on slavery, 75n, 83–84n; on "schooling" of slavery, 81
Turner, Nat, 36n, 96n, 152, 173

Ullman, Victor, 91n, 92n, 93n, 94n, 96n, 146n
Union Missionary Society, 139–40
Universal Negro Improvement Association, 180

Vashon, John B., 58, 62, 66, 105
Vine (ship), 32

Violence, 151–52, 154–55
Virginia Normal and Collegiate Institute, 151n
Voluntaryism, 14

Wade, Richard C., 36n
Walker, David, 48, 68, 71n, 76, 77n, 105, 110n, 121–22, 128n, 164; attacks Jefferson, 95, 133; on black moral superiority, 113; on American Indians, 87n
Walters, Alexander, 80n, 102n, 176
War of 1812, 49, 54
War of Independence, 15, 49
Ward, John William, 17n
Ward, Samuel Ringgold, 76, 99n, 107, 109, 113, 130n, 137n, 142, 143n, 145, 157n; architect of Albany National Convention, 142; on black moral superiority, 113; on black religious nature, 115–17; cessation of separatist activities discussed, 143; on "right of Revolution," 153; on self-improvement, 134n; views on amalgamation, 100
Washington, Booker T., 3, 72n, 81, 111, 132n, 147, 171, 174, 182; advocates designation "Negro," 50n; and black nationalism, 171; colonization and mercenary motives behind, 82; on "nation within a nation," 170; on Providence and slavery, 81
Washington, D.C., 7, 72n, 78, 158, 159
Washington, George, 152
Washington, Madison, 173
Watkins, William J., 40, 41, 45
Wattles, Augustus, 135, 136
Webster, Daniel, 37, 79n
Wecter, Dixon, 180n
Weekly Advocate, 49, 52, 55n, 125, 127, 128n, 133
Weekly Anglo-African, 50, 103n, 127n, 131n, 155n
Wesley, Charles H., 174
West Indian Emancipation, 134
Western Reserve College, 86n
Wheatley, Phyllis, 25–26, 32, 69, 70n; quoted, 69
Whigs, 10, 21
Whipper, William, 107n, 126, 128, 144, 145; advocates abandonment of term "colored," 101; proposal of, at 1835 black convention, 51–52
Whitfield, James M., 149n, 196
Whitman, Walt, 170
Wilberforce Settlement (Upper Canada), 57n, 87
Wilberforce University, 146
Wilkinson, James Garth, 123
Willard, Emma, 35n
Williams, George Washington, 72–73, 119n, 150, 174; oration of, 80n; on origin of Civil War, 164; on record of blacks in military, 150; on wickedness of slavery, 72
Williams, Kenny J., 122n
Williams, Lorraine K., 17n
Williams, Peter, 41, 56n; on cause of slavery, 110; on double standard for blacks, 55; on Paul Cuffe, 79–80; optimism of, 61–62
Williams, Roger, 8, 12
Williams, William Appleton, 18n

Wilson, Joseph T., 156, 165
Wilson, Woodrow, 11, 13, 15, 17, 18, 20,
  176, 179
Women, 40n, 118, 130n, 138, 154, 160
Woodson, Carter G., 92n, 95n, 105n,
  114n, 151n, 156n, 157n, 159n, 160n
Woodson, Lewis, 61n, 101, 105, 133, 135n,
  141–42, 160n
Woodward, C. Vann, 118, 177
World Tomorrow, 121n
World War I, 1, 6, 177–78
Wright, H. C., 160

Wright, Theodore S., 63, 72, 106, 130n,
  142; on benefits of agricultural
  vocation, 137; denunciation of
  colonization, 42
Wyatt-Brown, Bertram, 41n, 99n, 100n,
  140n

Yale College, 23
Yamma, Bristol, 23, 25
Young, Robert Alexander, 164
Young Men's Colonization Society, 65n